THE PRAGMATIC BASIS OF APHASIA

A Neurolinguistic Study of Morphosyntax Among Bilinguals

NEUROPSYCHOLOGY AND NEUROLINGUISTICS

a series of books edited by **Harry A. Whitaker**

BRUYER:
The Neuropsychology of Face Perception and Facial Expression

DELOCHE/SERON:
Mathematical Disabilities: A Cognitive Neuropsychological Perspective

GIVON:
Mind, Code, and Context: Essays in Pragmatics

KELLER/GOPNIK:
Motor and Sensory Processes of Language

KNEZEVIC/MAXIMILIAN/MUBRIN/PROHOVNIK/WADE:
Handbook of Regional Cerebral Blood Flow

NESPOULOS/PERRON/LECOURS:
The Biological Foundations of Gesture: Motor and Semiotic Aspects

PARADIS:
The Assessment of Bilingual Aphasia

SCHNITZER:
The Pragmatic Basis of Aphasia: A Neurolinguistic Study of Morphosyntax Among Bilinguals

VAID:
Language Processing in Bilinguals: Psycholinguistic and Neuropsychological Perspectives

THE PRAGMATIC BASIS OF APHASIA

A Neurolinguistic Study of Morphosyntax Among Bilinguals

Marc L. Schnitzer
University of Puerto Rico

Routledge
Taylor & Francis Group
LONDON AND NEW YORK

First published 1989 by Lawrence Erlbaum Associates, Inc.

Published 2016 by Routledge
2 Park Square, Milton Park, Abingdon, Oxfordshire OX14 4RN
711 Third Avenue, New York, NY 10017, USA

First issued in paperback 2016

Routledge is an imprint of the Taylor & Francis Group, an informa business

Library of Congress Cataloging in Publication Data

Schnitzer, Marc L.
The pragmatic basis of aphasia.

Bibliography: p.
Includes index.
1. Aphasics—Language. 2. Neurolinguistics.
3. Bilingualism. I. Title. [DNLM: 1. Aphasia.
2. Neuropsychology. 3. Psycholinguistics.
WL 340.5 S361p]
RC425.S28 1989 616.85'52 88-24373

ISBN 13: 978-1-138-98971-9 (pbk)
ISBN 13: 978-0-8058-0191-0 (hbk)

Publisher's Note
The publisher has gone to great lengths to ensure the quality of this reprint but points out that some imperfections in the original may be apparent.

Para Nicolás

Contents

Foreword

The title of this work is misleading in several ways. First, it is nowhere claimed that the basis of aphasia is pragmatic. Rather, the data presented herein suggest that aphasia represents a regression *to* a pragmatic basis of communication. Second, the study includes monolingual hispanophones as well as bilinguals among its subjects. Finally, although it is obvious that all the tests deal with morphology or syntax, there are none that focus on a combination of both. Consideration of morphology and of syntax remains distinct in this research, although the phenomena are normally inseparable, particularly in Spanish.

The preparation of this work had many stages and the author is indebted to many people for facilitating them. For her complete cooperation in the recruitment of subjects for the earliest pilot phase, the author wishes to express his gratitude to Sra. Luz T. Brignoni, Administrator of the home for the aged "Centro de Envejecientes Condominio Leopoldo Figueroa" of Río Piedras, Puerto Rico, as well as to the three ladies who participated, who must remain anonymous.

Barbara Bilder, Principal of the High School of the Baldwin School of Puerto Rico (Guaynabo) is gratefully acknowledged (along with her colleagues Kay Ellis and Harry McKay) for providing bilingual students from the sixth and seventh grades as subjects for the validation phase of this study. I am likewise obliged to the students and their parents.

For patient referrals and medical records for the principal investigation, I am indebted to the staff of the Neurological Outpatient Clinic (Clínica Externa de Neurología), especially to its head, Dr. Luis Sánchez Longo; to the staff of the neurosurgery unit of the Hospital Municipal, especially to Dr. José V. Santos; to

Ana Cintrón, R.N., Supervisor of the Casa de Salud; and to Alison Lladó, R.N., Head Nurse at the University District Hospital (Centro Médico de Puerto Rico).

For their aid in data collection, I am very grateful to my former speech pathology students Nancy Segarra, Raquel Anderson, and Carmen Ana Ramos; and for their aid in the analysis of data I am grateful to Joe Carroll, Nancy Vergara, and most especially José Orench.

Thanks go to Emily Krasinski, Gail Tosto-Geiger, and Richard Cameron for their help in managing the huge number of data. To the Facultad of Humanidades of the University of Puerto Rico, I am grateful for a sabbatical year in which to write up this investigation. I am grateful for a grant from FIPI that enabled me to complete the study. Thanks to Gene Mohr and Judith Suben for their useful comments.

Harry Whitaker has been giving me good advice for a good many years. Most recently, his numerous insightful comments and suggestions have helped improve this manuscript significantly.

The person to whom I feel most indebted is Nicolás Linares, former Head of the Departamento de Trastornos Comunicológicos at the Medical Sciences Campus of the U.P.R. He persuaded me to come to Puerto Rico, assuring me that I would be able to work on bilingual aphasia and that he would collaborate with me. He made all the contacts necessary for locating subjects and for testing them in the various units of the Centro Médico de Puerto Rico. He is coauthor of the test battery used in this study. He has been a great help and constant inspiration. It is to him that this work is dedicated. Gracias, Nico, por todo.

1 Introduction

Aphasic errors do not carry their linguistic interpretation with them.
—John C. Marshall

Most studies of bilinguals and polyglots afflicted with aphasia have focused attention on differential cerebral localization or hemispheric lateralization (e.g., Albert & Obler, 1978; Galloway, 1983), or patterns of recovery (e.g., Paradis, 1977; Paradis, Goldblum, & Abidi, 1982; also see Paradis (1983) for reissue of older case reports). The present study differs from previous studies of bilingual aphasia in that it is concerned primarily not with the characteristics of the aphasics (12 Spanish–English bilinguals and 9 monolingual hispanophones) in relation to their linguistic performance, but rather with the detailed nature of their linguistic performance in a variety of ''natural'' and metalinguistic tasks. It is a study of *language* rather than of aphasia, in the tradition of Harold Goodglass (e.g., Goodglass, 1968; Goodglass & Berko, 1960; Goodglass & Hunt, 1958), in which aphasics are subjected to a variety of formal tests, but different from Goodglass's work in that its primary purpose is to use aphasic performance to understand language rather than to use linguistic analysis to understand aphasia. The present study is not primarily a linguistic analysis of aphasia, but rather an aphasiological analysis of language.

As Jason Brown (1977, 1979, 1980, 1982) has claimed, pathology *reveals* function at a lower neurological and cognitive level, in his theory of ''microgenesis,'' which adopts the position that ''a set of psychological and brain levels forms a substructure within a behavior as it unfolds over evolutionary and maturational stages'' (1982, p. 44). Distinguishing among four phylogenetic and ontogenetic levels of neuroanatomical form and cognitive function—sensorimotor (subcortical), presentational (limbic), representational (neocortical), and symbolic (asymmetric, neocortical)—he claims that each higher level is a ''differentiation of an earlier less specified stage'' (1977, p. 24). He also states that neuropathology can reveal the mode in which more primitive stages function, because for Brown a symptom, rather than being viewed as a deficiency, is "like a window into the component the damaged area supports" (1982, p. 448). I use the word "mode" because, although it is not Brown's term, it underlines the kinship between Brown's levels and Talmy Givón's (1979) communicative continuum.

Givón, whose principal concern is not brain function, distinguishes among three communicative modes: monopropositional, pragmatic, and syntactic, which constitute the three cardinal points in a phylogenetic and ontogenetic continuum. The monopropositional mode is used by canines, pongids, and human babies and may be used by normal adult human beings under special circumstances. This mode is found as well in severe aphasia. The monopropositional mode is restricted in time and space to the "here and now." It is restricted with respect to subject–agent to *you* and *I,* (agent and recipient–benefactive are not coded, but rather presupposed), and with respect to referents, to currently perceivable concrete objects. In illocutionary force it is restricted to the imperative, or more properly speaking, the manipulative.

The pragmatic mode, which is the communicative mode of pidgins, evolves into the syntactic mode as pidgins evolve into creoles. This pragmatic mode, according to Givón, is intermediate in child language development between the monopropositional stage and the full-fledged syntactic mode. It begins as the child begins to use two-word utterances. In the pragmatic mode, there is a tendency to use topic-comment structure, rather than the subject-predicate structure typical of the syntactic mode. Conjunction is the more common approach to combination of clauses in the pragmatic mode, with little or no subordination, the latter process being restricted to the syntactic mode.

Other characteristics of Givón's pragmatic mode are slow rate of delivery with multiple intonation contours (as opposed to the rapid rate of the syntactic mode in which utterances are contained within a single contour). Word order is controlled by the pragmatic principle of old information first, new information last (as compared to the syntactic mode, in which thematic and semantic relations govern word order). In the pragmatic mode, there is roughly a one-to-one ratio of verbs to nouns, with the proportion of nouns predominating in the syntactic mode. Inflectional morphology is characteristic of the syntactic mode and is not found in the pragmatic mode.

In addition to these salient features that characterize the three communicative modes, Givón discusses a process that he calls *morphologization,* a process of change in the syntactic mode, in which syntactic elements become cliticized into bound morphemes. There is then a further tendency for these morphemes to become gradually eroded by phonological processes, which then necessitates the introduction of new syntactic elements—presumably to preserve intelligibility and prevent information loss.

The two languages that the present study is concerned with illustrate this phenomenon. The phonologically more conservative dialects of Spanish tend not to use subject pronouns, because verb endings signal person and number, but in Puerto Rican Spanish, which tends to elide final /s/s[1] (which distinguish second person from third person singular when at the end of appropriate verb forms), there is a marked tendency to use personal subject pronouns, especially for second person in the present, imperfect, future, and conditional indicative, and present and past subjunctive forms, where the elimination of final /s/ leads to ambiguity. Modern English, which has very little person-marking morphology on verbs *requires* the use of explicit pronouns.

This hierarchical evolutionary approach to language is paralleled by the neurological approaches of Brown (1977, 1979, 1980, 1982) noted earlier, Lamendella (1976, 1977a, 1977b, 1979), and Goldstein (1933, 1948, 1959). These three share the view that the nervous system is organized hierarchically (cf. Hayek, 1952; Jackson, 1958) and that brain damage can reveal function at a more primitive level of neuropsychological organization. Thus for Brown, who takes issue with the "modular" localizationist approach to interpretation of aphasic symptomatology, it makes no sense to speak of the "loss" of a function that may be "regained" a few minutes later. Rather, neuropathology gives rise to the operation of the nervous system at a lower evolutionary or maturational level.

In a similar vein, Lamendella (op. cit.) views the linguistic system as part of a hierarchy in which neopallial systems exercise control over the limbic system, inhibiting certain functions in the latter (1977a, p. 196). He believes that the forebrain limbic systems constitute the basic level of human communication (somewhat along the lines of Givón's monopropositional mode). By about 1 year of age, children develop neocortically based conceptual systems that involve thematic relations (this level akin to Givón's pragmatic mode). From about 20 months of age, the child begins to use morphosyntactic means to encode the lower level conceptualizations (Lamendella, 1976, 1977b). The child has at this point arrived at the equivalent of Givón's syntactic mode.

Goldstein (1933, 1948, 1959) had long argued along lines similar to these regarding neuropathology. Although not antilocalizationist in the sense of believing neuropathology in any area equally likely to result in a given kind of symptomatology, Goldstein believed that aphasia was attributable to what he called a "basic defect" in which the patient was reduced to functioning in terms of "concrete" rather than "abstract" language, due to an inability to assume the "abstract attitude." This conception of the problem obviously parallels a conception involving a regression to a representational or even presentational level in Brown's system, to a limbic level in Lamendella's system, and to the pragmatic mode in Givón's system.

---

[1]See López Morales (1983), Poplack (1977), Terrell (1976, 1978a, 1978b), Uber (1981), Hammond (1982) and Hochberg (1986, 1987).

Recently Lebrun and Buyssens (1982) have proposed revising Goldstein's terminology from *concrete* and *abstract* attitudes to *language* and *metalanguage*, respectively, Thus, for Lebrun and Buyssens, the "basic defect" is an inability to use metalanguage. In spie of their stated definition of metalanguage as "use of language to refer to language itself or to any part of it" (p. 21), in fact their use of the term goes beyond what is generally meant in the literature by "metalinguistic performance". For example, for Lebrun and Buyssens, object naming would constitute a metalinguistic task if it were clear to the subject that (s)he was involved in a task of object naming. Thus they refer to a patient cited by Goldstein (1948, p. 61–63) who could not name animals on request, yet could do so when imagining the animals at the local zoo. In the latter situation she did not name the category "bear", but rather "polar bear," "brown bear," and so on.

Clearly Goldstein, Brown, Lamendella, and Givón are not making identical claims. I present them here together because they are obviously alike in their Jacksonian postulation that observed normal language behavior is at the summit of a hierarchy of functions.[2] A disruption of the hierarchy can result in symptoms that represent a lower overall level of function. Of the four, Givón has not made specific neurological claims. Draizar (1982) however, has recently carried the Givónian approach into the realm of aphasiology and experimental neurolinguistics.

Because one of Givón's prime concerns is language change (as much in the traditional sense of historical-comparative linguistic studies, as in the related senses of language acquisition and creolization), Draizar studied two groups of aphasics, each of which performed a picture-description task and a free discourse "task." Each group was subjected to Melodic Intonation Therapy (Sparks, Helm, & Albert, 1974), a kind of deblocking procedure (e.g., Weigl, 1968, 1970, 1974; Weigl & Bierwisch, 1970) in which the clinician began by singing or humming a melody. The clinician then sang the melody using the words of a target phrase or sentence. The patient then sang along with the clinician, and the latter gradually stopped participating to let the patient complete the phrase alone. The patient then *repeated* the phrase. Finally a normal intonation contour was substituted for the melody, and all the procedures were repeated with the normal intonation. In the Draizar study, the experimental group used narrative contexts for the sentences used in the Melodic Intonation Therapy, whereas the Control group used arbitrary sentences. Draizar compared the two groups, consisting of nine aphasics with left frontal and/or temporal-lobe lesions, before and after 15 weeks of therapy along the lines just described, with respect to seven categories relevant to Givón's pragmatic-syntantactic mode distinction:

---

[2]Garrett (1975, 1976, 1980, 1984) has argued for a model of speech production based on errors made by normal speakers. Although presented as stages in speech production, rather than as phylogenetic levels, his "message level" and "functional and positional levels" appear to correspond in nontrivial ways to Givón's pragmatic and syntactic modes, respectively.

1. Quantity of verbalization (less [pragmatic] vs. more [syntactic]).
2. Word order (topic-comment [pragmatic] vs. subject-predicate [syntactic]).
3. Syntactic complexity (conjunction [pragmatic] vs. subordination [syntactic]).
4. Noun to verb ratio ($N \leq V$ [pragmatic] vs. $N > V$ [syntactic]).
5. Use of grammatical morphemes (used in syntactic mode only).
6. Use of anaphora (greater in syntactic mode).
7. Intonation pattern (more cohesive with increased syntacticization).

The results of the study tended to support Givón's approach to language change as applied to linguistic evolution of aphasics. The categories of word order, syntactic complexity, and noun-to-verb ratio were found to increase significantly over the 15-week period (ANOVA, p = .03, .005, .025, respectively). Furthermore, the use of the narrative (i.e., *pragmatic*) context in the experimental group yielded increases significantly greater than those for the control group for the categories of syntactic complexity ($p = .012$) and use of anaphora ($p = .021$).

The present investigation differs profoundly from Draizar's in that it was not originally intended to examine Givón's continuum. Indeed, it was conceived more than a year before the publication of Givón's work. Thus the analyses of the test items in such terms have been post hoc, and the investigation reported and discussed herein may be best thought of as an extended pilot study, which offers sufficient food for thought to warrant future studies of Givón's approach to language evolution as applied to aphasic linguistic dissolution.

The investigation reported herein was originally intended to study the effects of various personal and neuropathological characteristics of bilingual aphasics on their linguistic and metalinguistic behavior, and the author began the study with a strict localizationist bias (Schnitzer, 1978a, 1982, 1986). But as will become obvious, the interpretation of the data as indicative of regression along Givón's continuum is quite persuasive. And although such analysis by no means obviates the need for close correlation of lesion site with psychological symptom, and in no sense makes a claim for overall equipotentiality, nonetheless, the data strongly support a vertical (i.e., hierarchical) approach as complementary to a horizontal (i.e., localizationist) one.[3]

Certain of the functions of the syntactic mode can be seen to be more automatic, less "computational" than others. These low-level phenomena (such as certain kinds of agreement, concord, and other morphological manifestations of syntactic redundancy) are acquired early and tend to be resistant to linguistic

[3]The reader should note that this distinction between "vertical" and "horizontal" does not correspond to Fodor's (1983) distinction between horizontal and vertical faculties. Fodor's vertical faculties are modular, and the horizontal ones are the least localizable.

dissolution.[4] In chapter 6 (''Interpretation''), it is argued that in the tests taken by the aphasics in this study, significant differences in performance on items with differing linguistic characteristics can be traced either to:

1. The fact that a pragmatic-mode strategy is being employed in a task requiring syntactic-mode processing.
2. The fact that certain items can be dealt with successfully by means of pragmatic-mode processing, whereas other cannot.
3. The fact that certain low-level syntactic-mode phenomena are over-learned, automatic, and resistant to dissolution. (See footnote [4].)

It should be noted at the outset that the word ''pragmatic'' is used throughout this work in a systematically ambiguous manner. ''Pragmatic'' in the sense of Givón's communicative continuum refers to a cardinal point specified by the characteristics mentioned previously, at which speakers behave with relative insensitivity to the purely morphosyntactic properties of language. But this insensitivity to properties of the syntactic mode will entail a *comparative* enhancement of sensitivity to pragmatic factors in a more general sense of the term, including, for example, general knowledge of the world, Grice's maxims (Grice, 1975), awareness of the communicative setting and participants. Hence, lin-

---

[4]Givón, in more recent work, considers this distinction between automatic, routinized or unattended processing and controlled, analytic or attended processing (Givón, Kellogg, Posner, & Yee, 1985, Givón, in preparation). Givón et al. (1985) present an analysis of discourse processing by normal subjects, in which the authors argue for a distinction between automated versus attended components of the tracking of (pronominal and nonpronominal) referents in a discourse. Grammatical coding of referents as pronouns, indefinite nouns, or definite nouns triggers automatic processing responses. But other, nonautomatic, context-sensitive processing is also integrated into the overall process of tracking referents. This distinction has been proposed for nonlinguistic tasks as well, comparing slow, effortful approaches to novel tasks (generally involving some sort of serial processing) to fast, relatively effortless performance of tasks not under conscious control, and accessible to parallel processing (Schneider, 1985; Schneider & Shiffrin, 1977). Posner and Snyder (1975) discuss in some detail the role of attention and awareness with respect to how conscious strategies interact with automatic processes in performance.

Givón's more recent terminologies of ''pregrammaticized'' (unroutinized) versus ''grammaticized'' (routinized) (Givón et al., 1985) and ''pregrammatical mode'' versus ''grammatical mode'' (Givón, in preparation) tend to suggest a dichotomy rather than a continuum. Nonetheless, reported results in this work suggest a continuum in which the first system is preferred for certain kinds of tasks and the second works as a kind of backup. At the opposite end of the continuum, the propositions that the two systems contribute are reversed. This interpretation is consistent with the approach to aphasia of the present work as a regression along a continuum.

Although as noted, the more automatic linguistic functions appear to be more resistant to dissolution than the more conscious ones, this distinction should not be confused with Goldin-Meadow's (1982) distinction between resilient and fragile properties of language. For her, resilient properties are those likely to develop in language acquisition in spite of a degraded linguistic input.

guistic performance by aphasics that shows greater sensitivity to pragmatic elements in this more general sense (in comparison to demonstrated insensitivity for morphosyntactic elements) will be considered as evidence of regression in the direction of the pragmatic mode.

A caveat is in order here, I believe, concerning the use of the word "regression" in this book. First, it is nowhere implied nor do I wish to imply that aphasic language regresses to an earlier stage of linguistic ontogeny. There is ample evidence in the literature that it does not (e.g., Caramazza & Zurif, 1978; Dennis & Wiegel-Crump, 1979). My aim is emphatically not to resurrect a Jakobsonian regression hypothesis (e.g., Jakobson, 1968). What I do wish to suggest is that aphasic language represents a regression *along the Givonian communicative continuum,* a regression to a more primitive *form* not to an earlier *stage*. In the words of Brown (1980, p. 299), the regression is "*micro*structural, not ontogenetic. Pathological symptoms refer to levels in cognition, not stages in cognitive development." Aphasics tend to function at a level more characteristic of the pragmatic mode than do normal speakers. Although this mode is found in certain stages of child language, certain kinds of pidgins, etc. (see Chapter 7), this fact does not entail that aphasic speech should closely resemble children's speech or pidgins.

Second, it is important to emphasize that *appropriate* use of the pragmatic mode is *not* an indicator of a more primitive system of communication. On the contrary, the fact that many important aspects of communication must be analyzed in terms of discourse pragmatics may indicate that these aspects are in fact too complex to be syntacticized: That is why they remain as discourse phenomena. It is only when pragmatic processes are used instead of syntactic processes because the speaker lacks (adequate control of) the appropriate syntactic processes, that one can speak of the use of a more primitive system. Thus, in this book it is argued that in aphasia, pragmatic-mode strategies tend to be used for tasks that in normals have become syntacticized. Hence, aphasics tend to fail on tasks that force the use of the syntactic mode. It is in this sense only that I am claiming that aphasic language is more primitive than normal language and that it constitutes a regression.

In this study of Spanish–English bilinguals and monolingual hispanophones it becomes clear that aphasia affects the two languages in much the same way. This is especially so in the sentence comprehension tests in which identical pragmatic factors are shown to correlate in the same way with the test results in the two languages. Although the differing grammatical structures of the two languages do not permit the analysis of identical factors in the majority of the morphological and syntactic tests considered herein, nonetheless, it is shown that pragmatic-mode factors of similar kinds relate to aphasic dissolution in both languages of the bilinguals. In both languages we find the kind of performance which can be analyzed as regression along the communicative continuum.

In the last two chapters, evidence is adduced for the claims made in previous chapters, based on other research in aphasiology, as well as on research in the fields of first and second language acquisition, pidgin and creole studies, the phenomenon of language death, and attempts to teach language to nonhuman primates. In conclusion, the implications of the present study for linguistic theory are discussed.

2 Instrument

DESCRIPTION OF THE TEST BATTERY

The test battery used in this study consisted of two types of syntax tests and four types of morphology tests. Each type of test had a variant in each of the four combinations of input (listening or reading) and output (speaking or writing) modalities. Each type of test had a variant in each of the two languages, Spanish and English (with certain necessary differences, owing to the dissimilarities between the two languages). No test item presented in one modality combination was repeated in any test in a different modality combination (or in the same one), in order to eliminate any possible effects of learning or prior familiarity with test items. Nonetheless, there was an attempt made to *balance* test items among the four modality combinations with respect to type and difficulty of item. In the sentence-comprehension tests, an attempt was made for balance across the two languages as well.

Syntax

Sentence Comprehension

Each of the eight sentence-comprehensions tests (one for each of the four input–output modality combinations in each of the two languages) consisted of eight sentences about each of which the subject was required to answer three questions. Thus for those subjects who took all eight tests, there were 192 items to which to respond (24 items × 4 modality combinations × 2 languages). In the

English versions, the eight sentences presented in each of the four modality combinations included simple declarative sentences, reversible passives, various types of embeddings, including indirect commands and questions, relative clauses, and infinitive, gerundive and tensed complement clauses, as well as coordinate clauses.

For Spanish, in addition to the simple declaratives, passives, relatives, coordinate clauses, and indirect commands and questions, there were complement sentences in both indicative and subjunctive modes, as well as infinitives. There were a number of gapping constructions in the test sentences in both languages.

Syntax Correction

The eight syntax-correction tests (four in each language, one in each modality combination) each consisted of nine sentences of which the subject was required to judge the grammaticality, and correct the sentence if ungrammatical. Each of the eight tests contained two grammatically correct and seven grammatically incorrect sentences. In the English tests, the errors involved use of articles, prepositions, word order (auxiliary fronting, for example), tense, and auxiliary *do*. In the Spanish tests, they involved prepositions, articles, subject-verb agreement, tense-aspect, mode, negative concord, and sequence of tenses.

Morphology

Verb Paradigm Completion

Each of the four English tests (for each modality pair) consisted of eight items (five regular verbs, three irregular) in which a phrase of the form

SUBJECT PRONOUN - PRESENT TENSE VERB

was presented, followed by:

"Yesterday," SAME SUBJECT PRONOUN ______.

After a response by the patient, this was followed by:

SAME SUBJECT PRONOUN - APPROPRIATE FORM OF "have" ______.

The patient was required to provide the appropriate past tense and past participle forms in the positions of the blanks (e.g., "He runs. Yesterday, he ______. He has ______." The patients were expected to respond with "ran; run.") There were thus a total of 64 responses made by patients who took all four tests of English verb paradigm completion.

Each of the four Spanish tests consisted of 15 items of which 10 involved regular verbs and 5 involved irregular forms. Verb forms were randomly distributed among the four modalities with respect to person, number, and tense-aspect. On presentation of a verb in conjugation with two persons in a given tense-aspect (along with the appropriate subject pronouns), the patient was required to respond with the correct verb form for an additional person presented (e.g., "Yo corto, tú cortas, ellas ______." The patient was expected to respond with "cortan"). There were a total of 60 items of this form.

Spanish Number and Gender Agreement

Each of the four tests consisted of six noun phrases of the form

DEFINITE ARTICLE - NOUN - ADJECTIVE

in which (for four of the items) the article and adjective had the wrong gender (Spanish nouns have two genders—masculine and feminine) and (for the other two) the article and the adjective had the wrong number (Spanish has two numbers—singular and plural). The patient was required fo determine if the phrase was grammatically correct or incorrect and to correct it if incorrect (all items presented were incorrect).

Each of the four tests included an item with a marked gender (e.g., in *mesa,* the final *a* indicates the likelihood of feminine gender), an item with unmarked gender (e.g., in *calle* there is no phonological or orthographic clue as to the gender), and an item with paradoxically marked gender (e.g., in *clima* the final *a* misleadingly indicates the likelihood of feminine gender for this masculine noun). The subjects were expected to respond to the phrase *una clima cálida* with *un clima cálido.*

English Plural Inflection

In each of the modality combinations, subjects had to convert six singular nouns to plural. The test format was:

"I see one" SINGULAR NOUN. "I see two" ______.

In each test there were three regular and three irregular plurals. The regular plurals consisted of one /s/ allomorph, one /z/ allomorph, and one /əz/ allomorph.

English Possessive and Third Person Singular Present Verb Inflection[1]

In each of the four modality combinations, there were two items of the form

"This" $NOUN_1$ "belongs to" $NOUN_2$. "Whose" $NOUN_1$ "is it?"

in which the subject was to respond with the genitive form of $Noun_2$. In addition, there were two items of the form:

"Two" PLURAL $NOUN_3$—PRESENT TENSE VERB.
"One" SINGULAR $NOUN_3$ ______.

in which the subject was required to supply the third person singular present form of the verb. The correct responses to these items were distributed among /s/, /z/, and /əz/ allomorphs. These two morphemes were grouped together because of their identical allomorphy.

PREPARATION AND VALIDATION OF THE TEST BATTERY

In 1978, Nicolás Linares and the author decided to try to develop an instrument that would test language skills in all their ramifications. It was to be a clinical instrument for use with language disrupted adults, that would include tests of phonology, graphemics, morphology, syntax, lexical semantics (definitions, synonymy, antonomy, hyponomy), comprehension of texts, and pragmatics. It was to measure these abilities in all relevant combinations of input–output modalities. Further, it was to permit pointing to correct answers chosen from sets of alternatives for those patients who were limited in control of their speech or writing modalities. It was to require no special materials such as objects or pictures to identify so that the listening–speaking (and in some cases listening–writing) portions could be administered to visually impaired patients.

The test was constructed (with equal participation by Linares and Schnitzer) along the lines described, and piloted with three normal female residents of a San Juan area home for the aged who had completed 5 to 9 years of formal education and who were natively bilingual. The three subjects took an average of 14 hours to complete the test battery, which led to the decision to focus only on the

---

[1]The reader will note a similarity between many of these tests of English inflection and those used in some of Goodglass's early work (e.g., Goodglass 1968, Goodglass & Berko 1960; Goodglass & Hunt 1958).

morphological and syntactic portions of the test in the present study of aphasics. Because of the excessive time taken by normal subjects to complete the battery, it was deemed infeasible to administer the entire test battery to a population of aphasics. Based on the results of the pilot, the morphology and syntax sections were amended, taking into account the errors made by the three subjects: any item scored as incorrect for any one of the three was eliminated or replaced.

The second phase of test validation involved 10 sixth- and seventh-grade students (aged 11 to 13) at a private school in the San Juan metropolitan area at which all classes are given in English, except Spanish classes. All 10 students were considered to be bilingual by the faculty. They each took approximately 4 hours to complete the morphology and syntax tests in the two languages.

The results of one of the students on the English tests were eliminated from consideration, as were the results from another student on the Spanish tests: These two subjects were deemed by the investigator to be deficient in English and Spanish, respectively. The results of the remaining 9 sets of tests in the two languages were used in the following manner: Any test item answered incorrectly by more than two subjects was reconsidered; any item answered incorrectly by two subjects only, in which the two subjects made the same error, was also reconsidered. Reconsideration resulted in three outcomes: (1) The item was eliminated altogether, (2) the item was altered or replaced by a similar one, (3) a response previously considered to be incorrect was accepted as correct.

The test battery as thus modified was the one given to the aphasic subjects in this study and presented in the following section.

Thus the test battery was not normalized or standardized on any sort of normal or aphasic population (as is usually done for clinical tests of aphasia). Nonetheless, because all problematic items were eliminated or in some way ameliorated before the test was presented to the aphasics, one could assume (taking into account that human variability and fallibility being as they are, there is virtually *no* test to which a normal population will respond without *any* error) that virtually all errors were due to neuropathology. There is one (unfortunate) reservation that must be made to this statement: Because the test was validated with a group of sixth and seventh graders, errors made by patients with less than a sixth-grade education could conceivably be due to educational level, rather than pathology. (We had not anticipated there being aphasic subjects with so little formal education.) It seems unlikely, however, that this reservation would apply to tests taken in the listening–speaking modality combination.

THE ENGLISH TEST BATTERY

Acceptable correct responses are given in parenthesis. Other reasonable paraphrases and alternatives were accepted as well.

English Sentence Comprehension

Listening–Speaking

1. The woman brought him the bricks in a truck.
   a. Who received the bricks? (He did; the man; the boy)
   b. What did the woman do? (brought the bricks)
   c. Where were the bricks? (in a truck; in the truck)
2. The woman was served pork and beans by the man.
   a. Who received the pork and beans? (the woman)
   b. Who served the pork and beans? (the man)
   c. What did the woman serve? (nothing)
3. The boy's going to the movies without his girlfriend was a mistake.
   a. Where did the boy go? (to the movies)
   b. Where did the girl go? (nowhere, don't know)
   c. What was the mistake? (the boy's going to the movies without his girlfriend
4. The lady saw the picture with her friend.
   a. What did the lady see? (the picture)
   b. Who saw the picture? (the lady and her friend)
   c. What did the friend do? (saw the picture)
5. The husband liked the wife's leaving every morning.
   a. Who left every morning? (the wife)
   b. What did the husband do? (nothing; liked the wife's leaving)
   c. When did the wife leave? (every morning; in the morning)
6. The man who went to the store set fire to the woman's house.
   a. Where did the man go? (to the store)
   b. Who set fire to the house? (the man [who went to the store])
   c. Name two things the man did. (1. went to the store) (2. set fire to the (woman's) house)
7. The girl asked the man to fry the chicken that she plucked.
   a. Who plucked the chicken? (the girl)
   b. Who was asked to do something? (the man)
   c. What did the girl ask the man to do? (fry the chicken)
8. The policeman realized that the woman did not rob the bank.
   a. Who robbed the bank? (don't know; nobody; some one else)

b. What did the policeman realize? (that the woman did not rob the bank)

c. What did the woman do? (nothing; don't know)

Reading–Speaking

1. The teacher gave some cheese to the boy from the city.
   a. What happened to the cheese? (The teacher gave it to the boy from the city; It was given to the boy (from the city))
   b. Who got the cheese? (the boy [from the city])
   c. Where was the teacher from? (don't know)
2. The boy was chased around the block by the dog.
   a. What did the dog do? (chased the boy around the block)
   b. Where did the boy chase the dog? (He didn't; nowhere)
   c. Who was chased? (the boy)
3. That the doctor gave five dollars to the clerk surprised the girl.
   a. What did the doctor do? (gave five dollars [to the clerk])
   b. What happened to the girl? (she was surprised)
   c. What did the doctor give the girl? (nothing)
4. The father went to the party and the mother did too.
   a. Who went to the party? (The father and the mother)
   b. What did the mother do? (Went to the party)
   c. Where did the mother go? (To the party)
5. The policeman knew that the boy went to the game.
   a. Where did the boy go? (to the game)
   b. Who went to the game? (the boy)
   c. What did the policeman know? (that the boy went to the game)
6. The child who the woman looked at jumped down.
   a. Who jumped down? (the child [that the woman looked at])
   b. What did the woman do? (looked at the child [that jumped down])
   c. Who looked at the woman? (nobody)
7. The sergeant told the soldier to mop the floor that the cook messed up.
   a. What did the sergeant order? (that the floor be mopped; that the soldier mop the floor)
   b. Who received the order? (the soldier)
   c. What did the sergeant say that the cook did? (messed up the floor; nothing)

8. The waiter does not know that the cook is at home.
   a. Where is the cook? (at home)
   b. What does the waiter know? (don't know; nothing)
   c. Who knows that the cook is at home? (no one; don't know)

Listening–Writing

1. In the kitchen, the milkman showed the child a book.
   a. Who showed something? (the milkman)
   b. What did the child do? (nothing; looked at the book; don't know)
   c. Where did all this take place? (in the kitchen)
2. The soldier was pushed out the window by the firemen.
   a. What did the soldier do? (nothing; fell out the window)
   b. Who pushed somebody? (the fireman)
   c. Who did the soldier push? (nobody)
3. For the clerk to eat lunch at Joe's restaurant is a habit.
   a. Who eats at Joe's restaurant? (the clerk)
   b. Which meal of the day does the clerk usually eat at Joe's restaurant? (lunch)
   c. Where does the clerk usually eat lunch? (at Joe's restaurant)
4. The man fried eggs, and the woman, fish.
   a. Who fried fish? (the woman)
   b. What did the man do? (fried eggs)
   c. What did the woman do? (fried fish)
5. The farmer wanted for the girl to start grooming horses.
   a. What did the girl do? (nothing)
   b. What did the farmer want? (for the girl to start grooming horses)
   c. Whom did the farmer want to groom dogs? (nobody)
6. The baby tore the book which her father wrote.
   a. What did the baby do? (tore the book [which her father wrote])
   b. Who wrote the book? (the baby's father)
   c. What happened to the book? (the baby tore it; it got torn; it was torn)
7. The boy told the girl to stop lying on the bed he just made.
   a. Who made the bed? (the boy)
   b. What was the girl doing? (lying on the bed)
   c. What did the girl request? (nothing)

8. The maid could understand why the lady was not fired.
    a. What couldn't the maid understand? (nothing)
    b. Who was fired? (no one; don't know)
    c. What happened to the lady? (nothing)

Reading–Writing

1. The girl hit the ball to her grandfather on the beach.
    a. Who hit the ball? (the girl)
    b. What was done to the ball? (the girl hit it; the girl hit it to her grandfather; it was hit; it went to the girl's grandfather)
    c. Where was the grandfather? (on the beach)
2. The manager was sent home by the engineer.
    a. Where was the engineer sent? (nowhere)
    b. What did the engineer do? (sent home the manager)
    c. Who was sent home? (the manager)
3. Looking at the drunk makes the child ill.
    a. Who becomes ill? (the child)
    b. When does the child become ill? (when (s)he looks at the drunk; sentence doesn't say)
    c. What makes the child ill? (looking at the drunk)
4. The girl eats string beans because her mother wants her to.
    a. What does the girl's mother want? (for her to eat string beans)
    b. Who eats string beans? (the girl)
    c. What does the girl's mother eat? (don't know; doesn't say; nothing)
5. The employee enjoyed running around the block.
    a. Where did the employee run? (around the block)
    b. What did the employee enjoy? (running around the block)
    c. How did the employee feel about running around the block? (he/she enjoyed it)
6. The singer asked the actress about the record he heard.
    a. What did the actress do? (don't know; nothing)
    b. Who heard the record? (the singer)
    c. Who asked about the record? (the singer)
7. The father asked the mother not to leave her muddy boots on the kitchen floor.
    a. Who made the request? (the father)

b. What was the request? (for the mother not to leave her muddy boots on the kitchen floor)

c. Where does father want mother's muddy boots to be left? (don't know; doesn't say; someplace other than the kitchen floor)

8. The administration ordered the students to stop breaking windows.

a. Who ordered the students not to break windows? (the administration)

b. What did the students do? (broke windows)

c. What has the administration done? (ordered the students to stop breaking windows)

English Syntax Correction

Listening–Speaking

1. The man was hit by girl.
   (The man was hit by the girl.)
2. Fred gave the book at the man.
   (Fred gave the book to the man.)
3. The man's going to the movies was a mistake.
   (Correct)
4. Gives him eating pizza indigestion.
   (Eating pizza gives him indigestion.)
5. What the dancer ate?
   (What did the dancer eat?)
6. Drinking coffee gives insomnia him.
   (Drinking coffee gives him insomnia.)
7. Would have the girl been doing it?
   (Would the girl have been doing it?)
8. The actor went to New York and the actress did so too.
   (Correct)
9. She didn't went to school.
   (She didn't go to school.)

Reading–Speaking

1. Doctor Smith did not found the pencils.
   (Doctor Smith did not find the pencils.)
2. Should have been she learning?
   (She should have been learning.)
   (Should she have been learning?)

3. Who Mathilda kissed?
   (Who did Mathilda kiss?)
   (Who kissed Mathilda?)
4. It was a pity that the child missed the party.
   (Correct)
5. Bert made popcorn and so did Ken.
   (Correct)
6. Ann gave the bottle them.
   (Ann gave them the bottle.)
   (Ann gave the bottle to them.)
7. Locked Mary in the cell the jailer.
   (The jailer locked Mary in the cell.)
8. Philip borrowed $100 to the employee.
   (Philip borrowed $100 from the employee.)
   (Philip lent 100 to the employee.)
9. The council looked to mayor for guidance.
   (The council looked to the mayor for guidance.)

Listening–Writing

1. The mother was kissed by child.
   (The mother was kissed by the child.)
2. Martha received the gifts toward the man.
   (Martha received the gifts from the man.)
   (Martha received the gifts to the man.)
3. Makes him the car accident feel frightened.
   (The car accident makes him feel frightened)
   (Does the car accident make him feel frightened?)
4. Difficult situations makes nervous her.
   (Difficult situations make her nervous.)
5. Ruth cooked dinner and Peggy did too.
   (Correct)
6. For Jack to take the smaller part was peculiar.
   (Correct)
7. Where Billy went?
   (Where did Billy go?)
8. Can be John going away?
   (Can John be going away?)
9. Harry couldn't ate the whole cake.
   (Harry couln't eat the whole cake.)

Reading–Writing

1. Did he sang the song?
   (Did he sing the song?)
2. The horse ran away and the dog did so too.
   (Correct)
3. Would have eaten Mary the pie?
   (Would Mary have eaten the pie?)
4. Albert threw the ball her.
   (Albert threw her the ball.)
   (Albert threw the ball to her.)
5. What your sister did?
   (What did your sister do?)
6. Might be visiting relatives annoying?
   (Might visiting relatives be annoying?)
   (Visiting relatives might be annoying.)
7. Not to be able to go made Paul jealous.
   (Correct)
8. The man stole three thousand dollars to the bank.
   (The man stole three thousand dollars from the bank.)
9. The car was given to owner.
   (The car was given to the owner.)

English Verb Morphology

Listening–Speaking

1. He hides. Yesterday, he _____. He has _____.
   (hid, hidden)
2. He sleeps. Yesterday he _____. He has _____.
   (slept, slept)
3. They bring it. Yesterday they _____. They have _____.
   (brought it, brought it)
4. We go. Yesterday we _____. We have _____.
   (went, gone)
5. He has it. Yesterday he _____. He has _____.
   (had it, had it)
6. You like it. Yesterday you _____. You have _____.
   (liked it, liked it)

7. We laugh. Yesterday we _____. We have _____.
   (laughed, laughed)
8. She fears it. Yesterday she _____. She has _____.
   (feared it, feared it)

Reading–Speaking

1. I steal. Yesterday I _____. I have _____.
   stole, stolen)
2. We grow. Yesterday we _____. We have _____.
   (grew, grown)
3. You forgive him. Yesterday you _____. You have _____.
   (forgave him, forgiven him)
4. I make it. Yesterday I _____. I have _____.
   (made it, made it)
5. We speak. Yesterday I _____. We have _____.
   (spoke, spoken)
6. We envy her. Yesterday we _____. We have _____.
   (envied her, envied her)
7. They hate it. Yesterday they _____. They have _____.
   (hated it, hated it)
8. She notes it. Yesterday she _____. She has _____.
   (noted it, noted it)

Listening–Writing

1. She writes. Yesterday, she _____. She has _____.
   (wrote, written)
2. He takes it. Yesterday, he _____. He has _____.
   (took it, taken it)
3. I draw. Yesterday, I _____. I have _____.
   (drew, drawn)
4. We do it. Yesterday, we _____. We have _____.
   (did it, done it)
5. They mean to. Yesterday, they _____. They have _____.
   (meant to, meant to)
6. You reach it. Yesterday, you _____. You have _____.
   (reached it, reached it)
7. I miss him. Yesterday, I _____. I have _____.
   (missed him, missed him)

8. He revises it. Yesterday, he ____. He has ____.
(revised it, revised it)

Reading –Writing

1. She teaches. Yesterday, she ____. She has ____.
(taught, taught)
2. He comes. Yesterday, he ____. He has ____.
(came, come)
3. They eat. Yesterday, they ____. They have ____.
(ate, eaten)
4. She says it. Yesterday, she ____. She has ____.
(said it, said it)
5. He swears. Yesterday, he ____. He has ____.
(swore, sworn)
6. You allow it. Yesterday, you ____. You have ____.
(allowed it, allowed it)
7. I load it. Yesterday, I ____. I have ____.
(loaded it, loaded it)
8. He invades. Yesterday, he ____. He has ____.
(invaded, invaded)

English Plural Formation

Listening–Speaking

1. I see one boy. I see two ____. (boys)
2. I see one church. I see two ____. (churches)
3. I see one foot. I see two ____. (feet)
4. I see one woman. I see two ____. (women)
5. I see one wife. I see two ____. (wives)
6. I see one brick. I see two ____. (bricks)

Reading–Speaking

1. I see one cup. I see two ____. (cups)
2. I see one pill. I see two ____. (pills)
3. I see one child. I see two ____. (children)
4. I see one sheep. I see two ____. (sheep)

5. I see one judge. I see two ______. (judges)
6. I see one thief. I see two ______. (thieves)

Listening–Writing

1. I see one bus. I see two ______. (buses, busses)
2. I see one cat. I see two ______. (cats)
3. I see one bug. I see two ______. (bugs)
4. I see one ox. I see two ______. (oxen)
5. I see one man. I see two ______. (men)
6. I see one wolf. I see two ______. (wolves)

Reading–Writing

1. I see one glove. I see two ______. (gloves)
2. I see one witch. I see two ______. (witches)
3. I see one hat. I see two ______. (hats)
4. I see one mouse. I see two ______. (mice)
5. I see one knife. I see two ______. (knives)
6. I see one goose. I see two ______. (geese)

English Possessive and Third Person Singular Present Inflections

Listening–Speaking

1. This book belongs to the man.
   Whose book is it? (the man's)
2. This pen belongs to the boss.
   Whose pen is it? (the boss's)
3. Two girls pay. What does one girl do? (pays)
   (cue: Two girls pay. One girl ______.)
4. Two children fuss. What does one child do? (fusses)
   (cue: Two children fuss. One child ______.)

Reading–Speaking

1. This cap belongs to the chief.
   Whose cap is it? (the chief's)

2. This robe belongs to the judge.
   Whose robe is it? (the judge's)
3. Two ladies knit. One lady ______.
   (knits)
4. Two boys push. One boy ______.
   (pushes)

Listening–Writing

1. This stall belongs to the cow.
   Whose stall is it? (the cow's)
2. This cap belongs to the nurse.
   Whose cap is it? (the nurse's)
3. Two boys hide. What does one boy do? (hides)
   (cue: Two boys hide. One boy ______.)
4. Two planes crash. What does one plane do? (crashes)
   (cue: Two planes crash. One plane ______.)

Reading–Writing

1. This hat belongs to the woman.
   Whose hat is it? (the woman's)
2. This book belongs to the church.
   Whose book is it? (the church's)
3. Two girls sew. One girl ______. (sews)
4. Two friends kiss. One friend ______. (kisses)

THE SPANISH TEST BATTERY

Spanish Sentence Comprehension

Listening–Speaking

1. El hombre le trajo las medias en la bolsa a ella.
   a. ¿Quién recibió las medias? (ella)
   b. ¿Qué hizo el hombre? (le trajo las medias a ella)
   c. ¿Dónde estaban las medias? (en una (la) bolsa)
2. A la niña le fue dada una ración de arroz y habichuelas por el muchacho.
   a. ¿Quién recibió la ración de arroz y habichuelas?
      (la niña)

b. ¿Quién dio la ración de arroz y habichuelas?
(el muchacho)
c. ¿Qué dio la niña?
(nada)

3. La salida del hombre al campo sin su novia fue una sorpresa.
   a. ¿Qué hizo el hombre? (salió, fue al compo)
   b. ¿A dónde fue la novia del hombre? (a ningún sitio)
   c. ¿Cuál fue la sorpresa? (que el hombre no fuera con su novia al campo)
4. La joven escuchó el concierto con su abuela.
   a. ¿Qué eschuchó la joven? (el concierto)
   b. ¿Quién eschuchó el concierto? (la joven y su abuela)
   c. ¿Qué hizo la joven? (eschuchó el concierto)
5. El señor quería que su hija comiera cada tarde.
   a. ¿Qué quería la hija del señor? (nada, no sé)
   b. ¿Qué quería el señor? (que la hija comiera cada tarde)
   c. Para el señor, ¿cuándo debía comer la hija? (Cada tarde)
6. El muchacho que visitó el museo miró la tienda de la señora.
   a. ¿A dónde fue el muchacho? (al museo)
   b. ¿Quién miró la tienda? (el muchacho)
   c. ¿Qué dos cosas hizo el muchacho? (visitó el museo y miró la tienda)
7. La muchacha le pidió al carnicero que horneara el lechón que ella había matado.
   a. ¿Quién mató el lechón? (la muchacha)
   b. ¿Quién recibió la orden? (el carnicero)
   c. ¿Qué le pidió la muchacha al carnicero que hiciera? (que horneara el lechón)
8. La mamá se dio cuenta de que el hijo no chocó el carro.
   a. ¿Quién chocó el carro? (no se sabe; nadie)
   b. ¿De qué se dio cuenta la mamá? (de que el hijo no chocó el carro)
   c. ¿Qué hizo el hijo? (nada; no chocó el carro)

Reading–Speaking

1. El hombre en el pasillo le pidió el dinero a la empleada en el ascensor.
   a. ¿Qué pasó con el dinero? (no se sabe; se lo pidió a la empleada)
   b. ¿Quién tenía el dinero? (la empleada en el ascensor; no se sabe)
   c. ¿Dónde estaba el hombre? (en el pasillo)

2. El gato fue perseguido hacia la azotea por el lagartijo.
   a. ¿Qué hizo el lagartijo? (persiguió al gato; subió a la azotea)
   b. ¿Dónde persiguió el gato al lagartijo? (no lo hizo)
   c. ¿Quién fue perseguido? (el gato)
3. El que el payaso hubiera perdido su pantalón verde fue agradable para la nena.
   a. ¿Qué pasó con el payaso? (perdió el pantalón)
   b. ¿Cómo se sintió la nena? (contenta, feliz, agradada, etc.)
   c. ¿Qué encontró el payaso? (nada)
4. El sacerdote fue a la tienda y el abogado también lo hizo.
   a. ¿Quién fue a la tienda? (el sacerdote y el abogado)
   b. ¿Qué hizo el abogado? (fue a la tienda)
   c. ¿A dónde fue el abogado? (a la tienda)
5. El alumno supo que la profesora fue al baile.
   a. ¿A dónde fue la profesora? (al baile)
   b. ¿Quién fue al baile? (la profesora)
   c. ¿Qué supo el alumno? (que la profesora fue al baile)
6. La muchacha que el soldado empujó comió mantecado.
   a. ¿Quién comió mantecado? (la muchacha que el soldado empujó)
   b. ¿Qué hizo el soldado? (empujó a la muchacha)
   c. ¿Quién empujó al soldado? (nadie)
7. El gerente le dijo a la secretaria que corrigiera la carta que escribió el conserje.
   a. ¿Qué ordenó el gerente? (que la secretaria corrigiera la carta que escribió el conserje)
   b. ¿Quién escribió la carta? (el conserje)
   c. ¿Qué dijo el gerente que había hecho el conserje? (escribir la carta)
8. El policía evitó que el hombre se diera en la rodilla.
   a. ¿Dónde se dio el hombre? (en ningún sitio)
   b. ¿Quién evitó el golpe? (el policía)
   c. ¿Qué hizo el policía? (evitó que el hombre se diera en la rodilla)

Listening–Writing

1. La maestra le dio una botella de leche al cartero en el pasillo.
   a. ¿Quién dio algo? (la maestra)
   b. ¿Qué hizo el cartero? (nada o recibió la botella de leche)
   c. ¿Dónde ocurrió todo esto? (en el pasillo)

2. La criada fue sacada del cuarto por el cantinero.
   a. ¿Qué hizo la criada? (nada; salió del cuarto)
   b. ¿Quién saco a quién? (el cantinero sacó a la criada)
   c. ¿A quién sacó la criada? (a nadie)
3. El que el niño vaya a jugar a casa de la secretaria los viernes es una costumbre.
   a. ¿A dónde va el niño los viernes normalmente? (a casa de la secretaria)
   b. ¿Qué es lo que hace el niño en casa de la secretaria? (jugar)
   c. ¿Cuál es la costumbre que tiene el niño? (ir a jugar a casa de la secretaria los viernes)
4. El alto pintó casas y el bajo verjas.
   a. ¿Quién pintó casas? (el alto)
   b. ¿Qué pintó el bajo? (verjas)
   c. ¿Qué hizo el alto? (pintó casas)
5. El obrero quiso que el estudianto cogiera las herramientas.
   a. ¿Qué quiso el estudiante? (nada)
   b. ¿Qué quiso el obrero? (que el estudiante cogiera las herramientas)
   c. ¿Quién quiso el obrero que cogiera las herramientas? (el estudiante)
6. El atleta manchó el traje que compró su mamá.
   a. ¿Qué hizo el atleta? (manchó el traje)
   b. ¿Quién compró el traje? (la mamá del atleta)
   c. ¿Qué le pasó al traje? (fue manchado por el atleta; el atleta lo manchó)
7. La mujer le dijo al señor que dejara de pisar la grama que ella acababa de recortar.
   a. ¿Quién recortó la grama? (la mujer)
   b. ¿Qué estaba haciendo el hombre? (pisando la grama)
   c. ¿Qué pidió la mujer? (que el hombre dejara de pisar la grama)
8. El padre sabía por qué el niño no fue invitado.
   a. ¿Qué sabía el padre? (por qué el niño no fue invitado)
   b. ¿Quién fue invitado? (nadie; no se sabe)
   c. ¿Qué le pasó al niño? (no fue invitado)

Reading–Writing

1. El niño empujó el escritorio a la pared del cuarto de estudios.
   a. ¿Quién empujó el escritorio? (el niño)

   b. ¿Qué le pasó al escritorio? (fue empujado a la pared)
   c. ¿Dónde quedaba la pared? (en el cuarto de estudios)
2. La maestra fue empujada hacia el piso por el estudiante.
   a. ¿A dónde fue empujada la maestra? (hacia el piso)
   b. ¿Qué hizo el estudiante? (empujó a la maestra)
   c. ¿Quién fue empujado? (la maestra)
3. El comer la pizza del jefe pone enfermo al guardia.
   a. ¿Quién se enferma? (el guardia)
   b. ¿Cuándo es que el guardia se pone enfermo? (cuando come la pizza del jefe)
   c. ¿Qué es lo que enferma al jefe? (nada; no se sabe)
4. El muchacho arregla las camas porque su papá así se lo ordena.
   a. ¿Qué es lo que ordena el papá del muchacho? (que el muchacho arregle las camas)
   b. ¿Quién arregla las camas? (el muchacho; el hijo)
   c. Qué es lo que arregla el papá del muchacho? (nada)
5. A la nena le alegró ver la película en televisión.
   a. ¿Qué le alegró a la nena? (ver la película en televisión)
   b. ¿Dónde vió la nena la película? (en televisión)
   c. ¿Cómo se sintió la nena? (alegre)
6. El artista le habló a la maestra sobre la obra de teatro que él vio.
   a. ¿Qué hizo la maestra? (nada; no sabemos)
   b. ¿Quién vio la obra de teatro? (el artista)
   c. ¿Quién habló acerca de la obra de teatro? (el artista)
7. El esposo le dijo a su mujer que no pusiera el plato frío en el horno caliente.
   a. ¿Quién hizo la petición? (el esposo)
   b. ¿Cuál fue la petición? (que la esposa no pusiera el plato frío en el horno caliente)
   c. ¿Qué quería el esposo? (que la esposa no pusiera el plato frío en el horno caliente)
8. El entrenador les ha pedido a los jugadores que no tomen cerveza.
   a. ¿Quién les pidió a los jugadores que no tomen cerveza? (el entrenador)
   b. ¿Qué hicieron los jugadores? (nada)
   c. ¿Qué hizo el entrenador? (les pidió a los jugadores que no tomen cerveza)

Spanish Syntax Correction

Listening–Speaking

1. El hombre fue golpeado por niña.
   (El hombre fue golpeado por la niña.)
2. Juan le dio el libro hacia el hombre.
   (Juan le dio el libro al hombre.)
3. La ida de Pedro al cine fue un error.
   (correcta)
4. El muchacho tengo que ir a la escuela.
   (El muchacho tiene que ir a la escuela.)
5. ¿Qué tú comiendo?
   (¿Qué (tú) estás comiendo? o ¿Qué (tú) comes?)
6. Tomar café dale insomnio a la muchacha.
   (Tomar café le da insomnio a la muchacha.)
7. Isabel leyó una novela y Raquel lo hizo también.
   (está correcta)
8. No pudo levantó el baúl.
   (No pudo levantar el baúl.)
9. Nunca no vino a la escuela.
   (Nunca vino a la escuela.)

Reading–Speaking

1. El doctor Sánchez no debió encontró los papeles.
   (El doctor Sánchez no debió encontrar los papeles.)
2. ¿A quién Matilda basado?
   (¿A quién ha besado Matilda? o ¿A quién Matilda besó?)
3. Que nadie más lo supiera era improbable.
   (está correcta)
4. Ellos comieron plátanos nunca.
   (Ellos nunca comieron plátanos; ellos no comieron plátanos nunca.)
5. Humberto preparó pan y Nicolás también.
   (está correcta)
6. Le Ana dio la botella al compañero.
   (Ana le dio la botella al compañero.)
7. Espero que Juan va.
   (Espero que Juan vaya.)

8. Felipe le pidió prestado cien dólares sobre el empleado.
   (Felipe le pidió prestado cien dólares al empleado.)
9. El consejo le pidió ayuda a profesora.
   (El consejo le pidió ayuda a la profesora.)

Listening–Writing

1. La mamá fue besada por hijo.
   (La mamá fue besada por el hijo.)
2. Marta recibió regalos desde el hombre.
   (Marta recibió regalos del hombre.)
3. Deseó que cocería el arroz.
   (Deseó que cociera el arroz.)
4. Las situaciones difíciles ponen la pensativa.
   Las situaciones defíciles la ponen pensativa.)
5. Ruth cocinó la comida y Margarita lo hizo también.
   (está correcta)
6. Nadie no llegó a la fiesta.
   (Nadie llegó a la fiesta.)
7. Fue raro que José cogiera la parte más pequeña.
   (está correcta)
8. ¿Dónde Guillermo ido?
   (¿Dónde se ha ido Guillermo?)
9. Arturo no pudo comió el bizcocho entero.
   (Arturo no pudo comer el bizcocho entero.)

Reading–Writing

1. La mujer estaba parada el hombre.
   (La mujer estaba parada al lado del hombre.)
2. El había cantaba la canción. (El había cantado la canción; El cantaba la canción.)
3. El caballo se fue y el perro hizo lo mismo.
   (está correcta)
4. Eugenio lo haciendo había estado.
   (Eugenio lo había estado haciendo.)
5. ¿Cómo tú estando?
   (¿Cómo tú estas? o ¿Cómo estás tú?)
6. La niña mire el televisor.
   (La niña mira el televisor.)

7. No haber podido ir puso celoso a Pablo.
   (está correcta)
8. Gilberto sacó $3,000 al banco.
   Gilberto sacó $3,000 del banco.)
9. El carro fue prestado por dueño.
   (El carro fue prestado por su dueño o por el dueño.)

Spanish Verb Morphology

Listening–Speaking

1. Nosotros comemos; ella come; yo ____.
   (como)
2. El trabajaba; yo trabajaba; nostros ____.
   (trabajábamos)
3. Yo subí; ustedes subieron; él ____.
   (subió)
4. Yo hablaré; ella hablará; tú ____.
   (halarás)
5. Tú decidirías; nosotros decidiríamos; ellos ____.
   (decidirían)
6. El ha bebido; ella ha bebido; yo ____.
   (he bebido)
7. Yo brinco; tú brincas; nosotros ____.
   (brincamos)
8. Nosotros corrimos; yo corrí; tú ____.
   (corriste)
9. You tenía; ella tenía; ellos ____.
   (tenían)
10. Yo viviré; ellos vivirán; él ____.
    (vivirá)
11. Ustedes pueden; nosotros podemos; tú ____.
    (puedes)
12. Nosotros cupimos; él cupo; tú ____.
    (cupiste)
13. Ellos dirán; ustedes dirán; tú ____.
    (dirás)
14. Nosotros vendríamos; ustedes vendrían; yo ____.
    (vendría)

15. Yo he puesto; ellos han puesto; tú _____.
    (has puesto)

Reading–Speaking

1. Tú tomarías; ellos tomarían; yo _____.
   (tomaría)
2. Tú has oído; yo he oído; nosotros _____.
   (hemos oído)
3. Yo escribo; ella escribe; tú _____.
   (escribes)
4. El deseó; ella deseó; ellos _____.
   (desearon)
5. Ellos abrían; nosotros abríamos; yo _____.
   (abría)
6. Yo caería; ustedes caerían; tú _____.
   (caerías)
7. Yo he tocado; ellos han tocado; usted _____.
   (ha tocado)
8. El leerá; ellos leerán; nosotros _____.
   (leeremos)
9. Yo rompo; ustedes rompen; ella _____.
   (rompe)
10. Nosotros cerramos; ellas cerraron; yo _____.
    (cerré)
11. Yo apuesto; nosotros apostamos; usted _____.
    (apuesta)
12. Nosotros hicimos; él hizo; yo _____.
    (hice)
13. Yo iba; nosotros íbamos; tú _____.
    (ibas)
14. Tú sabrás; yo sabré; ellos _____.
    (sabrán)
15. Ellos habrían; usted habría; nosotros _____.
    (habríamos)

Listening–Writing

1. El acordaba; nosotros acordábamos; tú _____.
   (acordabas)

2. Tu andarías; ellos andarían; usted _____.
   (andaría)
3. Usted cosió; tú cosiste; nosotros _____.
   (cosimos)
4. Nosotros hemos sentido; tú has sentido; ellos _____.
   (han sentido)
5. Nosotros adquiriremos; ustedes adquirirán; yo _____.
   (adquiriré)
6. Ellos han hervido; yo he hervido; tú _____.
   (has hervido)
7. Nosotros saltamos; yo salto; ellos _____.
   (saltan)
8. Ustedes herirían; tú herirías; nosotros _____.
   (heriríamos)
9. Usted venderá; yo venderé; ellos _____.
   (venderán)
10. Yo detenía; nosotros deteníamos; él _____.
    (detenía)
11. El ha muerto; ella ha muerto; ellos _____.
    (han muerto)
12. El era; tú eras; nosotros _____.
    (éramos)
13. Nosotros hemos cubierto; ustedes han cubierto; ella _____.
    (ha cubierto)
14. Yo veía; nosotros veíamos; ustedes _____.
    (veían)
15. Nosotros valdremos; tú valdrás; él _____.
    (valdrá)

Reading–Writing

1. Ustedes descubren; ella descubre; yo _____.
   (descubro)
2. Nosotros describimos; yo describí; ellos _____.
   (describieron)
3. Ellos confesaban; nosotros confesábamos; yo _____.
   (confesaba)
4. Yo caminaré; tú caminarás; ustedes _____.
   (caminarán)

5. Nosotros entendíamos; tú entendías; él _____.
   (entendía)
6. Ustedes han cambiado; ella ha cambiado; nosotros _____.
   (hemos cambiado)
7. Yo complacería; tú complacerías; ellos _____.
   (complacerían)
8. Yo medía; usted medí; nosotros _____.
   (medíamos)
9. El ha dado; ellas han dado; yo _____.
   (he dado)
10. Ellos pensarán; tú pensarás; nosotros _____.
    (pensaremos)
11. Tú trajiste; él trajo; nosotros _____.
    (trajímos)
12. Nosotros estuvimos; tú estuviste; ellas _____.
    (estuvieron)
13. Nosotros colgamos; él cuelga; yo _____.
    (cuelgo)
14. Tú querrías; yo querría; ustedes _____.
    (querrían)
15. Yo caliento; nosotros calentamos; ellos _____.
    (calientan)

Spanish Number and Gender Agreement

Listening–Speaking

1. El cama bonito.
   (La cama bonita.)
2. Las problemas sencillas.
   (Los problemas sencillos.)
3. El silla ancho.
   (La silla ancha.)
4. Las edificios altas.
   (Los edificios altos.)
5. Los salón limpios.
   (Los salones limpios o El salón limpio.)
6. Las pared rotas.
   (Las paredes rotas o La pared rota.)

Reading–Speaking

1. Unos fotos viejos.
   (Unas fotos viejas.)
2. Los flores rojos.
   (Las flores rojas.)
3. Un mesa nuevo.
   (Una mesa nueva.)
4. Una teléfono blanca.
   (Un teléfono blanco.)
5. Unas calle estrechas.
   (Unas calles estrechas o Una calle estrecha.)
6. Los almacén vacíos.
   (El almacén vacío o Los almacenes vacíos.)

Listening–Writing

1. Una clima cálida.
   (un clima cálido.)
2. Un nota prolongado.
   (Una nota prolongada.)
3. Los plumas negros.
   (Las plumas negras.)
4. Las cielos bellas.
   (Los cielos bellos.)
5. Las persona viejas.
   (La persona vieja o Las personas viejas.)
6. Unos cajón sucios.
   (Un cajón sucio o Unos cajones sucios.)

Reading–Writing

1. Una sistema completada.
   (Un sistema completado.)
2. El gente sabio.
   (La gente sabia.)
3. Unos cortinas claros.
   (Unas cortinas claras.)
4. Unas techos pequeñas.
   (Unos techos pequeños.)

5. Unas mujer lindas.
   (Unas mujeres lindas o Una mujer linda.)
6. Los plato calientes.
   (El plato caliente o Los platos calientes.)

3 Procedures

GENERAL REMARKS

All tests were administered in one or more sessions of 1 to 4 hours with no patient's testing time extending beyond a 3-week period. Tests were administered to hospitalized patients at the subject's bedside, and to outpatients at the Clínica Externa de Patología del Habla (Speech Pathology Outpatient Clinic) at the Centro Médico de Puerto Rico (Puerto Rico Medical Center). All Spanish tests were administered completely in Spanish. All English tests were administered completely in English.

Before formal testing began, each subject was interviewed in Spanish. Bilinguals were interviewed in English as well. In addition, in many cases patients were administered informal nonstandardized tests in naming and following commands of varying complexity to determine whether a putative aphasic was indeed aphasic, as well as to check for gross auditory and visual impairment.

All stimuli for reading tasks were presented on 5 × 8 inch cards held horizontally. The *x*-height of lower case letters was ¼ in. and the height of capital letters was ½ in. Letters were spread horizontally at approximately three per inch. A space of one *x*-height was left between the descendings of the line above and the ascendings of the line below. Standard orthographic and printing conventions (roman type) were observed in the two languages. This format was intended to provide optimal legibility and to minimize the effects of visual field cuts. In the case of the deaf subject, all instructions were presented in writing.

For each subtest, after instructions as to the nature of the task were given, a demonstration item was provided to insure that the subject understood the task required. No test was administered to any patient who did not show mastery of the task by means of the demonstration item.

ADMINISTRATION OF THE INDIVIDUAL TESTS

Sentence Comprehension

For each of the four modality combinations in each of the two languages, there were eight content sentences presented. The subject was required to answer three questions about each content sentence. (See "Description of the Test Battery" in chapter 2 for details.) The administration procedures were identical for the two languages. They are presented here in English only, with statements made by the examiner for the Spanish tests given in brackets.

Listening–Speaking

Instructions

The examiner (E) says to the subject (S):

"I am going to say some sentences to you. I would like for you to answer some questions about the sentences. Do you understand? ("Yo le voy a decir algunas oraciones y quiero que usted me conteste ciertas preguntas sobre las mismas. ¿Entendió?") (In case of a negative response or no response, the examiner repeats instructions. If S gives a second negative response, E proceeds to demonstration item.) E proceeds to demonstration item.

Demonstration Item

E says to S:

"The dog is on the floor. Where is the dog?" ("El perro está en el piso. ¿Dónde está el perro?") and elicits an oral response by whatever means necessary. E will proceed with the test only if S shows evidence of understanding the task, e.g., if S answers the question in some way, or tries to. In no case should the time dedicated to the demonstration item and the learning of the task be allowed to exceed 1 minute.

Administration

E says each sentence twice at first and after waiting 10 seconds asks question *a*. If no response is emitted in 30 seconds, E asks question *a* one more time. E then says the sentence once again and waits 10 seconds before asking question *b*. If there is no immediate response, E waits 30 seconds again before repeating question *b* one more time. E does likewise with question *c*, saying the sentence once again and waiting 10 seconds before presenting the question, and waiting 30 seconds for a response before repeating question *c*.

Sample Items

The lady saw the picture with her friend. Who saw the picture?
El hombre le trajo las medias en la bolsa a ella. ¿Dónde estaban las medias?

Reading–Speaking

Instructions

E says the following to S:

"I am going to show you some sentences. I am going to show you some questions about the sentences and I want you to tell me the answer. Do you understand? ("Yo le voy a presentar algunas oraciones escritas y quiero que usted me conteste ciertas preguntas sobre las mismas. ¿Entendió?") (In case of a negative response or no response, E repeats instructions. In case of second negative response, E proceeds to the demonstration item.) E proceeds to demonstration item.

Demonstration Item

E places the card that says "The dog is on the floor" ("El perro está en el piso") on the table and and allows S to read it. He then places the card that says "Where is the dog?" beneath and says "Answer this question." (Entonces presenta la tarjeta con la pregunta "¿Dónde está el perro?" y sonsaca una respuesta oral del sujeto usando cualquier medio que sea necesario.) E will elicit an oral response by whatever means are necessary. E will proceed with the test only if S shows evidence of understanding the task, e.g., if S answers the question orally in some way or tries to. In no case should the time dedicated to the demonstration item and the learning of the task be allowed to exceed 2 minutes.

Administration

E places sentence card on table and allows time for S to read it. E then places question *a* beneath it and says "Answer this question" (Y dice que el S conteste la pregunta). When a response is emitted, or if no response is emitted after 30 seconds, E removes the card with question *a* and places question *b* beneath the sentence. E repeats the procedures for question *a* with questions *b* and *c*.

Sample Items

The boy was chased around the block by the dog. What did the boy do?
El alumno supo que la profesora fue al baile. ¿Quién fue al baile?

Listening–Writing

Instructions

E says to S:

"I'm going to say some sentences to you and ask you questions about them. I want you to write down the answer to the questions. Do you understand?" ("Yo le voy a decir algunas oraciones y quiero que usted me escriba contestaciones a algunas preguntas sobre las mismas. ¿Entendió?") (In case of a negative response or no response, E repeats instructions. If S gives a second negative response, E proceeds to demonstration item.) E proceeds to demonstration item.

Demonstration Item

E says to S:

"The dog is on the floor. Where is the dog? Write the answer." ("El perro está en el piso. ¿Dónde está el perro? Escriba la contestación.") E elicits a written response from S by whatever means are necessary. E will proceed with the test only if S shows evidence of understanding the task, e.g., if S writes the answer to the question or tries to. In no case should the time dedicated to the demonstration item and the learning of the task be allowed to exceed 3 minutes.

Administration

E says each sentence twice at first and after 10 seconds asks question *a*. If S does not begin to write within 30 seconds, E asks question *a* one more time. E says the sentence once again and waits 10 seconds before asking question *b*. If S does not begin to write within 30 seconds, E repeats question *b* one more time. E does likewise with question *c*, saying the sentence again and waiting 10 seconds before stating the question, and waiting 30 seconds for E to begin writing before repeating question *c*.

Sample Items

The man fried eggs, and the woman, fish. What did the woman do?
El atleta manchó el traje que compró su mamá. ¿Qué le pasó al traje?

Reading–Writing

Instructions

E says to S:

"I am going to show you some sentences. I am also going to show you some questions about the sentences. I want you to write down the answer to the questions. Do you understand?" ("Yo le voy a presentar algunas oraciones escritas. También le voy a presentar algunas preguntas sobre las mismas. Quiero que me escriba las contestaciones. ¿Entendió?'') (In case of a negative response or no response, E repeats instructions. If S gives a second negative response, E proceeds to demonstration item.) E proceeds to demonstration item.

Demonstration Item

E places the card that says ''The dog is on the floor'' (''El perro está en el piso'') on the table and allows S to read it. He then places the card that says ''Where is the dog?'' (¿Dónde está el perro?) beneath it and says ''Write the answer to this question'' (''Escriba la contestación a esta pregunta''). E will elicit a written response by whatever means necessary. E will proceed with the task only if S shows evidence of understanding the task, e.g., if he writes the answer to the question or tries to. In no case should the time dedicated to the demonstration item and the learning of the task be allowed to exceed 3 minutes.

Administration

E places sentence card on table and allows time for S to read it. E then places question *a* beneath it and tells S to write the answer to it. If S does not begin to write within 30 seconds, E removes the question card. E does likewise with question *b* and *c* allowing S 30 seconds to start his written response.

Sample Items

The singer asked the actress about the record he heard. Who heard the record?
El comer la pizza del jefe pone enfermo al guardia. ¿Quién se enferma?

Correction of Syntax

Each of the tests administered in each of the four modality combinations in the two languages consisted of 2 grammatically correct sentences and seven sentences with various types of syntactic errors (as discussed in ''Description of the Test Battery'' in chapter 2). As in the case of the Sentence Comprehension tests, the administration procedures were identical in the two languages. They are thus described herein in English only, with statements made by the examiner for the Spanish tests given in brackets (72 items).

Listening–Speaking

Instructions

E says to S:

''I am going to say some sentences. You will listen to each one and correct any that are grammatically wrong. Do you understand?'' (''Yo le voy a decir algunas oraciones. Usted va a escuchar cada oración y la va a corregir si hay algo incorrecto. ¿Entendió?") (In case of a negative response or no response, E repeats instructions. In case of a second negative response, E proceeds to the demonstration item.) E proceeds to demonstration item.

Demonstration Item

E says to S:

"They are a good time having" ("Espero que ella viene") and elicits an oral response by whatever means necessary. E will proceed with the test only if S shows evidence of understanding the task, e.g., S corrects the sentence or tries to.

In no case should the time dedicated to the demonstration item and the learning of the task be allowed to exceed 3 minutes.

Administration

E says each sentence twice. If no response is emitted in 30 seconds, or if S requests repetition, E will present the sentence one more time.

Sample Items

What the dancer ate? No pudo levantó el baúl.

Reading–Speaking

Instructions

E says to S:

"I am going to show you some written sentences. I want you to look at each one and tell me if it is grammatically correct or not. If the sentence is not correct, I want you to tell me how it should be. Do you understand?" ("Yo le voy a presentar algunas oraciones escritas. Usted va a mirar cada oración y va a decir si hay algo incorrecto. Si la oración no está correcta, quiero que me diga como se debe decir. ¿Entendió?") (In case of a negative response or no response, E repeats instructions. In case of a second negative response, E proceeds to the demonstration item.) E proceeds to demonstration item.

Demonstration Item

E presents the card to S that says "They are a good time having" ("Espero que ella viene") and elicits an oral response by whatever means necessary. E proceeds with the test only if S shows evidence of understanding the task, e.g., if S orally corrects the sentence or tries to. In no case should the time dedicated to the demonstration item and the learning of the task be allowed to exceed 3 minutes.

Administration

E places sentence card on table. If S does not begin to respond within 30 seconds, E proceeds to the next item. S will be allowed no more than 2 minutes to respond *once he begins to respond.*

Sample Items

Ann gave the bottle them. ¿A quién Matilda besado?

Listening–Writing

Instructions

E says to S:

"I am going to say some sentences. You will listen to each one and correct any that are grammatically wrong, *in writing.* Do you understand?" ("Yo le voy a decir algunas oraciones. Usted va a escuchar cada oración y la va a corregir por escrito si hay algo incorrecto. ¿Entendió?") (In case of a negative response or no response, E repeats instructions. In case of a second negative response, E proceeds to the demonstration item.) E proceeds to demonstration item.

Demonstration Item

E says to S:

"They are a good time having" ("Espero que ella viene") and elicits a written response by whatever means necessary. E will proceed with test only if S shows evidence of understanding the task, e.g., if S corrects the sentence in writing or tries to. In no case should the time dedicated to the demonstration item and the learning of the task be allowed to exceed 3 minutes.

Administration

E says each sentence twice. If S does not begin to write within 30 seconds, or if S requests repetition, E will present the sentence one more time.

Sample Items

Can be John going away? Deseó que cocería el arroz.

Reading–Writing

Instructions

E says to S:

"I am going to show you some written sentences. I want you to look at each one and correct any that are grammatically wrong, *in writing.* Do you understand?'' (''Yo le voy a presentar algunas oraciones escritas. Usted va a leer cada oración y la va a corregir por escrito si hay algo incorrecto. ¿Entendió?'') (In case of a negative response or no response, E repeats instructions. In case of a second negative response, E proceeds to the demonstration item.) E proceeds to the demonstration item.

Demonstration Item

E presents the card to S that says ''They are a good time having'' (''Espero que ella viene'') and elicits a written response by whatever means necessary. E will proceed with the test only if S shows evidence of understanding the task, e.g., if S corrects the sentence in writing, or tries to. In no case should the time dedicated to the demonstration item and the learning of the task be allowed to exceed 3 minutes.

Administration

E places sentence card on table. If S does not begin to respond within 30 seconds, E proceeds to the next item.

Sample Items

The man stole three thousand dollards to the bank. La niña mire el televisor.

English Verb Morphology

For each of the four modality combinations, there were eight items, which were English verbs presented in a present-tense context. For each item, the subject was to respond with a past tense and a past participle. Thus, there were a maximum total of 64 responses to this test. (See ''Description of the Test Battery'' in chapter 2 for details.)

Listening–Speaking

Instructions

E says to S:

''I am going to tell you about people doing different things at different times. I will say the first one and you complete the next two. For example: If I say 'He runs, yesterday', then you say 'ran'. Do you understand?'' (In case of a negative response or no response, E repeats instructions. If S gives a second negative response, E proceeds to the demonstration item.) E proceeds to demonstration item.

Demonstration Item

E says:

"You run, yesterday you ____," and elicits an oral response from S by whatever means necessary. He then says "you have ____" and elicits an oral response to this as well. E will proceed with the test only if S shows evidence of understanding the task, e.g., if the subject utters some form of the presented verb (*run*) or tries to. In no case should the time dedicated to the demonstration item and the leaning of the task be allowed to exceed 7 minutes.

Administration

E will attempt to elicit each response once. If no response is emitted in 10 seconds, E will try one more time.

Sample Item

We go. Yesterday, we ____. We have ____.

Reading–Speaking

Instructions

E says to S:

"I am going to show you some sentences about people doing different things at different times. The first one will be complete and the next two will have two blank spaces. Your task will be to tell me what word belongs in the blank." E shows S the written sentences "He runs. Yesterday he ____. He has ____." and says, "He runs, yesterday he ran" (pointing at first blank while saying *ran*), "He has run" (pointing at second blank while saying *run*), and then "Do you understand?" (In case of a negative response or no response, E repeats instructions, including illustration. If S gives a second negative response, E proceeds to demonstration item.) E proceeds to demonstration item.

Demonstration Item

E shows S the sentences "He runs. Yesterday, he ____." and elicits an oral response by whatever means are necessary. E then shows S the sentence "He has ____." and elicits an oral response to this as well. E will proceed with the test only if S shows evidence of understanding the task, e.g., if S utters some form of the presented verb (*run*) or tries to. In no case should the time dedicated to the demonstration item and the learning of the task exceed 7 minutes.

Administration

E will attempt to elicit each response once. If no response is emitted in 10 seconds, E will try one more time.

Sample Item

I steal. Yesterday, I _____. I have _____.

Listening–Writing

Instructions

E says to S:

"I am going to tell you about people doing different things at different times. I will say the first one and you complete the next two *in writing*. For example, if I say 'He runs. Yesterday he _____,'' then you write "ran." Do you understand?'' (In case of a negative response or no response, E repeats instructions. If S gives a second negative response, E proceeds to the demonstration item.) E proceeds to the demonstration item.

Demonstration Item

E says:

"You run. Yesterday you _____,'' and elicits a written response from S by whatever means necessary. E then says "you have'' and elicits a written response to this as well. E will proceed with the test only if S shows evidence of understanding the task, e.g., if S writes some form of the presented verb (*run*) or tries to. In no case should the time dedicated to the demonstration item and the learning of the task exceed 7 minutes.

Administration

E will attempt to elicit each response once. If S does not begin to write within 10 seconds, E will try one more time.

Sample Item

You reach it. Yesterday, you _____. You have _____.

Reading–Writing

Instructions

E tells S:

"I am going to show you some sentences about people doing different things at different times. The first one will be complete and the next two will have a blank space. Your task will be to write the word which belongs in the blank space. Do you understand?'' (In case of a negative response or no response, E proceeds to demonstration item.) E proceeds to demonstration item.

Demonstration Item

E shows S the sentences "He runs. Yesterday, he ____." and elicits a written response by whatever means are necessary. E then shows S the sentence "He has ____." and elicits a written response to this as well. E will proceed with the test only if S shows evidence of understanding the task, e.g., if S writes some form of the presented verb (*run*) or tries to. In no case should the time dedicated to the demonstration item and the learning of the task exceed 7 minutes.

Administration

E will attempt to elicit each response once. If S does not begin to write in 10 seconds, E will try one more time.

Sample Item

She teaches. Yesterday, she ____. She has ____.

English Plural Formation

In each of the four modalities, there were 6 nouns that the patient was requested to pluralize (24 items). For details, see "Description of the Test Battery" in chapter 2.

Listening–Speaking

Instructions

E says to S:

"I am going to tell you about some things that I see. If I tell you that I see *one* of something, I want you to complete a sentence about *two* of something. For example, if I say 'I see one bench' you would say 'I see two benches'. Do you understand?" (In case of a negative response or no response, E repeats instructions. If S gives a second negative response, E proceeds to the demonstration item.) E proceeds to demonstration item.

Demonstration Item

E says, "I see one bench; I see two ____," and elicits an oral response from S by whatever means are necessary. E will proceed with the test only if S shows evidence of understanding the task, e.g., if S utters some form of the noun in question (i.e., "bench") or tries to. In no case should the time dedicated to the demonstration item be allowed to exceed 3 minutes.

Administration

E will attempt to elicit each response once. If no response is emitted within 10 seconds, E will try one more time.

Sample Item

I see one foot. I see two _____.

Reading–Speaking

Instructions

E says to S:

"I am going to show you some sentences about things that I see. If the sentence says that I see *one* of something, I want you to complete the next sentence about *two* of something. For example (E presents the demonstration item), this sentence says "I see one bench." The next one says 'I see two' so you would say 'benches.' Do you understand?" (In case of a negative response or no response, E repeats instructions. If S gives a second negative response, E proceeds to demonstration item.) E proceeds to demonstration item.

Demonstration Item

E shows S the demonstration item, "I see one bench. I see two _____." and elicits an oral response by whatever means are necessary. E will proceed with test only if S shows evidence of understanding the task, e.g., if S utters some form of the noun in question (i.e., "bench") or tries to. In no case should the time dedicated to the demonstration item be allowed to exceed 3 minutes.

Administration

E will attempt to elicit each response once. If no response is emitted within 10 seconds, E will try one more time.

Sample Item

I see one sheep. I see two _____.

Listening–Writing

Instructions

"I am going to tell you about some things that I see. If I tell you that I see *one* of something, I want you to complete the next sentence about *two* of something, *in writing*. For example, if I say "I see one bench; I see two," you would write "benches." Do you understand?" (In case of a negative response or no response, E repeats instructions. If S gives a second negative response, E proceeds to the demonstration item.) E proceeds to demonstration item.

Demonstration Item

E says, "I see one bench; I see two _____," and elicits a written response from S by whatever means are necessary. E will proceed with the test only if S shows evidence of understanding the task, e.g., If S writes some form of the noun in question (i.e., 'bench') or tries to. In no case should the time dedicated to the demonstration item be allowed to exceed 3 minutes.

Administration

E will attempt to elicit each response once. If S does not begin to write within 10 seconds, E will try one more time.

Sample Item

I see one cat. I see two _____.

Reading–Writing

Instructions

E says to S:

"I am going to show you some sentences about things that I see. If the sentence says that I see *one* of something, I want you to complete the next sentence about *two* of something, *in writing*. For example (E presents the demonstration item), this sentence says 'I see one bench.' The next one says 'I see two' so you would write 'benches.' Do you understand?" (In case of a negative response or no response, E repeats instructions. If S gives a second negative response, E proceeds to demonstration item.) E proceeds to demonstration item.

Demonstration Item

E shows S the demonstration items "I see one bench. I see two _____." and elicits a written response by whatever means are necessary. E will proceed with the test only if S shows evidence of understanding the task, e.g., if S writes some form of the noun in question (i.e., 'bench') or tries to. In no case should the time dedicated to the demonstration item be allowed to exceed 3 minutes.

Administration

E will attempt to elicit each response once. If S does not begin to write within 10 seconds, E will try one more time.

Sample Item

I see one witch. I see two _____.

English Possessives and Third Person Singular Present

In each modality combination, there were two items requiring response with possessive inflection and two requiring response with third person singular present inflection. These two tasks were presented in a single test in the speaking modality and as two tests in the writing modality. For details, see "Description of the Test Battery" in chapter 2.

Listening–Speaking

Instructions

E says to S:

"I am going to ask you some questions about things that I tell you about and I want you to answer them. Do you understand?" (In case of a negative response or no response, E repeats instructions. If S gives a second negative response, E proceeds to demonstration item.) E proceeds to demonstration item.

Demonstration Item

E says: "This chair belongs to the teacher. Whose chair is it?" and elicits an oral response from S by whatever means are necessary. E will proceed with test only if S shows evidence of understanding the task, e.g., if S utters the possessive form of the noun phrase in question (i.e., "the teacher's") or tries to. In no case should the time dedicated to the demonstration item be allowed to exceed 5 minutes.

Administration

For items 1 and 2 (Possessives): E will attempt to elicit each response once. If no response is emitted within 10 seconds, E will try one more time.

For items 3 and 4 (Third Person Singular Present): E will make the statement and ask the question. If no response is emitted within 10 seconds, E will ask the question one more time. If an uninflected verb form is emitted, E will elicit the inflected form by saying the subject noun phrase of a full-sentence correct response, e.g., "Two men fight. What does one man do?" If S says "fight," E cues with "Two men fight. One man _____".

Sample Items

This book belongs to the man. Whose book is it?
Two children fuss. What does one child do?

Reading–Speaking (Possessives)

Instructions

E says to S:

I am going to show you some sentences and questions about them. I want you to answer the questions. Do you understand?'' (In case of a negative response or no response, E repeats instructions. If S gives a second negative response, E proceeds to the Demonstration Item.) E proceeds to the Demonstration Item.

Demonstration Item

E shows S the sentences:

''This chair belongs to the teacher. Whose chair is it?'' and elicits an oral response from S by whatever means are necessary. E will proceed with test only if S shows evidence of understanding the task, e.g., if S utters the possessive form of the noun phrase in question (i.e., ''the teacher's'') or tries to. In no case should the time dedicated to the demonstration item be allowed to exceed 5 minutes.

Administration

E will attempt to elicit each response once. If no response is emitted in 10 seconds, E will try one more time.

Sample Item

This robe belongs to the judge. Whose robe is it?

Reading–Speaking (Third Person Singular Present)

Instructions

E says to S:

''I am going to show you some sentences and I want you to fill in the blank with the correct word. For example in these two sentences (E shows S demonstration item) 'Two dogs eat. One dog' you would fill in the blank with the word 'eats.' Do you understnad?'' (In case of a negative response or no response, E proceeds for demonstration item.) E proceeds to demonstration item.

Demonstration Item

E shows S the item:

'Two dogs eat. One dog ______'' and elicits an oral response from S by whatever means are necessary. E will proceed with test only if S shows evidence of understanding the task, i.e., if S utters the correct form of the verb in question (i.e., ''eats'') or tries to. In no case should the time dedicated to the demonstration item be allowed to exceed 5 minutes.

Administration

E will attempt to elicit each response once. If no response is emitted in 10 seconds, E will try one more time.

Sample Item

Two ladies knit. One lady ______.

Listening–Writing

Instructions

E says to S:

''I am going to ask you some questions about things that I tell you about and I want you to answer them *in writing*. Do you understand?'' (In case of a negative response or no response, E repeats instructions. In case of a second negative response, E proceeds to demonstration item.) E proceeds to demonstration item.

Demonstration Item

E says ''This chair belongs to the teacher. Whose chair is it?'' and elicits a written response from S by whatever means are necessary. E will proceed with the test only if S shows evidence of understanding the task, i.e., if S writes the possessive form of the noun phrase in question (''the teacher's'') or tries to. In no case should the time dedicated to the demonstration item be allowed to exceed 5 minutes.

Administration

For items 1 and 2, E will attempt to elicit each response once. If S does not begin to write within 10 seconds, E will try one more time.

For items 3 and 4, E will make the statement and ask the question. If S does not begin to write within 10 seconds, E will repeat the item one more time. If S writes an uninflected verb form, E will elicit the inflected form by saying the subject noun phrase of a full-sentence correct response, e.g., "Two men fight. What does one man do?" If S writes "fight," E cues with "Two men fight. One man ______."

Sample Items

This stall belongs to the cow. Whose stall is it?
Two boys hide. What does one boy do?

Reading–Writing (Possessives)

Instructions

E says to S:

"I am going to show you some sentences and questions about them. I want you to write the answers to the questions. Do you understand?" (In case of a negative response or no response, E proceeds to demonstration item.) E proceeds to demonstration item.

Demonstration Item

E shows S the sentences:

"This chair belongs to the teacher. Whose chair is it?" and elicits a written response by whatever means are necessary. E will proceed with the test only if S shows evidence of understanding the task, i.e., if S writes the possessive form of the noun phrase in question (i.e., "the teacher's") or tries to. In no case should the time dedicated to the demonstration item be allowed to exceed 5 minutes.

Administration

E will attempt to elicit each response once. If S does not begin to write within 10 seconds, E will try one more time.

Sample Item

This hat belongs to the woman. Whose hat is it?

Reading–Writing (Third Person Singular Present)

Instructions

E says to S:

"I am going to show you some sentences and I want you to write the word that correctly fills the blank. For example, in these first sentences (E shows S the demonstration item) 'Two dogs eat. One dog, you would fill in the blank with the word 'eats.' Do you understand?'' (In case of a negative response or no response, E proceeds to demonstration item.) E proceeds to demonstration item.

Demonstration Item

E shows S the item:

''Two dogs eat. One dog ______'' and elicits a written response from S by whatever means are necessary. E will proceed with the test only if S shows evidence of understanding the task, i.e., if S writes the correct form of the verb in question (i.e., ''eats'') or tries to. In no case should the time dedicated to the demonstration item exceed 5 minutes.

Administration

E will attempt to elicit each response once. If S does not begin to write within 10 seconds, E will try one more time.

Sample Item

Two friends kiss. One friend ______.

Spanish Verb Morphology

For each modality, there were 15 items in which the subject was required to complete a verbal paradigm (60 items in total). The following examiner protocols are translated from the original Spanish. The statements made by the examiner are given in Spanish with English translation.

Listening–Speaking

Instructions

E says the following to S:

''Voy a hablarle de personas que hacen varias cosas. Le diré las primeras dos y usted completa la tercera. Por ejemplo, si yo le digo, 'El habla, yo hablo, ustedes ______,' entonces usted dice *hablan*. ¿Entendió?'' (''I am going to speak to you about persons who do various things. I will say the first two and you will complete the third. For example, if I say 'He speaks, I speak, you [plural] ______,' then you say *speak*. Do you understand?'') (If the S gives a negative response or does not respond, the instructions are repeated; if the S gives a negative response again, the E proceeds to demonstrate the task with the demonstration item.) E proceeds to the demonstration item.

Demonstration Item

The E says: "Yo corto, tú cortas, ellos ______" ("I cut (present), you (singular familiar) cut (present), they ______.") and elicits a response from the S, using whatever means may be necessary. The E continues with the test only if the S gives evidence of understanding the task (for example, if the S attempts or achieves completion of the phrase). The time dedicated to the demonstration item and the learning of the task should not be allowed to exceed 5 minutes.

Administration

E says each stimulus one time. If a response is not given in 10 seconds, the E will say the stimulus only one more time.

Sample Item

Nosotros corrimos; yo corrí; tú ______.

Reading–Speaking

Instructions

The E says the following to the S:

"Voy a presentarle material escrito sobre personas que hacen varias cosas. Le presentaré las primeras dos y usted completa la tercera. ¿Entendió?" ("I am going to present to you written material about persons that do various things. I will present the first two to you and you complete the third. Do you understand?") (If the subject gives a negative response or does not respond, the instructions are repeated; if [the subject] gives a negative response again, the E proceeds to demonstrate the task with the demonstration item.) E proceeds to the demonstration item.

Demonstration Item

The E presents the phrases: "Yo canto, tú cantas, ellos ______" ("I sing, you [singular familiar] sing, they ______") and elicits a response from the S using whatever means may be necessary.

The E continues with the test only if the S gives evidence of understanding the task (e.g., the subject attempts or achieves completion of the phrase). The time dedicated to the demonstration item and the learning of the task should not be allowed to exceed 5 minutes.

Administration

E says each stimulus one time. If the S does not give a response in 10 seconds, the E will say the stimulus only one more time.

Sample Item

Tú tomarías; ellas tomarían; yo ____.

Listening–Writing

Instructions

The E says the following to the S:

"Voy a hablarle de personas que hacen varias cosas. Le diré las primeras dos y usted escribe y completa la tercera. ¿Entendió?" ("I am going to speak to you about people who do various things. I will tell you the first two and you write and complete the third. Do you understand?") (If the S gives a negative response or does not respond, the instructions are repeated; if the S gives a negative response again, the E proceeds to demonstrate the task with the demonstration item.) The E proceeds to the demonstration item.

Demonstration Item

The E says: "Yo salgo, él sale, tú ____" ("I go out, he goes out, you (singular familiar) ____") and elicits a response from the S using whatever means may be necessary. The E continues with the test only if the S gives evidence of understanding the task (e.g., the S attempts or achieves completion of the phrase in writing.) The time dedicated to the demonstration item and learning of the task should not be allowed to exceed 5 minutes.

Administration

The E says each stimulus one time. If the S does not begin to answer in 10 seconds, the E says the stimulus only one more time.

Sample Item

Usted venderá; yo venderé; ellos ____.

Reading–Writing

Instructions

The E says the following to the S:

"Voy a presentarle material escrito sobre personas que hacen varias cosas. Leerá las primeras dos y usted escribe y completa la tercera. ¿Entendió?" ("I am going to present written material to you about persons who do various things. You will read the first two and you write and complete the third. Do you understand?") (If the S gives a negative response or does not respond, the instructions are repeated; if the S gives a negative response again, the E proceeds to demonstrate the task with the demonstration item.) The E proceeds to the demonstration item.

Demonstration Item

The E presents the following:

"Yo salgo, él sale, tú ______" ("I go out, he goes out, you [singular familiar] ______) and elicits a response from the S using whatever means may be necessary. The E continues with the test only if the S shows evidence of understanding (e.g., that the S attempts or achieves completion of the phrase in writing). The time dedicated to the demonstration item and learning of the task should not be allowed to exceed 5 minutes.

Administration

The E presents each stimulus one time. If the S does not begin to respond in 10 seconds, the E presents the stimulus one more time.

Sample Item

Nosotros colgamos; él cuelga; yo ______.

Correction of Spanish Number and Gender Agreement

These tests contain 6 items in each of the four modality combinations. Each item requires the subject to correct both a determiner and an adjective with respect to either gender or number. There are thus a total of 48 responses to the tests. The following examiner protocols are translated from Spanish. Examiner statements are given in Spanish with English translation.

Listening–Speaking

Instructions

The E says the following to the S:

"Le voy a decir algunas frases. Usted va a corregirlas si están incorrectas. ¿Entendió?" ("I am going to say some phrases to you. You are going to correct them if they are incorrect. Do you understand?") (If the subject gives a negative response or does not respond, the instructions are repeated; if the subject gives a negative response again, the E proceeds to demonstrate the task with the demonstration item.) The E proceeds to the demonstration item.

Demonstration Item

The E says:

" 'El lápiz larga.' ¿Cree usted que esta frase esté correcta? No lo está. Hágala correcta." ('The [masculine] long [feminine] pencil.' ["pencil" is a feminine noun.] Do you think that this phrase is correct? It isn't. Make it correct.) The E then elicits an oral response from the S using whatever means may be necessary. The E continues with the test only if the S gives evidence of understanding the task (e.g., the S tries to correct or succeeds in correcting the phrase). The time dedicated to the demonstration item and learning of the task should not be allowed to exceed 5 minutes.

Administration

The E says each stimulus once. If no response is given in 10 seconds, the E says the stimulus only one more time.

Sample Item

El silla ancho

Reading–Speaking

Instructions

The E says the following to the S:

"Le voy a presentar unas frases escritas. Usted va a corregirlas si están incorrectas. ¿Entendió?" ("I am going to present some written phrases to you. You are going to correct them if they are incorrect. Do you understand?") (If the S gives a negative response or does not respond, the instructions are repeated; if the S gives a negative response again, the E proceeds to demonstrate the task with the demonstration item.) The E proceeds to the demonstration item.

Demonstration Item

The E presents the phrase "El gato linda" ("The [masculine] pretty [feminine] cat [masculine]") and says "¿Cree usted que esta frase esté correcta? No lo está. Hágala correcta." ("Do you think that this phrase is correct? It isn't. Make it correct.") and elicits an oral response using whatever means may be necessary. The E continues with the test only if the S gives evidence of understanding the task (e.g., the subject tries to correct or succeeds in correcting the phrase). The time dedicated to the demonstration item and learning of the task should not be allowed to exceed 5 minutes.

Administration

The E presents each stimulus once. If no response is given in 10 seconds the E presents the stimulus one more time only.

Sample Item

Los almacén vacíos.

Listening–Writing

Instructions

The E says the following to the S:

"Le voy a decir algunas frases. Usted va a corregirlas por escrito si están incorrectas. ¿Entendió?" ("I am going to say some phrases to you. You are going to correct them in writing if they are incorrect. Do you understand?") (If the subject gives a negative response or does not respond, the instructions are repeated; if the subject gives a negative response again, the E proceeds to demonstrate the task with the demonstration item.)

Demonstration Item

The E says: " 'La lápiz larga' " ('The [feminine] long [feminine] pencil' ['Pencil' is a masculine noun.]) "¿Cree usted que esta frase esté correcta? No lo está. Hágala correcta." ("Do you think that this phrase is correct? It isn't. Make it correct.") and elicits a written response from the S using whatever means may be necessary. The E continues with the test only if the S gives evidence of understanding the task (e.g., the subject tries to correct or succeeds in correcting the phrase). The time dedicated to the demonstration item and learning of the task should not be allowed to exceed 5 minutes.

Administration

The E says each stimulus one time. If the S does not begin to answer in 10 seconds, the E says the stimulus only one more time.

Sample Item

Una clima cálida.

Reading–Writing

Instructions

The E says the following to the S:

"Le voy a presentar unas frases escritas. Usted va a corregirlas por escrito si están incorrectas. ¿Entendió?" ("I am going to present to you some written phrases. You are going to correct them in writing if they are incorrect. Do you understand?") (If the S gives a negative response or does not respond, the instructions are repeated; if the S gives a negative response again, the E proceeds to demonstrate the task with the demonstration item.) The E proceeds to the demonstration item.

Demonstration Item

The E presents the written phrase "La barco pequeña" ("The [feminine] little [feminine] boat" ["Boat" is a masculine noun.]) and says, "¿Cree usted que esta frase esté correcta? No lo está. Escríbala correctamente." ("Do you think that this phrase is correct? It isn't. Write it correctly.") and elicits a response from the S using whatever means may be necessary. The E continues with the test only if the S gives evidence of understanding the task (e.g., the S attempts to correct or succeeds in correcting the phrase in writing). The time dedicated to the demonstration item and learning of the task should not be allowed to exceed 5 minutes.

Administration

The E presents each stimulus once. If the S does not begin to write in 10 seconds, the E presents the stimulus one more time only.

Sample Item

Unas techos pequeñas.

4 Subjects

The aphasic patients used as subjects in this study were not *selected* in the usual sense of the term; they were not chosen from a population. In fact, every suitable subject in the entire population available was used. From September 1981 until June 1983, weekly rounds were made of the Hospital Municipal, the University District Hospital, the Casa de Salud, and the Clínica Externa de Neurología at the Centro Médico de Puerto Rico (CMPR). Envelopes containing blank referral forms were placed at critical locations in the various hospital units so that doctors and nurses could notify the investigator and his assistants of the existence of the aphasic patients. In addition, aphasics from outside the Centro Médico were referred to the Clínica Externa de Patología del Habla (Speech Pathology Outpatient Clinic) from a variety of sources. Administration of the test battery was attempted with every aphasic encountered in these ways during the period stated. Of more than 100 patients interviewed (of whom a number were eliminated who turned out not to be aphasic), 21 were able to pass the demonstration item on at least one subtest of the test battery. These 21 aphasics are the subjects of this study.

The patients, 15 men and 6 women, ranged in age from 18 to 74 with a median of 48. They had from 2 to 20 years of formal education, with a median of 10. They had been aphasic from 1 to 160 weeks at the time testing began (with a median of 15 weeks), with etiologies of CVA, trauma, neoplasm, and infection, with lesions localized in the left frontal, temporal, parietal, and occipital lobes and right frontal lobe, as well as subcortically. Based on residential and educational histories, as well as prepathologic evaluations by the patients themselves (whenever possible) and family members, the subjects were divided into three groups with respect to level of bilingualism:

1. Monolingual Hispanophones (9 subjects). These patients had never

learned more than a few words or sentences in English and had never had occasion to use the language.

2. Spanish Dominant (7 subjects). These patients were native speakers of Spanish who had used English on a regular basis prior to the onset of neuropathology, but who had never acquired the same facility in English as they had (had) in Spanish.
3. Balanced Bilinguals (5 subjects). These were patients for whom there was sufficient reason to believe that they had had equal prepathologic abilities in English and Spanish. It is possible that one or two may have slightly preferred English.

The following case descriptions each end with a summary of the results that the subject obtained on each subtest (s)he took. Patients did not take certain subtests for a variety of reasons:

1. The subject was a monolingual hispanophone and could therefore not take any test in English.
2. The subject was unable to pass the demonstration item on one or more tests. Failure to demonstrate understanding of the task required, by means of answering correctly (with cueing and repeated explanation if necessary) the demonstration item (or at least attempting to do so in such a way as to show that the task was understood) resulted in the subject's not being administered that subtest.
3. The subject was discharged before the test battery could be completed and could not or would not return to complete testing.
4. The patient could not be located after having taken one or more tests.

Note that completion of the full test battery in both languages took an average of 12 hours and was administered in up to 4 sessions over a 3-week period. The figures on ''Duration of Aphasia at Time of Evaluation'' thus refer to the length of time the patient had been aphasic as of the initiation of testing. Most patients took only a subset of the test battery, and monolingual Spanish speakers, of course, took none of the English tests.

As a final note, it should be mentioned that the patients have not been classified into traditional types (Broca's, Wernicke's, etc.) for reasons noted in Schwartz (1984) and Caramazza (1984). Virtually none of the subjects presented with what could be called a ''textbook example'' of a syndrome, and clinical impressions such as ''fluent,'' ''dysfluent,'' ''logarrheic,'' etc. were thought to be too imprecise to be included among the independent variables. Even if one were not to consider Schwartz's and Caramazza's critiques of traditional classification, the reasonably objective ''phrase length ratio'' of Goodglass et al. (1964) would have been inappropriate because it was calculated for English speakers only, and 9 of the 21 subjects in this study were monolingual Spanish speakers. The morphosyntax of Spanish differs sufficiently from that of English to call into question what would count as a ''word'' in Spanish for purposes of word-group counts. Also, a number of the aphasics were so mild as to invalidate the phrase-length-ratio criterion. Furthermore, it would be undesirable to group aphasics together according to syndrome because the use of group data would involve an implicit and illegitimate claim as to the homogeneity of the group, given the uncontrolled nature of neuropathology (See Caramazza, 1986). The only grouping used for computational purposes in the present study is the grouping of *test items* according to their independently determined characteristics.

In the following case reports, unattributed material enclosed in double quotation marks comes directly from the medical reports.

PATIENT 1

Patient 1, a 41-year-old ambidextrous housewife, with a history of arterial hypertension, was given a neurological examination at the Clínica Externa de Patología del Habla of the Centro Médico de Puerto Rico (CMPR) in Río Piedras on December 8, 1981. She had been in good condition until the previous June when she developed fever, general malaise, and severe headache. She was hospitalized with a diagnosis of meningitis. At that time she had displayed dysphasic symptoms and right-side weakness. After discharge, the patient had two brief episodes of loss of consciousness and of visual hallucinations. At the present neurological examination, the patient presented ''dysphasia without apraxia or agnosia'' and ''paraphasia without neologisms.'' She was assessed as having had encephalitis with focal clues indicative of a left frontoposterior lesion.

Patient 1 was born in Puerto Rico and learned Spanish in her home. She attended the first grade of school in Puerto Rico. At 7 years of age, she moved with her family to New York, where she lived until age 23. She attended school in New York through the 10th grade. Subsequent to her return to Puerto Rico, she completed the 11th grade; she had planned to take courses in order to graduate when she was stricken with meningitis and was unable to continue.

The patient described herself as having been able to read and write ''very well'' in both Spanish and English. In spontaneous speech during the testing sessions, she displayed a mild anomia and very occasional grammatical mistakes, as well as some slurring and dysfluencies involving repetition (e.g., she said ''todo mala'' instead of ''todo malo'', and ''Por eso yo estaba llorando mañana'' instead of ''Por eso, yo estaba llorando por la mañana'' [''That's why I was crying morning'' instead of ''That's why I was crying in the morning'']; ''in the foot'' instead of ''on the foot''; ''on the purse'' instead of ''in the purse''). Occasionally she used Spanish nouns when speaking English.

Summary of Independent Variables for Patient 1

Sex: Female
Age: 41

Duration of aphasia at time of evaluation: 35 weeks
Level of bilingualism: Balanced
Lateralization of lesion: Left
Site of lesion: Fronto-posterior
Etiology: Infection
Handedness: Ambidextrous
Education: Eleventh grade

Summary of Results of Tests Administered

Spanish		*Number of Correct Responses*		
Sentence Comprehension				
Listening–Speaking	(24 items)	17 (71%)		
Reading–Speaking	(24 items)	6 (25%)		
Listening–Writing	(24 items)	2 (8%)		
Reading–Writing	(24 items)	0 (0%)		
Syntax Correction				
Listening–Speaking	(9 items)	5 (56%)		
Reading–Speaking	(9 items)	3 (33%)		
Listening–Writing	(9 items)	0 (0%)		
Reading–Writing	(9 items)	0 (0%)		
Verb Morphology				
Listening–Speaking	(15 items)	3 (20%)		
Reading–Speaking	(15 items)	2 (13%)		
Listening–Writing	(15 items)	0 (0%)		
Reading–Writing	(15 items)	2 (13%)		
Number and Gender Agreement		*Total*	*Articles*	*Adjectives*
Listening–Speaking	(12 items)	10 (83%)	5 (83%)	5 (83%)
Reading–Speaking	(12 items)	6 (50%)	3 (50%)	3 (50%)
Listening–Writing	(12 items)	0 (0%)	0 (0%)	0 (0%)
Reading–Writing	(12 items)	0 (0%)	0 (0%)	0 (0%)

English		*Number of Correct Responses*		
Sentence Comprehension				
Listening–Speaking	(24 items)	20 (83%)		
Reading–Speaking	(24 items)	6 (25%)		
Listening–Writing	(24 items)	2 (8%)		
Reading–Writing	(24 items)	2 (8%)		
Syntax Correction				
Listening–Speaking	(9 items)	2 (22%)		
Reading–Speaking	(9 items)	1 (11%)		
Listening–Writing	(9 items)	0 (0%)		
Reading–Writing	(9 items)	1 (11%)		
Verb Morphology		*Total*	*Past Tenses*	*Past Participle*
Listening–Speaking	(16 items)	3 (19%)	1 (13%)	2 (25%)
Reading–Speaking	(16 items)	1 (6%)	1 (13%)	0 (0%)
Listening–Writing	(16 items)	0 (0%)	0 (0%)	0 (0%)
Reading–Writing	(16 items)	2 (13%)	2 (25%)	9 (0%)

Plurals			
Listening–Speaking	(6 items)		4 (67%)
Reading–Speaking	(6 items)		3 (50%)
Listening–Writing	(6 items)		1 (17%)
Reading–Writing	(6 items)		2 (33%)
Possessives and 3rd Person Singular Present		*Possessives*	*3rd Person Singular Present*
Listening–Speaking	(4 items)	1 (50%)	1 (50%)
Reading–Speaking	(4 items)	0 (0%)	0 (0%)
Listening–Writing	(4 items)	0 (0%)	0 (0%)
Reading–Writing	(4 items)	0 (0%)	0 (0%)

PATIENT 2

Patient 2, a 24-year-old male law student was referred to the Clínica Externa de Patología del Habla by the neurosurgery department of the Hospital Municipal of the CMPR, where he was evaluated on September 1, 1982. In May of the same year, the patient had suffered a blow to the head that resulted in a subdural hematoma and a large left fronto-temporal lesion, which resulted in a total aphasia for 3 weeks following the trauma.

This patient, born and raised in Puerto Rico, had studied English in school for 16 years but had never lived in an English-speaking community and had had few occasions to use oral English. Nonetheless, it must be assumed that his reading knowledge of English had been of a superior level, because he had been admitted to law school (Universidad de Puerto Rico). He reported that although he had not spoken English frequently, prior to the accident he had been able to make himself understood without difficulty. He stated that his written English had been better than his spoken English. He reported that in Spanish he had been able to communicate both orally and in writing without difficulty. An uncle of the patient reported that the patient had stuttered during childhood and adolescence.

At the time of the evaluation, the patient reported that although his speech had improved markedly since the accident, he nonetheless continued to experience difficulty understanding certain people in his town, newscasters on television, "because they speak very fast" (in Spanish), and some words in the (Spanish language) newspaper.

In spontaneous speech in Spanish, the patient spoke in simple sentences, which were generally grammatically correct. He showed some difficulty with verb conjugation and selection (e.g., "Cuánto tiempo voy" [instead of "va"], "a hacer para estar bien?" "Eso es lo más que me gustaba" [instead of "gustaría"] a mí).

In English, the patient could respond only to simple questions, and to these with some difficulty (e.g., to "Where were you born?", he responded with his date of birth).

Summary of Independent Variables for Patient 2

Sex: Male
Age: 24
Duration of aphasia at time of evaluation: 15 weeks
Level of bilingualism: Spanish dominant
Lateralization of lesion: Left
Site of lesion: Frontal and temporal lobes
Etiology: Trauma
Handedness: Right
Education: College graduate

Summary of Results of Tests Administered

Spanish		*Number of Correct Responses*		
Sentence Comprehension				
Listening–Speaking	(24 items)	16 (67%)		
Reading–Speaking	(24 items)	16 (67%)		
Reading–Writing	(24 items)	15 (63%)		
Syntax Correction				
Listening–Speaking	(9 items)	4 (44%)		
Reading–Speaking	(9 items)	6 (67%)		
Verb Morphology				
Listening–Speaking	(15 items)	11 (73%)		
Reading–Speaking	(15 items)	8 (53%)		
Listening–Writing	(15 items)	1 (7%)		
Reading–Wrting	(15 items)	9 (60%)		
Number and Gender Agreement		*Total*	*Articles*	*Adjectives*
Listening–Speaking	(12 items)	8 (67%)	4 (67%)	4 (67%)
Reading–Speaking	(12 items)	10 (83%)	5 (83%)	5 (83%)
Listening–Writing	(12 items)	11 (92%)	6 (100%)	5 (83%)
Reading–Writing	(12 items)	8 (67%)	4 (67%)	4 (67%)

English		*Number of Correct Responses*
Sentence Comprehension		
Listening–Speaking	(24 items)	0 (0%)
Reading–Speaking	(24 items)	3 (13%)
Reading–Writing	(24 items)	2 (8%)

PATIENT 3

Patient 3, a 58-year-old man who had worked as a truck driver, a security guard, and a factory worker, suffered from a left parietal undifferentiated malignant tumor. On September 1, 1983 a parietal craniotomy and gross total excision of tumor were performed. The neurological record at the Hospital Municipal of the CMPR noted a "right hemiparesis, disorientation in time and space, and incoherent speech but no dysarthria."

This patient was born and raised in Puerto Rico, where he completed the eighth grade. He reported that he did some additional studying by means of a correspondence school in California. He spent 20 years of his adult life (beginning at age 22) in Chicago, and Gary, Indiana, 14 of them as a psychiatric patient (according to a cousin).

On Setpember 8, 1983, this patient was evaluated at his bedside in the neurosurgery ward. In spontaneous conversation, he spoke fluently and generally grammatically in both languages (although he did show the noted disorientation), with a few grammatical mistakes (e.g., "with friend" instead of "with a friend", "era veintiún años" instead of "tenía veintiún años". (This latter error may have been due to influence from English.) He tended to respond to English questions in Spanish, unless reminded to use English.

Summary of Independent Variables for Patient 3

Sex: Male
Age: 58
Duration of aphasia at time of evaluation: Unknown
Level of bilingualism: Spanish dominant
Lateralization of lesion: Left
Site of lesion: Parietal lobe
Etiology: Neoplasm
Handedness: Right
Education: Eighth grade

Summary of Results of Tests Administered

Spanish			*Number of Correct Responses*	
Sentence Comprehension				
Listening–Speaking	(24 items)		16 (67%)	
Reading–Speaking	(24 items)		14 (58%)	
Syntax Correction				
Listening–Speaking	(9 items)		5 (56%)	
Reading–Speaking	(9 items)		6 (67%)	
Verb Morphology				
Listening–Speaking	(15 items)		3 (20%)	
Reading–Speaking	(15 items)		1 (7%)	
Number and Gender Agreement		*Total*	*Articles*	*Adjectives*
Listening–Speaking	(12 items)	12 (100%)	6 (100%)	6 (100%)
Reading–Speaking	(12 items)	8 (67%)	4 (67%)	4 (67%)

English		*Number of Correct Responses*
Sentence Comprehension		
Listening–Speaking	(24 items)	10 (42%)
Syntax Correction		
Listening–Speaking	(9 items)	2 (22%)

Verb Morphology		*Total*	*Past Tenses*	*Past Participles*
Listening–Speaking	(16 items)	6 (38%)	4 (50%)	2 (25%)
Reading–Speaking	(16 items)	0 (0%)	0 (0%)	0 (0%)

Plurals		
Listening–Speaking	(6 items)	4 (67%)

Possessives and 3rd Person Singular Present		*Possessives*	*3rd Person Singular Present*
Listening–Speaking	(4 items)	0 (0%)	0 (0%)

PATIENT 4

Patient 4, a 34-year-old male chef, was referred to the Clínica Externa de Patología del Habla at the CMPR (Río Piedras) from the Centro Médico de Mayagüez, for language evaluation. He had received a blow to the left side of the head with a pick axe on December 5, 1981, which caused a 2-day loss of consciousness, followed by an extended period of jargon aphasia, during which he was treated for his head wound at the Mayagüez facility.

The patient reported gradual improvement in his speech during the period between the accident and his evaluation at the CMPR on March 10, 1982. At this evaluation, the neurologist found the patient "alert and with coherent speech with dysphasia, paraphasic syllables, and no agnosia or apraxia." He was diagnosed as having "dysfunction" in the left frontoparietal area. The Mayagüez records were not made available.

The patient was born and raised in Puerto Rico. At the age of 18, he moved to New York where he lived until he was 25. Although he attended school through the 10th grade, he claimed that he had not learned to read and write English in school. During his 7 years in New York, he learned to read a bit of English but never learned to write it.

In spontaneous conversation, the patient showed fluent command of Spanish, with mild oral apraxia and phonemic paraphasias in a few infrequently used words of more than two syllables. His English was halting and showed evidence of influence from Spanish (e.g., "The little have 8 month" instead of "The little one is 8 months old").

Summary of Independent Variables for Patient 4

Sex: Male
Age: 34
Duration of aphasia at time of evaluation: 13 weeks
Level of bilingualism: Spanish dominant
Lateralization of lesion: Left

Site of lesion: Fronto-parietal
Etiology: Trauma
Handedness: Right
Education: 10th grade

Summary of Results of Tests Administered

Spanish		*Number of Correct Responses*		
Sentence Comprehension				
Listening–Speaking	(24 items)	11 (46%)		
Reading–Speaking	(24 items)	16 (67%)		
Listening–Writing	(24 items)	15 (63%)		
Reading–Writing	(24 items)	15 (63%)		
Syntax Correction				
Listening–Speaking	(9 items)	4 (44%)		
Reading–Speaking	(9 items)	6 (67%)		
Listening–Writing	(9 items)	4 (44%)		
Reading–Writing	(9 items)	4 (44%)		
Verb Morphology				
Listening–Speaking	(15 items)	8 (53%)		
Reading–Speaking	(15 items)	4 (27%)		
Listening–Writing	(15 items)	1 (7%)		
Reading–Writing	(15 items)	3 (20%)		
Number and Gender Agreement		*Total*	*Articles*	*Adjectives*
Listening–Speaking	(12 items)	11 (92%)	6 (100%)	5 (83%)
Reading–Speaking	(12 items)	12 (100%)	6 (100%)	6 (100%)
Listening–Writing	(12 items)	7 (58%)	4 (67%)	3 (50%)
Reading–Writing	(12 items)	10 (83%)	6 (100%)	4 (67%)

English		*Number of Correct Responses*		
Sentence Comprehension				
Listening–Speaking	(24 items)	9 (38%)		
Verb Morphology		*Total*	*Past Tenses*	*Past Participles*
Listening–Speaking		2 (13%)	1 (13%)	1 (13%)
Plurals				
Listening–Speaking		0 (0%)		

PATIENT 5

Patient 5, a 25-year-old college student and housewife with a history of migraine, lost consciousness on July 4, 1982, subsequent to a severe headache. Loss of consciousness following migraine attacks had occurred three times in the previous 5 years, each episode requiring hospitalization.

During her last stay at the University District Hospital of the CMPR, the patient had been given 2 CT scans, which revealed a right inferofrontal hemorrhage, a left parieto-temporal infarct, and a left occipital infarct, as well as an anterior cerebral aneurysm. An echocardiogram revealed a mild left ventricular dilatation. She presented with a right hemiplegia and right facial debility. She was diagnosed as having central VII nerve palsy.

On November 24, 1982, the patient was evaluated at the Clínica Externa de Patología del Habla. With the aid of her husband, she reported that her speech had improved since her hospitalization, that she had previously preseverated on a few stereotyped words and phrases, but that she still had the feeling that she could "think but not explain" what she was thinking. They noted that she had previously been able to speak English but no longer could. She had been a senior majoring in social sciences and had had to use English frequently in her studies. She had never lived outside Puerto Rico and had learned English at school.

On the day of her evaluation, her spontaneous speech was notably agrammatic. She also showed a marked problem in word retrieval, as well as a verbal apraxia. There was a tendency not to use verbs, for example, on being asked what had happened to her, she responded, "No sé porque yo, yo después acostada en la cama, y pronto un dolor de cabeza y nada más" ("I don't know because I, I after lying-down [adjective] in bed, and soon a headache and nothing more," that is, she lost consciousness).

Summary of Independent Variables for Patient 5

Sex: Female
Age: 25
Duration of aphasia at time of evaluation: 20 weeks
Level of bilingualism: Spanish dominant
Lateralization of lesions: Left, right
Site of lesions: Right frontal lobe, left parietal, temporal, occipital lobes
Etiology: CVA
Handedness: Right
Education: Three years of college

Summary of Results of Tests Administered

Spanish		*Number of Correct Responses*		
Sentence Comprehension				
Listening–Speaking	(24 items)	8 (33%)		
Syntax Correction				
Listening–Speaking	(9 items)	2 (22%)		
Verb Morphology				
Listening–Speaking	(15 items)	6 (40%)		
Reading–Speaking	(15 items)	1 (7%)		
Number and Gender Agreement		*Total*	*Articles*	*Adjectives*
Listening–Speaking	(12 items)	1 (8%)	0 (0%)	1 (17%)
Reading–Speaking	(12 items)	4 (33%)	1 (17%)	3 (50%)

English	*Number of Correct Responses*
Sentence Comprehension	
Listening–Speaking	1 (4%)

PATIENT 6

Patient 6, a 53-year-old electrical engineer, was born in Italy. At age 18 he migrated to Venezuela where he lived and studied for a year and where he learned Spanish. At age 19 he moved to New York, where he studied engineering for 4 years and learned English. The patient reported that he currently used English at work and both Spanish and English at home, and that he rarely used Italian, his native language.

On February 4, 1983, the patient suffered a CVA, sequela to a deficiency in an artificial aortic valve, which had been inserted 20 years previously. Among symptoms was a transient global aphasia with rapid recovery. On March 24 the patient suffered a second CVA with aphasia and hemiplegia. By the time of this evaluation (September, 1983) the hemiplegia was no longer present.

A CT scan taken on March 28, 1983 at Deborah Hospital in Browns Mills, New Jersey revealed several low-density areas involving the left frontal region as well as left temporal and parietal regions. Low density in left basal ganglia was also noted. The multiple areas of low density are consistent with infarctions and suggest the possibility of embolic events. All right hemisphere involvement was believed to be due to old lesions.

The patient was evaluated on September 14 and 21, 1983 at his home. At the first session approximately 1 hour was spent eliciting speech samples in Spanish and English.

The clinical picture presented by the patient in free discourse was one of mild fluent aphasia with good comprehension in both languages. Outside of a few neologisms and not a great many phonemic and verbal paraphasias, (e.g., ''estética'', [sistétika] instead of ''sintética'', ''I had to speech'' (instead of ''speak'') ''for an hour,'' ''So the doctor'' [gὲns héb] ''go look for the large''[súb] ''to hide the'' [súb], ''then it came over the'' [kæm]. . ''and it was all right''.), the patient presented relatively mild communicative difficulties.

Summary of Independent Variables for Patient 6

Sex: Male
Age: 53
Duration of aphasia at time of evaluation: 23 weeks
Level of bilingualism: Balanced

Lateralization of lesion: Left
Site of lesion: Frontal, temporal, parietal lobes
Etiology: CVA
Handedness: Right
Education: College graduate

Summary of Results of Tests Administered

Spanish		*Number of Correct Responses*
Sentence Comprehension		
Listening–Speaking	(24 items)	3 (13%)
Reading–Speaking	(24 items)	8 (33%)
Listening–Writing	(24 items)	13 (54%)
Reading–Writing	(24 items)	7 (29%)
Syntax Correction		
Listening–Speaking	(9 items)	2 (22%)
Reading–Speaking	(9 items)	2 (22%)
Listening–Writing	(9 items)	1 (11%)
Reading–Writing	(9 items)	3 (33%)
Verb Morphology		
Listening–Speaking	(15 items)	8 (53%)
Reading–Speaking	(15 items)	4 (27%)
Listening–Writing	(15 items)	3 (20%)
Reading–Writing	(15 items)	4 (27%)

Number and Gender Agreement		*Total*	*Articles*	*Adjectives*
Listening–Speaking	(12 items)	11 (92%)	5 (83%)	6 (100%)
Reading–Speaking	(12 items)	12 (100%)	6 (100%)	6 (100%)
Listening–Writing	(12 items)	9 (75%)	4 (67%)	5 (83%)
Reading–Writing	(12 items)	12 (100%)	6 (100%)	6 (100%)

English		*Number of Correct Responses*
Listening–Speaking	(24 items)	7 (29%)
Reading–Speaking	(24 items)	12 (50%)
Listening–Writing	(24 items)	6 (25%)
Reading–Writing	(24 items)	4 (17%)
Syntax Correction		
Listening–Speaking	(9 items)	0 (0%)
Reading–Speaking	(9 items)	6 (67%)
Listening–Writing	(9 items)	0 (0%)
Reading–Writing	(9 items)	2 (22%)

Verb Morphology		*Total*	*Past Tenses*	*Past Participles*
Listening–Speaking	(16 items)	12 (75%)	7 (88%)	5 (63%)
Reading–Speaking	(16 items)	8 (50%)	5 (63%)	3 (38%)
Listening–Writing	(16 items)	9 (56%)	6 (75%)	3 (38%)
Reading–Writing	(16 items)	6 (38%)	3 (38%)	3 (38%)

Plurals		*Number of Correct Responses*	
Listening–Speaking	(6 items)		3 (50%)
Reading–Speaking	(6 items)		4 (67%)
Listening–Writing	(6 items)		4 (67%)
Reading–Writing	(6 items)		3 (50%)
Possessives and 3rd Person Singular Present		*Possessives*	*3rd Person Singular Present*
Listening–Speaking	(4 items)	0 (0%)	0 (0%)
Reading–Speaking	(4 items)	0 (0%)	1 (50%)
Listening–Writing	(4 items)	0 (0%)	0 (0%)
Reading–Writing	(4 items)	2 (100%)	2 (100%)

PATIENT 7

Patient 7, a 62-year-old retired government official was referred to the Clínica Externa de Patología del Habla of the CMPR by his son, who along with the patient's wife provided the following information: On September 5, 1982, the patient suffered a CVA while visiting another son in Atlanta, Georgia. As a result, the patient was left with a right hemiparesis and a "severe mixed aphasia with heavy Wernicke's component; possible dyspraxia," according to a report from a speech/language pathologist at South Fulton Hospital, Atlanta, where the patient had been taken for treatment. This report was based on the patient's performance in English, which was described as "essentially not verbal except for automatisms (e.g., 'goodbye', 'yes')." He failed in receptive tests as well, giving echolalic responses to commands such as "open your mouth."

The patient holds a bachelor's degree in Education from the University of Puerto Rico. For 9 years, he worked as a teacher of industrial arts. Subsequently, he worked as Personnel Director in the Servicio de Empleos (Government Employment Office) of the Arecibo-Manatí District. His last job, from which he retired on account of his incapacity, was with the Agencia de Derecho al Trabajo (Right to Work Agency), where he had worked for 10 years. He had never lived in the United States and had only visited there on vacations. Nonetheless, he had studied English and had had a good command of it, as evidenced by the fact that his job required him to write proposals and reports in English.

A copy of the neurological report was not forwarded from Atlanta. Nevertheless, the right hemiparesis indicated a probable left hemisphere lesion.

On the day of his evaluation at the CMPR, December 8, 1982, the patient expressed himself in relatively fluent Spanish slightly affected by anomic lapses, and characterized by repetitions of words or phrases, prolongation of final sounds, and insertion of verbal pauses, usually "éste," (e.g., "Yo estaba a cargo [ðe:]. . . . Tenía 18 empleados que eran, éste. . . ."). His comprehension during conversation appeared to be normal. He was unable to use English in spontaneous speech and was unable to respond to questions in English.

Summary of Independent Variables for Patient 7

Sex: Male
Age: 62
Duration of aphasia at time of evaluation: 13 weeks
Level of bilingualism: Spanish dominant
Lateralization of lesion: Left (presumed)
Site of lesion: Not available
Etiology: CVA
Handedness: Right
Education: College graduate

Summary of Results of Tests Administered

Spanish		*Number of Correct Responses*		
Sentence Comprehension				
Listening–Speaking	(24 items)		1 (4%)	
Reading–Speaking	(24 items)		6 (25%)	
Reading–Writing	(24 items)		2 (8%)	
Verb Morphology				
Listening–Speaking	(15 items)		2 (13%)	
Reading–Speaking	(15 items)		7 (47%)	
Reading–Writing	(15 items)		2 (13%)	
Number and Gender Agreement		*Total*	*Articles*	*Adjectives*
Listening–Speaking	(12 items)	8 (67%)	5 (83%)	3 (50%)
Reading–Writing	(12 items)	7 (58%)	4 (67%)	3 (50%)

English		*Number of Correct Responses*
Reading–Speaking	(24 items)	3 (13%)

PATIENT 8

Patient 8, a 63-year-old Protestant minister, was brought to the Clínica Externa de Patología del Habla at the CMPR by his wife. He had suffered a CVA some years before, which left him with a marked oral apraxia. The patient's wife reported that he had been born and raised in Puerto Rico and had learned Spanish at home. He studied English in school in a rather intensive way, attending a school in which all subjects except Spanish were taught in English. At age 21 he moved to New York, where he lived and worked for 30 years. During this period the language of his home was always Spanish. His wife noted that the patient still read both languages with "good comprehension" and that he sometimes spoke English during conversations in Spanish "because certain things can be said better in English than in Spanish."

There was no neurological information available.

Because of the patient's apraxia, no tests involving oral tasks were attempted.

On the day of his evaluation, November 8, 1982, the patient was unable to say anything intelligible in English. In Spanish he uttered individual words only and always with severe distortion.

Summary of Independent Variables for Patient 8

Sex: Male
Age: 63
Duration of aphasia at time of evaluation: Not available
Level of bilingualism: Balanced
Lateralization of lesion: unknown
Site of lesion: unknown
Etiology: CVA
Handedness: Right
Education: College graduate

Summary of Results of Tests Administered

Spanish		*Number of Correct Responses*
Sentence Comprehension		
Listening–Writing	(24 items)	0 (0%)
Reading–Writing	(24 items)	0 (0%)
Syntax Correction		
Listening–Writing	(9 items)	0 (0%)
Reading–Writing	(9 items)	0 (0%)
Verb Morphology		
Listening–Writing		0 (0%)
Number and Gender Agreement		
Listening–Writing	(12 items)	0 (0%)
Reading–Writing	(12 items)	0 (0%)

English		*Number of Correct Responses*
Sentence Comprehension		
Listening–Writing	(24 items)	0 (0%)
Reading–Writing	(24 items)	0 (0%)
Syntax Correction		
Reading–Writing	(9 items)	1 (11%)
Verb Morphology		
Listening–Writing	(16 items)	0 (0%)
Reading–Writing	(16 items)	0 (0%)
Plurals		
Listening–Writing	(6 items)	0 (0%)
Reading–Writing	(6 items)	0 (0%)
Possessives and 3rd Person Singular Present		
Listening–Writing	(4 items)	0 (0%)
Reading–Writing	(4 items)	0 (0%)

PATIENT 9

Patient 9, a 58-year-old retired engineer who suffered a subdural hematoma as a result of head trauma due to a fall on January 17, 1982, was evaluated at his bedside at the Casa de Salud of the CMPR on January 27. No neurological records were available.

He was born and raised in Puerto Rico and attended college for 4 years in the United States, where he lived for 4 more years subsequent to his graduation from the Catholic University in Washington. He began to learn English at age 8. His wife is American, and he habitually spoke English with her, prior to his accident.

At the time of his evaluation, the patient was disoriented in time and space. His spontaneous speech was fluent and with a few distortions and verbal paraphasias in Spanish, and with an abnormal degree of hesitations indicative of a word-finding problem, (for example, ''dieciocho años'', then ''ocho minutos'', instead of ''ocho años'' (''eighteen years,'' then ''eight minutes,'' instead of ''eight years.''). In English, his spontaneous speech was marked by hesitations and verbal paraphasias, as well as by mild agrammatism (e.g., ''I knowledge everything in English'' instead of ''I studied everything in English''.)

Summary of Independent Variables for Patient 9

Sex: Male
Age: 58
Duration of aphasia at time of evaluation: 10 days
Level of bilingualism: Balanced
Lateralization of lesion: Not determined
Site of lesion: Not determined
Etiology: Trauma
Handedness: Right
Education: College graduate

Summary of Results of Tests Administered

Spanish			*Number of Correct Responses*	
Sentence Comprehension				
Listening–Speaking	(24 items)		15 (63%)	
Syntax Correction				
Listening–Speaking	(9 items)		5 (56%)	
Verb Morphology				
Listening–Speaking	(15 items)		11 (73%)	
Reading–Speaking	(15 items)		0 (0%)	
Number and Gender Agreement		*Total*	*Articles*	*Adjectives*
Listening–Speaking	(12 items)	2 (17%)	1 (17%)	1 (17%)

English		*Number of Correct Responses*		
Sentence Comprehension				
Listening–Speaking	(24 items)		11 (46%)	
Syntax Correction				
Listening–Speaking	(9 items)		1 (11%)	
Verb Morphology		*Total*	*Past Tenses*	*Past Participles*
Listening–Speaking	(16 items)	1 (6%)	1 (13%)	0 (0%)
Plurals				
Listening–Speaking	(6 items)		5 (83%)	
Possessives and 3rd Person Singular Present		*Possessives*		*3rd Person Singular Present*
Listening–Speaking		(0%)		0 (0%)

PATIENT 10

Patient 10, a 48-year-old white-collar worker of Puerto Rican parentage, was evaluated at his bedside in the neurosurgery ward of the Hospital Municipal of the CMPR on March 31, 1982. A lifelong resident of the United States, he was visiting relatives in Puerto Rico when he suffered a fall, which caused a fracture of his left parietal bone. Examination revealed ''displacement of the middle cerebral artery'' and a ''contused cerebral cortex.'' A left temporal craniotomy was performed, which revealed a left temporal intracerebral hematoma, which was subsequently evacuated.

The patient's wife, who had been born and raised in Puerto Rico, reported that they currently lived in California, where they were returning several days after the evaluation. She was unable to give useful information regarding the patient's acquisition of the two languages or his level of education in either language but did note that he had habitually spoken Spanish with her and English with virtually everyone else.

At the time of the evaluation, the patient tended to logarrheic and paragrammatic responses in which Spanish and English were freely mixed with neologisms and frequent preservation, for example:

Interviewer: Cómo se llama usted? (''What's your name?'')

Patient: My name? La [nem] es la [nem] la nena de la nena.

I: Can you speak English?

P: Yup.

I: Let's speak English.

P: Sí, la nena. ("Yes, the (little) girl.")

I: What's your name?

P: My name . . . It's um . . . Andy (not true). Pa' la nena es otro no me consiguió e [tumpakanóta]. They didn't have to. . . .

He responded in (mainly) Spanish jargon to all attempts to administer formal tests in English.

Summary of Independent Variable for Patient 10

Sex: Male
Age: 48
Duration of aphasia at time of evaluation: 2 weeks (estimate)
Level of bilingualism: Balanced
Lateralization of lesion: Left
Site of lesion: Temporal lobe
Etiology: Trauma
Handedness: Right
Education: Information not available

Summary of Results of Tests Administered

Spanish		*Number of Correct Responses*
Verb Morphology		
Listening–Speaking	(15 items)	2 (13%)

PATIENT 11

Patient 11, a 52-year-old physician with a private practice in Mayagüez, suffered a transient ischemic attack that led to aphasia. A CT scan was negative. The patient's wife reported that he had suffered eight previous aphasic episodes.

The patient was evaluated at his bedside in the men's ward of the University District Hospital of the CMPR on April 10, 1982. He revealed that he had been born and raised in the Dominican Republic, that he had studied medicine at the Universidad Autónoma de Santo Domingo, and that he had resided in Puerto Rico since 1967. He also stated that he spoke English with some difficulty but was able to read and write it well. This is typical of many physicians in Puerto Rico: Virtually all written professional communication in the medical profession is done in English; virtually all oral communication is done in Spanish.

At the time of his evaluation, the patient displayed no linguistic problem in his spontaneous speech in Spanish. He did, however, present with a moderate oral apraxia.

Summary of Independent Variables for Patient 11

Sex: Male
Age: 52
Duration of aphasia at time of evaluation: 1 week (estimate)
Level of bilingualism: Spanish dominant
Lateralization of lesion: not determined
Site of lesion: not determined
Etiology: Transient ischemic attack
Handedness: Right
Education: Doctor of medicine

Summary of Results of Tests Administered

Spanish			*Number of Correct Responses*	
Sentence Comprehension				
Listening–Speaking	(24 items)		19 (79%)	
Reading–Writing	(24 items)		20 (83%)	
Syntax Correction				
Listening–Speaking	(9 items)		9 (100%)	
Verb Morphology				
Listening–Speaking	(15 items)		14 (93%)	
Number and Gender Agreement		*Total*	*Articles*	*Adjectives*
Listening–Speaking	(12 items)	11 (92%)	6 (100%)	5 (83%)

English			*Number of Correct Responses*	
Sentence Comprehension				
Listening–Speaking	(24 items)		11 (46%)	
Reading–Writing	(24 items)		15 (63%)	
Verb Morphology		*Total*	*Past Tenses*	*Past Participles*
Listening–Speaking	(16 items)	2 (13%)	2 (25%)	0 (0%)
Plurals				
Listening–Speaking	(6 items)		4 (67%)	
Possessives and 3rd Person Singular Present		*Possessives*		*3rd Person Singular Present*
Listening–Speaking	(4 items)	2 (100%)		0 (0%)

PATIENT 12

Patient 12, a 74-year-old retired chef, was evaluated at his bedside at the Casa de Salud at the CMPR on June 18, 1982. He had been admitted because of problems "with balance and communication," which had begun a month earlier. Three and a half years previously, a left frontal craniotomy had been performed to remove a frontal meningioma. It was believed that the tumor had begun to grow again.

The patient reported that he had been born and raised in Arecibo, Puerto Rico, where he had attended school through the eighth grade. He subsequently attended a polytechnic institute. He had worked in the United States for 18 years.

His spontaneous speech appeared to be fluent and flawless in both languages on the day of his evaluation. Nonetheless, he was unable to pass the demonstration item in any English-language test.

Summary of Independent Variables for Patient 12

Sex: Male
Age: 74
Duration of aphasia at time of evaluation: 4 weeks
Level of bilingualism: Spanish dominant
Lateralization of lesion: Left
Site of lesion: Frontal lobe
Etiology: Neoplasm
Handedness: Right
Education: Eighth grade + polytechnical school

Summary of Results of Tests Administered

Spanish		*Number of Correct Responses*		
Sentence Comprehension				
Listening–Speaking	(24 items)	10 (42%)		
Verb Morphology				
Listening–Speaking	(15 items)	10 (67%)		
Number and Gender Agreement		*Total*	*Articles*	*Adjectives*
Listening–Speaking	(12 items)	12 (100%)	6 (100%)	6 (100%)

PATIENT 13

Patient 13, a 48-year-old housewife, was evaluated in the women's ward of the University District Hospital of the CMPR on March 9, 1983. A CT scan revealed that she had suffered a left Sylvian cerebral hemorrhage 6 days previously, and an arteriogram showed a "periferal [sic] embolism that originated from the left internal carotid artery, which could have been the cause." The patient presented with a right hemiplegia with left facial deviation, and "motor aphasia" for which she had been admitted 1 week previously.

On the day of the evaluation, the patient did not speak spontaneously. When required to answer questions, she responded with single words or short, halting, dysfluent phrases. Facial paralysis contributed to distortion in pronunciation. She reported that she had never known more than a few words of English.

Summary of Independent Variables for Patient 13

Sex: Female
Age: 48
Duration of aphasia at time of evaluation: 1 week
Level of bilingualism: Spanish monolingual
Lateralization of lesion: Left
Site of lesion: Sylvial fissure
Etiology: CVA
Handedness: Right
Education: Could not be determined

Summary of Results of Tests Administered

Spanish		*Number of Correct Responses*		
Sentence Comprehension				
Listening–Speaking	(24 items)	10 (42%)		
Reading–Speaking	(24 items)	1 (4%)		
Syntax Correction				
Listening–Speaking	(9 items)	4 (44%)		
Verb Morphology				
Listening–Speaking	(15 items)	6 (40%)		
Reading–Speaking	(15 items)	6 (40%)		
Number and Gender Agreement		*Total*	*Articles*	*Adjectives*
Listening–Speaking	(12 items)	8 (67%)	3 (50%)	5 (83%)
Reading–Speaking	(12 items)	5 (42%)	3 (50%)	2 (33%)

PATIENT 14

Patient 14, a 55-year-old unemployed laborer, was evaluated in the Clínica Externa de Patología del Habla at the CMPR on January 2, 1982. He had never lived outside of Puerto Rico. He had completed 4 years of elementary school and indicated that he knew no English.

His medical records were at a hospital in Ponce, where he had lived for the previous 45 years, and were unavailable. He presented with a right hemiparesis and therefore used his left hand for writing.

His spontaneous speech appeared to be basically normal, although it contained a few phonemic paraphasias (e.g., "Puerpo Nuevo" instead of "Puerto Nuevo").

Summary of Independent Variables for Patient 14

Sex: Male
Age: 55
Duration of aphasia at time of evaluation: unknown
Level of bilingualism: Spanish monolingual
Lateralization, site and etiology of lesion: not available
Handedness: Right
Education: Fourth grade

Summary of Results of Tests Administered

Spanish			*Number of Correct Responses*	
Sentence Comprehension				
Listening–Speaking	(24 items)		20 (83%)	
Reading–Speaking	(24 items)		19 (79%)	
Syntax Correction				
Listening–Speaking	(9 items)		4 (44%)	
Reading–Speaking	(9 items)		6 (67%)	
Verb Morphology				
Listening–Speaking	(15 items)		6 (40%)	
Reading–Speaking	(15 items)		6 (40%)	
Listening–Writing	(15 items)		4 (27%)	
Number and Gender Agreement			*Articles*	*Adjectives*
Listening–Speaking	(12 items)	12 (100%)	6 (100%)	6 (100%)
Reading–Speaking	(12 items)	5 (42%)	3 (50%)	2 (33%)

PATIENT 15

Patient 15, a 33-year-old man who had been working as a guard with a private security service prior to his accident, was evaluated at the Clínica Externa de Patología del Habla at the CMPR on April 14, 1982. Three years previously, he had suffered a gunshot wound to the left fronto-temporal region, which rendered him blind in the left eye.

He reported that he had completed the fifth grade and had never learned English, having spent his entire life in rural Puerto Rico. He presented with a mild right hemiparesis. He was currently living in Guayanilla; his medical records were in Ponce and not obtainable.

On the day of his evaluation, the only writing of which he was capable was his signature, which he appeared to draw rather than write. His spontaneous speech was dysfluent, without paraphasia. He showed some difficulty with word retrieval. The patient complained, "Olvido cosas. No hablo muy bien." (I forget things. I don't speak very well.)

Summary of Independent Variables for Patient 15

Sex: Male
Age: 33
Duration of aphasia at time of evaluation: 160 weeks
Level of bilingualism: Spanish monolingual
Lateralization of lesion: Left
Localization of lesion: information not available; probably fronto-temporal
Etiology: Trauma
Handedness: Right
Education: Fifth grade

Summary of Results of Tests Administered

Spanish		*Number of Correct Responses*
Sentence Comprehension		
Listening–Speaking	(24 items)	4 (17%)
Reading–Speaking	(24 items)	1 (4%)
Syntax Correction		
Listening–Speaking	(9 items)	4 (44%)
Verb Morphology		
Listening–Speaking	(15 items)	3 (20%)
Reading–Speaking	(15 items)	3 (20%)

Number and Gender Agreement		*Total*	*Articles*	*Adjectives*
Listening–Speaking	(12 items)	2 (17%)	1 (17%)	1 (17%)
Reading–Speaking	(12 items)	0 (0%)	0 (0%)	0 (0%)

PATIENT 16

Patient 16, a 32-year-old housewife, was admitted to the University District Hospital of the CMPR for a rheumatic heart condition on February 16, 1982. While there, she became dizzy and suffered a fall, after which she developed a right hemiparesis and "mild dysphasia of the motor type." Neurological examination revealed a left frontal lesion with involvement of Broca's Area and Exner's Center.

The patient indicated that she had always lived in Puerto Rico and never had learned English. On the day of her evaluation (March 3, 1982) her spontaneous speech appeared to be slightly dysfluent and extremely slow.

Summary of Independent Variables for Patient 16

Sex: Female
Age: 32
Duration of aphasia at time of evaluation: 3 weeks
Level of bilingualism: Spanish monolingual
Lateralization of lesion: Left
Site of lesion: Frontal lobe
Etiology: Trauma
Handedness: Right
Education: Fourth grade

Summary of Results of Tests Administered

Spanish		*Number of Correct Responses*		
Sentence Comprehension				
Listening–Speaking	(24 items)	11 (46%)		
Reading–Speaking	(24 items)	6 (25%)		
Syntax Correction				
Listening–Speaking	(24 items)	3 (33%)		
Verb Morphology				
Listening–Speaking	(15 items)	6 (40%)		
Reading–Speaking	(15 items)	6 (40%)		
Listening–Writing	(15 items)	1 (7%)		
Reading–Writing	(15 items)	0 (0%)		
Number and Gender Agreement		*Total*	*Articles*	*Adjectives*
Listening–Speaking	(12 items)	10 (83%)	5 (83%)	5 (83%)
Reading–Speaking	(12 items)	8 (67%)	4 (67%)	4 (67%)
Listening–Writing	(12 items)	5 (42%)	3 (50%)	2 (33%)
Reading–Writing	(12 items)	2 (17%)	0 (0%)	2 (33%)

PATIENT 17

Patient 17, an 18-year-old left-handed man who had begun to have hearing and language problems 1 year previous to his admission to the neurosurgery unit of the Hospital Municipal of the CMPR, was operated on on September 1, 1982. On August 12 he had been diagnosed as having bilateral acoustic neuromas with neurofibromatosis. A left suboccipital craniotomy and subtotal (95%) tumor resection on the left side were performed (leaving some of the tumor at the opening of the acoustic meatus). The VII nerve appeared displaced downward, and the tumor compressed the cerebellum, vermis, and pons. The lateral third of the cerebellar hemisphere was resected to prevent excessive retraction.

At his evaluation at the Casa de Salud on September 15, the patient was functionally deaf and spoke little. When he did speak, in response to written questions, it was with the flat intonation characteristic of deaf speakers, indicating that his hearing problems were probably of long duration.

His grandmother reported that he had always lived in Puerto Rico, had never learned English, and had spent 4 years in the seventh grade. He was expelled from school when his hearing had deteriorated to the point at which he could not function in a normal class.

Summary of Independent Variables for Patient 17

Sex: Male
Age: 18
Duration of aphasia at time of evaluation: 57 weeks
Level of bilingualism: Spanish monolingual
Lateralization of lesion: Bilateral
Site of lesion: Cerebellum, vermis, pons
Etiology: Neoplasm
Handedness: Left
Education: Seventh grade

Summary of Results of Tests Administered

Spanish		*Number of Correct Responses*
Sentence Comprehension		
Reading–Speaking	(24 items)	4 (17%)
Reading–Writing	(24 items)	0 (0%)

PATIENT 18

Patient 18, a 37-year-old upholsterer and furniture manufacturer, was evaluated at the Clínica Externa de Patología del Habla on November 20, 1982. He had been referred by the Rehabilitación Vocacional unit of the CMPR. He reported that 2½ years previously he had suffered a stroke, which had left him with a "communication problem" and with a right hemiparesis. He reported that therapy he had been receiving at the vocational rehabilitation center had helped him improve considerably. Nonetheless, he was referred for evaluation because several days previously he had found himself unable to understand what he read in the newspaper. He also found himself unable to write as he had done before.

The patient reported that he had been born and raised in Puerto Rico, graduated from high school, and had been able to read and write without difficulty. He stated that he had never learned English. Prior to his CVA, he had owned and operated a business that reupholstered, repaired, and manufactured furniture. The patient's medical records, which were apparently at a hospital in Carolina, were not available.

In spontaneous speech, this patient appeared to be normal. He did show a noticeable tendency to forget factual information (e.g., age, address, telephone number), but his speech was fluent and without anomia or paraphasia.

Summary of Independent Variables for Patient 18

Sex: Male
Age: 37
Duration of aphasia at time of evaluation: 2 1/2 years
Level of bilingualism: Spanish monolingual
Lateralization and site of lesion: not available
Etiology: CVA
Handedness: Right
Education: High school graduate

Summary of Results of Tests Administered

Spanish		*Number of Correct Responses*		
Verb Morphology				
Listening–Speaking	(15 items)	9 (60%)		
Reading–Speaking	(15 items)	7 (47%)		
Listening–Writing	(15 items)	3 (20%)		
Reading–Writing	(15 items)	2 (13%)		
Number and Gender Agreement		*Total*	*Articles*	*Adjectives*
Listening–Speaking	(12 items)	12 (100%)	6 (100%)	6 (100%)
Reading–Speaking	(12 items)	12 (100%)	6 (100%)	6 (100%)
Listening–Writing	(12 items)	5 (50%)	4 (67%)	2 (33%)

PATIENT 19

Patient 19, a 60-year-old occupationally incapacitated man, was evaluated at his bedside in the men's ward of the University District Hospital of the CMPR on December 15, 1982, where he had been admitted on December 6 because of aphasia and right hemiplegia, which had developed on December 5. A CT scan performed on December 7 revealed a left parietal low density that could represent an infarct. The following day he was placed on anticoagulants. An arteriogram taken on December 13 showed an occluded right internal carotid artery and atheromatosis in the left internal carotid artery. The patient had a history of progressive right leg spasticity since 1968, that caused him to be occupationally incapacitated.

The patient was born and raised in Puerto Rico, had completed the ninth grade, and had never learned English.

On the day of his evaluation, the patient's spontaneous speech was agrammatic, confined to single words and brief (two to three word) phrases, which he uttered only in response to specific questions. His speech was dysarthric and difficult to understand. He had moderate comprehension problems.

Summary of Independent Variables for Patient 19

Sex: Male
Age: 60
Duration of aphasia at time of evaluation: 2 weeks
Level of bilingualism: Spanish monolingual
Lateralization of lesion: Left
Site of lesion: Parietal lobe
Etiology: CVA
Handedness: Right
Education: Ninth grade

Summary of Results of Tests Administered

Spanish		*Number of Correct Responses*
Sentence Comprehension		
Listening–Speaking	(24 items)	7 (29%)
Reading–Speaking	(24 items)	1 (4%)

PATIENT 20

Patient 20, a 47-year-old housewife, was evaluated at the Clínica Externa de Patología del Habla at the CMPR on December 1, 1982. She had been referred from the University District Hospital, where she had been admitted on May 28 for a dilatation and curetage. Two days later, she suffered an occlusion due to an embolism in the middle cerebral artery, which rendered her mute and hemiplegic (right side), with her mouth deviated from the midline.

She had suffered from rheumatic fever as a child and because of cardiac insufficiency she had had a prosthetic mitral valve inserted in 1972.

She was born and raised in Puerto Rico and completed the first 4 years of elementary school. She had never learned English.

On the day of her evaluation, her verbalizations consisted of brief unintelligible phonations that were not recognizable lexically or segmentable phonologically. She could not repeat /pa/, /ta/, /ka/, or /s/. She responded to the one test she was able to take by writing with her left hand. She did not write more than two words at a time.

Summary of Independent Variables of Patient 20

Sex: Female
Age: 47
Duration of aphasia at time of evaluation: 27 weeks
Level of bilingualism: Spanish monolingual
Lateralization of lesion: Left
Site of lesion: Middle cerebral artery occlusion; lesion localization not reported
Etiology: CVA
Handedness: Right
Education: Fourth grade

Summary of Results of Test Administered

Spanish		*Number of Correct Responses*		
Number and Gender Agreement		*Total*	*Articles*	*Adjectives*
Reading–Writing	(12 items)	4 (33%)	0 (0%)	4 (67%)

PATIENT 21

Patient 21, a 51-year-old housewife, was evaluated in the neurosurgery ward of the Hospital Municipal of the CMPR on March 7, 1982, where she was hospitalized following an arteriogram of the brain, which revealed a right frontal mass. During the procedure, she suffered a CVA, which caused a left parieto-occipital lesion and right hemiparesis. She was unwilling to submit to an operation to remove the frontal mass.

The patient was born and raised in Puerto Rico, completed 2 years of school, and reported that although she had previously had been able to read and write "sin problema" ("without difficulty"), she presently was totally unable to do so. She stated that she had never learned English.

On the day of her evaluation, the patient's spontaneous speech was extremely slow and halting, but otherwise normal in intonation, morphosyntax, and segmental pronunciation. She was disoriented with respect to time.

Summary of Independent Variables for Patient 21

Sex: Female
Age: 51
Duration of aphasia at time of evaluation: 1 week
Level of bilingualism: Spanish monolingual
Lateralization of lesion: Left (plus right hemisphere tumor)
Site of lesion: Left: parieto-occipital / Right: frontal
Etiology: CVA (plus right hemisphere neoplasm)
Handedness: Right
Education: Second grade

Summary of Results of Tests Administered

Spanish		*Number of Correct Responses*	
Sentence Comprehension			
Listening–Speaking (24 items)		6 (25%)	
Syntax Correction			
Listening–Speaking (9 items)		3 (33%)	
Verb Morphology			
Listening–Speaking (15 items)		6 (40%)	
Number and Gender Agreement	*Total*	*Articles*	*Adjectives*
Listening–Speaking	2 (17%)	1 (17%)	1 (17%)

5 Results

OVERALL RESULTS

General Remarks

The scores of individual patients on individual tests are listed with each case description in chapter 4. The overall score, including number of subjects, mean, and median for each test are given in Tables 5.1 and 5.2.

Because of the small number of subjects and large degree of heterogeneity with respect to the various independent variables, the median score was calculated for each test and a Fisher Exact Probabilities Test was performed, comparing each independent variable with the number of subjects with scores below the median versus the number at the median and above, as dependent variable. Because the Fisher Test requires a 2 × 2 matrix, all the independent variables had to be coded as binary.

Independent Variables

The binary codification of these variables was as follows.

Sex

Fortunately, this is a naturally dichotomous category.

TABLE 5.1.
Overall Scores for Spanish Tests

Test	Modality	Number of Items	Number of Subjects	Total No. Correct Responses	Mean Score No.	Mean Score %	Median Score No.	Median Score %
Sentence comprehension	L-S	24	16	174	10.9	45%	10	42%
	R-S	24	12	98	8.2	34%	6	25%
	L-W	24	4	30	7.5	31%	7	29%
	R-W	24	8	59	7.4	31%	4.5	19%
Syntax correction	L-S	9	13	54	4.2	46%	4	44%
	R-S	9	6	29	4.8	54%	6	67%
	L-W	9	4	5	1.3	14%	0.5	6%
	R-W	9	4	7	1.8	19%	1.5	17%
Verb morphology	L-S	15	17	114	6.7	45%	6	40%
	R-S	15	13	55	4.2	28%	4	27%
	L-W	15	8	13	1.6	11%	1	7%
	R-W	15	7	22	3.1	21%	2	13%
Number and gender agreement	L-S	12	16	132	8.3	69%	10	83%
	R-S	12	11	82	7.5	62%	8	67%
	L-W	12	7	38	5.4	45%	6	50%
	R-W	12	8	43	5.5	45%	5.5	46%

Note: (L-S = Listening–Speaking; R-S = Reading–Speaking; L-W = Listening–Writing; R-W = Reading–Writing.)

Age

The age range was 18–74 years, with a median of 50. AGE was coded as under 50 versus over 50.

Duration of Aphasia

The duration of aphasia ranged from 1 week to 160 weeks at the time of first testing, with a median of 16 weeks. DURATION was coded as under 16 weeks versus over 16 weeks.

Level of Bilingualism

The three levels of bilingualisms described in chapter 4 were coded as follows:
For Spanish tests: Bilingual versus Monolingual
For English tests: Balanced versus Spanish dominant

Localization of Lesion

Only three lesion sites were found in a sufficient number of patients to make comparisons worthwhile. These were encoded as follows: (a) left frontal lobe

TABLE 5.2.
Overall Score for English Tests

Test	Modality	Number of Items	Number of Subjects	Total No. Correct Responses	Mean Score No.	Mean Score %	Median Score No.	Median Score %
Sentence comprehension	L-S	24	8	69	8.6	36%	9.5	40%
	R-S	24	4	24	6.0	25%	4.5	19%
	L-W	24	3	12	4.0	17%	6	25%
	R-W	24	5	23	4.6	19%	2	8%
Syntax correction	L-S	9	4	5	1.3	14%	1.5	17%
	R-S	9	2	7	3.5	39%	4.5	50%
	L-W	9	2	0	0	0%	0	0%
	R-W	9	3	4	1.3	15%	1	11%
Verb morphology	L-S	16	6	26	4.3	27%	2.5	16%
	R-S	16	3	9	3.0	19%	1	6%
	L-W	16	3	9	3.0	19%	0	0%
	R-W	16	3	8	2.7	17%	2	13%
Plural formation	L-S	6	6	20	3.3	56%	4	67%
	R-S	6	2	7	3.5	58%	3.5	58%
	L-W	6	3	5	1.7	28%	1	17%
	R-W	6	3	5	1.7	28%	2	33%
Possessive formation	L-S	2	5	3	0.6	30%	0	0%
	R-S	2	2	0	0	0%	0	0%
	L-W	2	3	0	0	0%	0	0%
	R-W	2	3	2	0.7	33%	0	0%
Third person singular present	L-S	2	3	1	0.3	17%	0	0%
	R-S	2	2	1	0.5	25%	0.5	25%
	L-W	2	2	0	0	0%	0	0%
	R-W	2	2	2	1.0	50%	1	50%

lesion versus no left frontal lobe lesion, (b) left temporal lobe lesion versus no left temporal lobe lesion, and (c) left parietal lobe lesion versus no left parietal lobe lesion.

Etiology

Only cerebrovascular accidents and trauma caused a sufficient number of cases to warrant comparison. They were encoded as CVA versus no CVA, and as trauma versus no trauma.

Education

The level of formal education ranged from 2 to 20 years, with a median of 10 years. Because of the unnatural position of this median in the Puerto Rican educational system, LEVEL OF EDUCATION was encoded in the following four ways, each of which was used for comparison with all the dependent variables:

1. Elementary education (eighth grade or lower) versus more than eighth-grade education.
2. College graduate versus not college graduate.
3. Elementary education (grade 8 or lower) versus high school education (grades 9 to 15).
4. College graduate versus graduate of elementary school (eighth grade) but not college (i.e., 8–15 years of formal education).

Handedness

Because 19 of the 21 subjects were right handed, this variable was omitted from the comparisons.

Overall Findings

There were only two significant interactions. It turned out that patients who had not suffered a CVA performed significantly better on Spanish Sentence Comprehension in the listening–speaking modality combination (Two-tailed Fisher Exact Test $p = .006$).

	CVA	No CVA
Below Median	6	2
Median or above	0	7

Although this result is not surprising since CVAs frequently cause more severe effects than tumors or infection (because in the latter types of cases the gradual progression may promote use of collateral pathways), it is surprising that no similar effect was found for trauma. A near significant interaction in the same direction ($p = .06$) between CVA etiology and performance on Syntax Correction in the listening–speaking modality combination was also found.

The second significant interaction was between level of bilingualism and performance on the Spanish Sentence Comprehension Test in the reading–speaking modality combination ($p = .03$).

	Monolingual	Bilingual
Below Median	4	0
Median or above	2	6

Apparently, knowledge of English helps in the performance of the Spanish reading task.

However, in view of the fact that there were 560 comparisons made, it is likely that these two "significant" effects were due to chance, because the probability of an effect at the .006 level being due to chance is one in 167 and the probability of a chance interaction at the .03 level is one in 33.

Although the comparisons made between the characteristics of the patients and their scores on the various tests were not very illuminating, one can detect an obvious trend in the results of the tests listed in Tables 5.1 and 5.2, viz. that there was a tendency to perform better in the speaking modality than in the writing modality. This trend was significant (two-tailed chi square) for all types of tests in Spanish.[1]

	Speaking	Writing		
Number of Correct Responses	272	89	361	$\chi^2 = 7.36$
Number of Incorrect Responses	400	199	599	df = 1
	672	288	960	$p < .01$

Spanish Sentence Comprehension

	Speaking	Writing		
Number of Correct Responses	83	12	95	$\chi^2 = 20.30$
Number of Incorrect Responses	88	60	148	df = 1
	171	72	243	$p < .001$

Spanish Syntax Correction

	Speaking	Writing		
Number of Correct Responses	169	35	204	$\chi^2 = 33.39$
Number of Incorrect Responses	281	190	471	df = 1
	450	225	675	$p < .001$

Spanish Verb Morphology

[1]All chi square calculations used herein include the Yates Correction Factor.

	Speaking	Writing		
Number of Correct Responses	214	79	293	$\chi^2 = 22.45$
Number of Incorrect Responses	110	101	211	df = 1
	324	180	504	$p < .001$

Spanish Number and Gender Agreement

For English, this trend was significant only for Sentence Comprehension:

	Speaking	Writing		
Number of Correct Responses	93	35	128	$\chi^2 = 10.94$
Number of Incorrect Responses	195	157	352	df = 1
	288	192	480	$p < .001$

A number of comparisons were made between characteristics of specific *items* and number of correct versus incorrect responses to these items, across all subjects. The remainder of this chapter is a discussion of these comparisons.

SENTENCE COMPREHENSION

Although the sentences used in the four Spanish and four English sentence comprehension tests were selected according to syntactic criteria noted in chapter 2, a close examination of the frequencies of correct and incorrect response to the 192 items in the eight tests failed to reveal an apparent correlation between a high or low proportion of correct answers and syntactic properties of the test sentences or the questions concerning them. What did appear to correlate with item scores were certain pragmatic or strategic properties of the sentences, of the questions, and of the relationship between the sentences and the questions concerning them.

Hypotheses

Transparency versus Opacity

For certain questions given in these tests, the information necessary for answering them was retrievable directly from the wording of the original sentence, without requiring any lexical or grammatical transformation on the part of the subject; these items are deemed to be transparent. Those that require some kind of syntactic transformation[2] or lexical recoding are considered to be opaque. For example, sentence 7 of the English listening–speaking test:

(7) The girl asked the man to fry the chicken that she plucked.

has a transparent question,

(7c) What did the girl ask the man to do?

and two opaque questions,

(7a) Who plucked the chicken? and

(7b) Who was asked to do something?

Question 7a requires recognition and understanding of the relative clause and the anaphoric use of "she," and 7b requires the recognition of the relationship of the passive question to the active sentence. Question 7c, on the other hand, can be answered without recourse to nonsuperficial linguistic structure. The answer to this question can be retrieved from the original sentence largely by quotation.

Sometimes questions were deemed opaque for lexical reasons, e.g., English reading–speaking, item 1b.

(1) The teacher gave some cheese to the boy from the city.

(1b) Who got the cheese?

Sentence 1b required knowledge of the relationship between *give* and *get*, and was thus considered to be opaque.

It was hypothesized that subjects would tend to answer a higher proportion of transparent items correctly than opaque ones.

Pragmatic Normality versus Strangeness

Many of the sentences and questions concerning them were contrived specifically to test the ability of the patients to make use of syntactic structure without relying on pragmatic cues or knowledge of the world. Thus, a sentence from Spanish reading–speaking, such as sentence 2:

(2) El gato fue perseguido hacia la azotea por el lagartijo.
("The cat was chased toward the roof by the lizard.")

[2]The term *transformation* is not being used here in the sense of contemporary theory. It is more akin to the surface-to-surface transformations of Harris (1952, 1957).

requires that a subject understand and attend to the passive structure upon answering the question:

(2a) ¿Que hizo el lagartijo?
("What did the lizard do?")

because a pragmatic or real-world based strategy would lead one to conclude that it was the cat that chased the lizard and not vice versa. Hence an item such as 2a would be considered pragmatically odd.

Similarly, sentence 8 from the English listening–writing test:

(8) The maid could understand why the lady was not fired.

has the question:

(8b) Who was fired?,

which requires the patient to realize that the information is not provided by sentence 8. This question is pragmatically odd, because the assumption (as stated explicitly in the instructions) was that the questions were to be *about* the presented sentences.

Some sentences were deemed pragmatically odd for sociocultural reasons, for example Spanish listening–speaking, sentence 7:

(7) La muchacha le pidió al carnicero que horneara el lechón que ella había matado.
("The girl asked the butcher to roast the pig that she had slaughtered.")

It would be normal for the butcher to slaughter the animal and for the girl to cook it.

Thus, questions (i) for which the information requested was not given in the original sentence or (ii) which concerned sentences that were pragmatically misleading or unusual, were considered pragmatically odd. All other items were considered to be pragmatically normal.

It was hypothesized that subjects would tend to answer a higher proportion of pragmatically normal items correctly than pragmatically odd ones.

No Apparent Alternative

For certain questions in the sentence comprehension tests, there is no obvious reasonable alternative to the correct answer. For example, in Spanish listening–speaking question 4c;

(4) La joven escuchó el concierto con su abuela.
("The young woman listened to the concert with her grandmother.")

(4c) ¿Que hizo la joven?
("What did the young woman do?")

there is no apparent alternative to the correct answer, "escuchó el concierto (con su abuela)" ("listened to the concert (with her grandmother)"). On the other hand, item 7a from English listening–writing:

(7) The boy told the girl to stop lying on the bed he just made.

(7a) Who made the bed?

requires one to decide between the boy and the girl.

It was hypothesized that subjects would tend to answer correctly a higher proportion of those questions to which there was no apparent alternative to the correct answer than those to which there was some reasonable alternative.

Short Answer versus Long Answer

Certain questions required longer answers than others. For example, English listening–writing (sentence 7a, just cited) requires a short answer ("the boy"), but English *reading*–writing, sentence 7b:

(7b) What was the request?

requires a long answer ("for the mother not to leave her muddy boots on the kitchen floor" or some reasonable paraphrase).

With long answers defined as those that require the use of three or more major-class lexical items and short answers as those requiring two or less, it was hypothesized that patients would tend to answer correctly questions requiring short answers more frequently than questions requiring long answers.

"¿Dónde?" and "Where?"

Some items asked *where* ("dónde" in Spanish) something happened, something or someone was, etc. These questions invariably required a short answer and usually had no apparent alternative to the correct one, were pragmatically normal, and were transparent. Hence it was hypothesized that *where* (*dónde*) questions would be very likely to be answered correctly, given the four previous hypotheses.

Tables 5.3–5.10 list the classifications of all 192 items in the eight sentence comprehension tests according to the five variables just described. In each case the marked (i.e., less frequent) value of these dichotomous variables is indicated with a check mark.

TABLE 5.3
Pragmatic Variables for Spanish Sentence-Comprehension:
Listening-Speaking

	Transparent	*Pragmatically Odd*	*No Obvious Alternative*	*Long Answer Required*	*Where?- ¿Dónde?*
1a.					
1b.	✓			✓	
1c.	✓		✓		✓
2a.					
2b.					
2c.		✓			
3a.					
3b.		✓			✓
3c.	✓			✓	
4a.	✓		✓		
4b.					
4c.	✓				
5a.		✓			
5b.	✓			✓	
5c.	✓		✓		
6a.					✓
6b.	✓				
6c.				✓	
7a.	✓	✓			
7b.		✓			
7c.	✓	✓			
8a.		✓			
8b.	✓			✓	
8c.		✓			

TABLE 5.4
Pragmatic Variables for Spanish Sentence Comprehension: Reading–Speaking

	Transparent	*Pragmatically Odd*	*No Obvious Alternative*	*Long Answer Required*	*Where?- ¿Dónde?*
1a.					
1b.					
1c.	✓				✓
2a.		✓			
2b.		✓			✓
2c.	✓	✓			
3a.					
3b.					
3c.		✓			
4a.					
4b.					
4c.			✓		✓
5a.	✓		✓		✓
5b.	✓				
5c.	✓			✓	
6a.	✓				
6b.					
6c.		✓			
7a.				✓	
7b.	✓	✓			
7c.					
8a.		✓			✓
8b.					
8c.	✓			✓	

TABLE 5.5
Pragmatic Variables for Spanish Sentence Comprehension:
Listening–Writing

	Transparent	*Pragmatically Odd*	*No Obvious Alternative*	*Long Answer Required*	*Where?- ¿Dónde?*
1a.	✓				
1b.		✓		✓	
1c.	✓		✓		✓
2a.		✓			
2b.				✓	
2c.					
3a.	✓		✓		✓
3b.	✓		✓		
3c.				✓	
4a.	✓				
4b.					
4c.	✓				
5a.		✓			
5b.	✓			✓	
5c.	✓		✓		
6a.	✓				
6b.					
6c.					
7a.					
7b.					
7c.				✓	
8a.	✓				
8b.		✓			
8c.			✓		

TABLE 5.6
Pragmatic Variables for Spanish Sentence Comprehension:
Reading–Writing

	Transparent	*Pragmatically Odd*	*No Obvious Alternative*	*Long Answer Required*	*Where?- ¿Dónde?*
1a.	✓		✓		
1b.					
1c.	✓		✓		✓
2a.	✓		✓		✓
2b.					
2c.	✓				
3a.					
3b.				✓	
3c.		✓			
4a.				✓	
4b.	✓				
4c.		✓			
5a.	✓			✓	
5b.	✓		✓		✓
5c.					
6a.		✓			
6b.					
6c.	✓				
7a.					
7b.				✓	
7c.				✓	
8a.	✓				
8b.		✓			
8c.	✓			✓	

TABLE 5.7
Pragmatic Variables for English Sentence Comprehension:
Listening–Speaking

	Transparent	*Pragmatically Odd*	*No Obvious Alternative*	*Long Answer Required*	*Where?- ¿Dónde?*
1a.				✓	
1b.	✓				
1c.	✓	✓			✓
2a.				✓	
2b.		✓			✓
2c.					
3a.	✓			✓	
3b.					
3c.	✓	✓			
4a.	✓				
4b.					
4c.			✓		✓
5a.			✓		✓
5b.					
5c.	✓				
6a.	✓			✓	
6b.	✓				
6c.		✓			
7a.					
7b.					
7c.	✓				
8a.			✓		✓
8b.	✓	✓			
8c.		✓			

TABLE 5.8
Pragmatic Variables for English Sentence Comprehension: Reading–Speaking

	Transparent	*Pragmatically Odd*	*No Obvious Alternative*	*Long Answer Required*	*Where?-¿Dónde?*
1a.				✓	
1b.					
1c.		✓			✓
2a.				✓	
2b.		✓			✓
2c.	✓				
3a.	✓			✓	
3b.					
3c.		✓			
4a.					
4b.					
4c.			✓		✓
5a.	✓		✓		✓
5b.	✓				
5c.	✓				
6a.	✓			✓	
6b.					
6c.		✓			
7a.					
7b.					
7c.					
8a.	✓		✓		✓
8b.		✓			
8c.		✓			

TABLE 5.9
Pragmatic Variables for English Sentence Comprehension:
Listening–Writing

	Transparent	*Pragmatically Odd*	*No Obvious Alternative*	*Long Answer Required*	*Where?- ¿Dónde?*
1a.	✓				
1b.		✓			
1c.			✓		✓
2a.		✓			
2b.					
2c.		✓			
3a.			✓		
3b.			✓		
3c.			✓		✓
4a.					
4b.	✓				
4c.					
5a.		✓			
5b.	✓			✓	
5c.		✓			
6a.	✓				
6b.					
6c.					
7a.					
7b.					
7c.		✓			
8a.		✓			
8b.		✓			
8c.		✓			

TABLE 5.10
Pragmatic Variables for English Sentence Comprehension:
Reading–Writing

	Transparent	*Pragmatically Odd*	*No Obvious Alternative*	*Long Answer Required*	*Where?- ¿Dónde?*
1a.	✓				
1b.					
1c.			✓		
2a.					✓
2b.				✓	
2c.	✓				
3a.					
3b.				✓	
3c.	✓				
4a.				✓	
4b.	✓				
4c.		✓			
5a.			✓		✓
5b.	✓		✓		
5c.			✓		
6a.		✓			
6b.					
6c.	✓				
7a.					
7b.				✓	
7c.		✓			✓
8a.					
8b.					
8c.	✓			✓	

Characteristic One: Transparency

Spanish

In the listening–speaking modality combination and in the reading–speaking modality combination there were significantly higher proportions (one-tailed chi square) of correct responses to items categorized as transparent than to those characterized as opaque.

	Opaque	Transparent		
Number of Correct Responses	81	93	174	$\chi^2 = 6.87$
Number of Incorrect Responses	127	83	210	df = 1
	208	176	384	$p < .005$

Listening–Speaking

	Opaque	Transparent		
Number of Correct Responses	15	41	56	$\chi^2 = 11.78$
Number of Incorrect Responses	69	55	124	df = 1
	84	96	180	$p < .0005$

Reading–Speaking

Although the results were not significant in the writing modality (perhaps for reasons to be discussed in the following chapter), the combined results of all four modality combinations were highly significant.

	Opaque	Transparent		
Number of Correct Responses	142	177	319	$\chi^2 = 16.06$
Number of Incorrect Responses	314	219	533	df = 1
	456	396	852	$p < .0005$

All Modalities Combined

English

In the listening–speaking modality combination there was a significantly higher proportion of correct responses to transparent items than to opaque items. Although in the other three modality combinations, results were not significant ($\chi^2 < 2.5.$), possibly because of the small number or patients taking the tests, nonetheless, the combination of the three remaining modality combinations[3] yielded a significantly higher proportion of correct answers to transparent questions than to opaque questions.

	Opaque	Transparent		
Number of Correct Responses	31	38	69	$\chi^2 = 7.13$
Number of Incorrect Responses	81	42	123	df = 1
	112	80	192	$p < .005$

Listening–Speaking

	Opaque	Transparent		
Number of Correct Responses	38	23	61	$\chi^2 = 3.78$
Number of Incorrect Responses	175	56	231	df = 1
	213	79	292	$p < .05$

All Other Modalities Combined

The combined results of all four combinations of modalities were highly significant.

	Opaque	Transparent		
Number of Correct Responses	69	61	130	$\chi^2 = 15.09$
Number of Incorrect Responses	256	98	354	df = 1
	325	159	484	$p < .0005$

All Modality Combinations Combined

[3]In anticipation of objections to the procedure of combining tests not taken by exactly the same subjects, a cross tabulation (chi square cum Fisher Exact Test) was run to see if any patient characteristics interacted with any of the item characteristics mentioned in this chapter. No significant effects or nearly significant effects (i.e., $p < .25$) were obtained.

Characteristic Two: Pragmatic Normality

Spanish

There was a significantly higher proportion of correct responses to pragmatically normal questions than to pragmatically odd ones in each of the four modality combinations.

Listening–Speaking

	Odd	Normal		
Number of Correct Responses	45	129	174	$\chi^2 = 7.77$
Number of Incorrect Responses	83	125	208	df = 1
	128	254	382	$p < .005$

Reading–Speaking

	Odd	Normal		
Number of Correct Responses	15	83	98	$\chi^2 = 12.82$
Number of Incorrect Responses	69	121	190	df = 1
	84	204	288	$p < .0005$

Listening–Writing

	Odd	Normal		
Number of Correct Responses	1	29	30	$\chi^2 = 4.28$
Number of Incorrect Responses	15	51	66	df = 1
	16	80	96	$p < .025$

Reading–Writing

	Odd	Normal		
Number of Correct Responses	2	56	58	$\chi^2 = 9.14$
Number of Incorrect Responses	30	104	134	df = 1
	32	160	192	$p < .005$

The overall results (all four modality combinations combined) were highly significant:

	Odd	Normal		
Number of Correct Responses	63	297	360	$\chi^2 = 26.33$
Number of Incorrect Responses	197	401	598	df = 1
	260	698	958	$p < .0005$

All Modalities Combined

English

There were significantly higher proportions of correct responses to pragmatically normal items than to odd ones in all combinations of input and output modalities except listening–writing (perhaps because of the small number of subjects who took the test in this modality combination).

	Odd	Normal		
Number of Correct Responses	7	62	69	$\chi^2 = 6.48$
Number of Incorrect Responses	33	90	123	df = 1
	40	152	192	$p < .01$

Listening–Speaking

	Odd	Normal		
Number of Correct Responses	0	24	24	$\chi^2 = 8.96$
Number of Incorrect Responses	24	48	72	df = 1
	24	72	96	$p < .005$

Reading–Speaking

	Odd	Normal		
Number of Correct Responses	0	23	23	$\chi^2 = 2.77$
Number of Incorrect Responses	15	82	97	df = 1
	15	105	120	$p < .05$

Reading–Writing

Overall (all four tests combined), the results were highly significant:

	Odd	Normal		
Number of Correct Responses	9	119	128	$\chi^2 = 21.81$
Number of Incorrect Responses	97	255	352	df = 1
	106	374	480	$p < .0005$

All Modalities Combined

Characteristic Three: Lack of Apparent Alternative

Spanish

There were significantly higher proportions of correct responses to questions to which there were no reasonable alternatives than to ones with alternatives, in three of the four modality combinations. In the listening–writing test, results were not significant ($\chi^2 < 1.5$), perhaps because of the fact that only four subjects took the test.

	Alternative	No Alternative		
Number of Correct Responses	142	32	174	$\chi^2 = 9.13$
Number of Incorrect Responses	194	16	210	df = 1
	336	48	384	$p < .005$

Listening–Speaking

	Alternative	No Alternative		
Number of Correct Responses	82	16	98	$\chi^2 = 10.89$
Number of Incorrect Responses	182	8	190	df = 1
	264	24	288	$p < .0005$

Reading–Speaking

	Alternative	No Alternative		
Number of Correct Responses	44	15	59	$\chi^2 = 3.84$
Number of Incorrect Responses	116	17	133	df = 1
	160	32	192	$p < .025$

Reading–Writing

Results were highly significant for the four tests combined:

	Alternative	No Alternative		
Number of Correct Responses	289	72	361	$\chi^2 = 24.41$
Number of Incorrect Responses	547	52	599	df = 1
	836	124	960	$p < .0005$

All Modalities Combined

English

For the English tests, there were significant results in the listening–speaking and reading–speaking modality combinations, with more correct responses to questions for which there were no reasonable alternative answers. In the writing modality, tests results were not significant ($\chi^2 < 1.1$), perhaps due to the low number of subjects, 3 and 5, respectively, for listening and reading.

	Alternative	No Alternative		
Number of Correct Responses	52	17	69	$\chi^2 = 4.07$
Number of Incorrect Responses	108	15	123	df = 1
	160	32	192	$p < .025$

Listening–Speaking

	Alternative	No Alternative		
Number of Correct Responses	15	9	24	$\chi^2 = 15.37$
Number of Incorrect Responses	69	3	72	df = 1
	84	12	96	$p < .0005$

Reading–Speaking

Overall results were again highly significant:

	Alternative	No Alternative		
Number of Correct Responses	94	33	127	$\chi^2 = 12.24$
Number of Incorrect Responses	309	43	352	df = 1
	403	76	479	$p < .0005$

All Modality Combinations Combined

Characteristic Four: Long versus Short Answer

It was hypothesized that there would be a higher proportion of correct responses to questions that required a short answer than to those that required a long answer (as defined earlier in "Short Answer versus Long Answer"). There were no significant results for any modality combination in either language for this test ($\chi^2 < 2.5$). A combination of the four Spanish tests with the four English tests did yield a significant result, however (see footnote 3).

	Short	Long		
Number of Correct Responses	415	74	489	$\chi^2 = 2.77$
Number of Incorrect Responses	768	178	946	df = 1
	1183	252	1435	$p < .05$

All English and Spanish Tests Combined

Characteristic Five: "¿Dónde? - Where?"

Spanish

Surprisingly, scores were not significant in any combination of modalities for this item characteristic, perhaps because of the relatively small number of "dónde" questions. Nevertheless, there was a significant effect for all four tests combined.

	Dónde	No Dónde		
Number of Correct Responses	56	295	351	$\chi^2 = 3.54$
Number of Incorrect Responses	68	526	594	df = 1
	124	821	945	$p < .05$

All Spanish Tests Combined

English

Results were significant only in the reading–speaking combination of modalities for this item characteristic:

	Where	Not Where		
Number of Correct Responses	9	15	24	$\chi^2 = 4.13$
Number of Incorrect Responses	11	61	72	df = 1
	20	76	96	$p < .025$

Reading–Speaking

Nonetheless, there was a significant effect when the results of the four tests were combined:

	Where	Not Where		
Number of Correct Responses	28	100	128	$\chi^2 = 3.54$
Number of Incorrect Responses	50	302	352	df = 1
	70	402	480	$p < .05$

All English Tests Combined

SYNTAX CORRECTION

In each of the eight tests (four for each language), there were two sentences that were perfectly correct grammatically, and seven that had some morphosyntactic error. The patient's task was to identify and correct the errors. It was hypothesized that subjects would respond more correctly to sentences that were morphosyntactically correct than to incorrect ones.

Spanish

The hypothesis was supported in the listening–speaking test, as well as in all four tests combined.

	Grammatical	Ungrammatical		
Number of Correct Responses	20	34	54	$\chi^2 = 11.19$
Number of Incorrect Responses	6	57	63	df = 1
	26	91	117	$p < .005$

Listening–Speaking

	Grammatical	Ungrammatical		
Number of Correct Responses	28	67	95	$\chi^2 = 4.08$
Number of Incorrect Responses	26	122	148	df = 1
	54	189	243	$p < .025$

All Modality Combinations Combined

English

Subjects tended to respond more correctly in their grammatical judgments to grammatically correct sentences in all modalities than to ungrammatical sentences. Because of the small number of grammatical sentences and the small number of subjects who took these tests, χ^2 could be calculated only for the combined results of the four tests.

	Grammatical	Ungrammatical		
Number of Correct Responses	8	8	16	$\chi^2 = 3.61$
Number of Incorrect Responses	14	49	63	df = 1
	22	57	79	$p < .05$

All Tests Combined

ENGLISH VERB MORPHOLOGY

The frame in which past tenses were elicited was "Yesterday [subject pronoun] ______." which can be interpreted as a pragmatic context. The frame in which past participles were elicited was "[subject pronoun] [appropriate form of 'have'] ______.", which is a purely syntactic context. It was hypothesized that the patients would perform better on past-tense responses than on past-participle responses.

The results were as follows: In each modality combination, the number of correct responses for past tense exceeded the number of correct responses for past participle by at least 50% (at least 100% in the nonlistening–speaking modality combinations). See Table 5.11.

For only one subject in only one of the four tests was the score for past participles greater than for past tenses. Of the 15 tests taken (6 in Listening–Speaking, 3 each in the other three combinations), 8 scores were higher for past tense than for past participle; of the remaining 7 tests, 6 had results in which past-

TABLE 5.11
Total Number of Correct Responses to English Verb Morphology Tests

	Total Number of Correct Responses	*Past Tenses*	*Past Participles*
Listening–Speaking	26	16	10
Reading–Speaking	9	6	3
Listening–Writing	9	6	3
Reading–Writing	7	5	2

TABLE 5.12
Number of Subjects for Whom Number of Correct Past-Tense Responses Exceeded, Equaled, and Fell Short of Correct Past-Participle Responses

	Past Tense > Past Participle	*Past Tense = Past Participle*	*Past Tense < Past Participle*
Listening–Speaking	4	1	1
Reading–Speaking	2	1	0
Listening–Writing	1	2	0
Reading–Writing	1	2	0

participle scores equalled past-tense scores. Of these 6, 5 were scores of *zero*. See Table 5.12. The hypothesis was supported at the .025 level for the four modality combinations combined:

	Past Tense	Past Participle		
Number of Correct Responses	33	18	51	$\chi^2 = 4.73$
Number of Incorrect Responses	103	118	221	df = 1
	136	136	272	$p < .025$

All Modalities

SPANISH VERB MORPHOLOGY

Analysis of Responses

Spanish has a highly inflected verb paradigm. There are three conjugation classes, two numbers, three persons (only two in the plural in New World Spanish), three aspects, three tenses, and three moods. In the tests given, correct answers (*expected,* not necessarily given by the patients) included all three conjugation classes (*-a-, -e-, -i-*); singular and plural; first, second, and third person; and preterite, imperfect, present perfect, present, conditional, and future tense-aspects, all in the indicative mode. No subjunctive forms were included because they do not normally occur in nonimperative main clauses.[4]

[4]The imperative mood was not included in these tests because of its distributional limitations and because of the rarity of verbs for which it is distinguished from both the indicative and the subjective forms (e.g., *pon, ven, haz, sal, ten,* etc.).

An examination of the data led to the following hypotheses: Subjects tended to respond correctly to items (a) in which the correct response was third person, or (b) in which the correct response was stressed on the penultimate syllable ("palabras llanas"). Furthermore, subjects tended to respond (c) more correctly to present tense items and (d) less correctly to future, conditional, and present perfect items.

The first two hypotheses failed to be supported in any modality ($\chi^2 < 2.2$.). The latter two were supported: The subjects performed significantly better on present tense items in the listening–speaking combination, and in the other three modality combinations considered together.

	Present	Not Present		
Number of Correct Responses	36	78	114	$\chi^2 = 15.99$
Number of Incorrect Responses	15	126	141	df = 1
	51	204	255	$p < .0005$

Listening–Speaking

	Present	Not Present		
Number of Correct Responses	22	68	90	$\chi^2 = 5.00$
Number of Incorrect Responses	46	284	330	df = 1
	68	352	420	$p < .025$

Listening–Writing, Reading–Speaking, and Reading–Writing Combined

Combined results from all four tests were highly significant:

	Present	Not Present		
Number of Correct Responses	58	146	204	$\chi^2 = 22.44$
Number of Incorrect Responses	61	410	471	df = 1
	119	556	675	$p < .0005$

All Modalities Combined

The last hypothesis was supported by significant results on the tests in the listening modality: Subjects performed worse on items in the future, conditional, or present perfect indicative tense-aspects than on other items.

	Future, Conditional, Present Perfect	Other Tenses		
Number of Correct Responses	40	74	114	$\chi^2 = 10.28$
Number of Incorrect Responses	79	62	141	df = 1
	119	138	255	$p < .005$

Listening–Speaking

	Future, Conditional, Present Perfect	Other Tenses		
Number of Correct Responses	1	12	13	$\chi^2 = 14.27$
Number of Incorrect Responses	71	36	107	df = 1
	72	48	120	$p < .0005$

Listening–Writing

The combination of all four tests yielded a highly significant result as well:

	Future, Conditional, Present Perfect	Other Tenses		
Number of Correct Responses	75	129	204	$\chi^2 = 14.15$
Number of Incorrect Responses	249	222	471	df = 1
	324	351	675	$p < .0005$

All Modalities Combined

Analysis of Errors

Because of the great number of inflectional categories in Spanish verb morphology, there are a great many sources of errors. Let us examine closely the kinds of errors that were made in the Spanish Verb-Morphology tests.

Listening–Speaking

Seventeen subjects took the test in the listening–speaking modality combination. The total score was 112/255, or 44.7% correct. Of five irregular verbs, four were regularized: 12 responses that were regular in form were emitted in cases in which irregular forms were required.

Person

There were 57 person mistakes. Thirteen of the 15 items were answered incorrectly with respect to person. Of the 2 items not answered incorrectly, both were first person.

There were 5 items that required a first-person response. There were 10 incorrect person responses to these items (an average of 2.0 per item). All 10 erroneous responses were in the form of third person.

There were 6 items that required a second-person response. There were 40 incorrect person responses to these items (an average of 6.7 per item). Of these errors, 28 were in the form of first person (4.7 per item) and 12 were in the form of third person (2.0 per item).

There were 4 items that required a third-person response. There were 7 incorrect person responses to these items (1.75 per item). Of these errors, 6 were first person in form (1.5 per item) and 1 was second person in form (0.25 per item).

There were thus a total of 34 erroneous first person responses (3.4 per item), one erroneous second-person response (0.1 per item), and 22 eroneous third-person responses (2.0 per item).

Number

There was a total of 30 number errors in this modality combination. Thirteen of the 15 items had number errors. To the 11 singular items there were 26 responses in plural form (2.4 per item). To the 4 plural items, there were 4 responses in singular form (1.0 per item).

Tense–Aspect

Table 5.13 represents the tense–aspect errors committed in this modality combination. The ordinate (row headings) lists the expected (i.e., correct) tense–aspects with the number of items of each tense–aspect in parenthesis. The column headings represent the tense–aspects with which the subjects responded.

TABLE 5.13
Distribution of Tense-Aspect Errors in the Listening–Speaking Modality Combination

		Responses							
Expected Tense-Aspect		*Preterite*	*Imperfect*	*Present Perfect*	*Present*	*Conditional*	*Future*	*Total*	*Errors/Item*
Preterite	(3)				7		2	9	3.0
Imperfect	(2)	13			2			15	7.5
Present Perfect	(2)	4			2		2	8	4.0
Present	(3)	5	1				1	7	2.3
Conditional	(2)	6			2		9	17	8.5
Future	(3)	3			5	2		10	3.3
TOTALS		31	1	0	18	2	14		

Reading–Speaking

Thirteen subjects took the Spanish Verb Morphology Test in the reading–speaking modality combination. The total score was 55/195 or 28.2%. All five irregular verbs were regularized. Thirteen responses that were regular in form were emitted in cases in which irregular forms were required.

Person

There were 46 person mistakes. Fourteen of the 15 items were answered incorrectly with respect to person. The one item not answered incorrectly was first person.

There were 6 items that required a first-person response. There were 17 incorrect person responses to these items (2.8 per item). All 17 erroneous responses were third person in form.

There were 3 items that required a second-person response. There were 16 incorrect person responses to these items (5.3 per item). Of these errors, 10 were first person in form (3.3 per item) and 6 were in the form of third person (2.0 per item).

There were 6 items that required a third-person response. There were 12 incorrect person responses to these items (2.0 per item). All 12 of these erroneous responses were first person in form.

Thus there were a total of 22 erroneous first-person responses (2.4 per item), no erroneous second-person responses, and 23 erroneous third-person responses (2.6 per item).

Number

There was a total of 44 number errors in this modality combination. Thirteen of the 15 items had number errors. To the 10 singular items there were 39 responses in plural form (3.9 per item). To the 5 plural items, there were 5 responses in singular form (1.0 per item).

Tense–Aspect

Table 5.14 represents the distribution of tense-aspect errors made in the reading–speaking modality combination. The columns and rows are as in Table 5.13.

Listening–Writing

Eight subjects took the Spanish Verb Morphology Test in the listening–writing modality combination. The total score was 15/120, or 12.5% correct. Of five irregular verbs, three were regularized. There were in fact only three such responses.

TABLE 5.14
Distribution of Tense-Aspect Errors in the Reading–Speaking Modality Combination

		Responses							
Expected Tense-Aspect		*Preterite*	*Imperfect*	*Present Perfect*	*Present*	*Conditional*	*Future*	*Total*	*Errors/Item*
Preterite	(3)				12		5	17	5.7
Imperfect	(2)	2			1	1	3	7	3.5
Present Perfect	(2)	8			1		3	12	6.0
Present	(3)	7					2	9	3.0
Conditional	(3)		1		3		4	8	2.7
Future	(2)	2	1		3			6	3.0
TOTALS		19	2	0	20	1	17		

Person

There were 6 person mistakes. Six of the 15 items were answered incorrectly (identifiably) with respect to person.

There were 4 items that required a first-person response. There were 2 responses in the form of second person and 1 in the form of third person to these items.

There were 2 items that required a second-person response, and only one incorrect response (in the form of first person) to these items.

There were 9 items requiring a third-person response, and 2 incorrect responses to these items (both in the form of first person).

Thus there were a total of 3 erroneous first-person responses (0.27 per item), 2 erroneous second-person responses (0.15 per item), and 1 erroneous third-person response (0.17 per item).

Number

There was a total of 4 errors in number. Four of the 15 items had a number error. To 3 of the 7 singular items, there was 1 response each in plural form. To 1 of the 8 plural items there was 1 response in singular form.

Tense–Aspect

Table 5.15 represents the distribution of tense–aspect errors in the listening–writing modality combination. The columns and rows are as in Tables 5.13 and 5.14.

Reading–Writing

Seven subjects took the test in the reading–writing modality combination. The total score was 20/105, or 19.0% correct. Three of the five irregular verbs were regularized and there were just 3 such regularizing responses.

Person

There were 19 person mistakes, in 11 of the 15 items.

There were 9 items that required a first-person response. There were 13 incorrect person responses to these items (1.4 per item), of which 7 were second person in form (0.8 per item) and 6 were third person in form (0.7 per item).

There were no items that required a second-person response. This resulted from the random assignment of person throughout stimulus items and expected responses considered together.

There were 6 items that required a third-person response. There were 6 incorrect person responses to these items (1.0 per item). Of these errors, 2 were

TABLE 5.15
Distribution of Tense-Aspect Errors in the Listening–Writing Modality Combination

		Responses							
Expected Tense-Aspect		*Preterite*	*Imperfect*	*Present Perfect*	*Present*	*Conditional*	*Future*	*Total*	*Errors/Item*
Preterite	(1)				1			1	1.0
Imperfect	(4)	3			1			4	1.0
Present Perfect	(4)	5			1			6	1.5
Present	(1)	1						1	1.0
Conditional	(2)	1			1			2	1.0
Future	(3)				4	2		6	2.0
TOTALS		10	0	0	8	2	0		

in first-person form (0.3 per item) and 4 were in second-person form (0.7 per item).

There were thus a total of 2 erroneous first-person responses (0.3 per item), 11 erroneous second-person responses (0.7 per item), and 6 erroneous third-person responses (0.7 per item).

Number

There were 18 number errors made in this modality combination. Nine of the 15 items had number errors. To the 5 singular items, there were 3 responses in plural form (0.6 per item). To the 10 plural items, there were 15 responses in singular form (1.5 per item).

Tense–Aspect

Table 5.16 represents the distribution of tense–aspect errors in the reading–writing modality combination. Columns and rows are as in the previous three tables.

Anomalies

In addition to the errors that could be accommodated by the parameters of the verbal morphology system of Spanish, there were a large number of paraphasic and anomalous responses. Table 5.17 ennumerates these anomalies by type and by modality combination.

SPANISH NUMBER AND GENDER AGREEMENT

Not surprisingly, in the Spanish agreement tests, there were proportionaly more correct responses in the speaking modality than in the writing modality (See Table 5.18). This follows the trend noted in the discussion of Table 5.1 and is significant at the .001 level.

	Speaking	Writing		
Number of Correct Responses	214	79	293	$\chi^2 = 22.45$
Number of Incorrect Responses	110	101	211	df = 1
	324	180	504	$p < .001$

Spanish Number and Gender Agreement

This result is significant for both number agreement and gender agreement.

	Speaking	Writing		
Number of Correct Responses	77	25	102	$\chi^2 = 12.98$
Number of Incorrect Responses	31	35	66	df = 1
	108	60	168	$p < .001$

Number Agreement

	Speaking	Writing		
Number of Correct Responses	137	54	191	$\chi^2 = 9.94$
Number of Incorrect Responses	79	66	145	df = 1
	216	120	336	$p < .01$

Gender Agreement

And it is significant for both articles and adjectives:

	Speaking	Writing		
Number of Correct Responses	107	41	148	$\chi^2 = 9.20$
Number of Incorrect Responses	55	49	104	df = 1
	162	90	252	$p < .01$

Agreement of Article with Noun

	Speaking	Writing		
Number of Correct Responses	107	41	147	$\chi^2 = 10.23$
Number of Incorrect Responses	55	50	105	df = 1
	162	90	252	$p < .01$

Agreement of Adjective with Noun

However, in the results of the four tests (48 items) given, another interesting fact stands out: In the speaking modality, correct agreement of both determiner and adjective was much more common than correct agreement of just determiner or just adjective, with a ratio of 4:1 of those responses in which both agreements

TABLE 5.16
Distribution of Tense-Aspect Errors in the Reading–Writing Modality Combination

		Responses							
Expected Tense-Aspect		*Preterite*	*Imperfect*	*Present Perfect*	*Present*	*Conditional*	*Future*	*Total*	*Errors/Item*
Preterite	(3)						1	1	0.3
Imperfect	(3)	6			2			8	2.7
Present Perfect	(2)	3			1			4	2.0
Present	(3)		2					2	0.7
Conditional	(2)	1			2			3	1.5
Future	(2)				1			1	0.5
TOTALS		10	2	0	6	0	1		

TABLE 5.17
Number and Type of Paraphasic and Anomalous Responses in the Spanish Verb Morphology Tests

	Modality Combination				
Type of Anomaly	*L - S*	*R - S*	*L - W*	*R - W*	*Total*
No response	5	13	18	21	57
Anomaly in root	8	4	9	3	24
Anomaly in ending	5	3	5	13	26
Neologism	10	10	47	5	72
Irrelevant response	12	4	8	1	25
Repetition of stimulus	10	29	1	3	43
Perseveration	2	0	1	0	3
Uninflected form	2	5	2	2	11

were correct to those in which only one was correct. In the writing modality, by contrast, the number of cases of correct agreement of both the determiner and the adjective exceeds the number of cases of only one of these correct by less than 50%. See Table 5.19. These results are significant at the .01 level:

	Speaking	Writing		
Correct agreement of both article and adjective	96	30	126	$\chi^2 = 8.38$
Correct agreement of only article *or* adjective (not both)	22	21	43	df = 1
	118	51	169	$p < .01$

Correct Agreement of Both Article and Adjective Compared With Correct Agreement of One Only

TABLE 5.18
Number and Percentage of Correct Responses to Spanish Agreement Tests

Modality Combination	*Number Agreement*	*Gender Agreement*	*Agreement of Article*	*Agreement of Adjective*
Listening–Speaking	49/64 (77%)	83/128 (65%)	66/96 (69%)	66/96 (69%)
Reading–Speaking	28/44 (64%)	54/88 (61%)	41/66 (62%)	41/66 (62%)
Listening–Writing	11/28 (39%)	27/56 (48%)	21/42 (50%)	17/42 (40%)
Reading–Writing	14/32 (43%)	27/64 (42%)	20/48 (42%)	23/48 (48%)

TABLE 5.19
Ratio of Correct Agreement of Both Article and Adjective With Head Noun to Correct Agreement of Either Article or Adjective but Not Both

Modality Combination	*Both Article & Adjective Correct*	*Only One Correct*	*Ratio Both : One Only*
Listening–Speaking	59	14	4.21
Reading–Speaking	37	8	4.63
Listening–Writing	14	10	1.40
Reading–Writing	16	11	1.45

ENGLISH PLURAL FORMATION

Subjects who took the English Plural Formation Tests were found to perform better on regular plurals than on irregular ones. This effect was found to be significant in the listening–speaking modality combination:

	Regular Pl.	Irregular Pl.		
Number of Correct Responses	14	6	20	$\chi^2 = 5.51$
Number of Incorrect Responses	4	12	16	df = 1
	18	18	36	$p < .02$

Listening–Speaking

Although in the other three modality combinations, the expected frequencies were too low to apply the chi square test, the result of combining the scores of the three remaining tests were significant:

	Regular	Irregular		
Number of Correct Responses	14	4	18	$\chi^2 = 7.2$
Number of Incorrect Responses	10	20	30	df = 1
	24	24	48	$p < .01$

Combined Results for Reading–Speaking, Listening–Writing and Reading–Writing

The combined results of all four tests were highly significant:

	Regular	Irregular		
Number of Correct Responses	28	10	38	$\chi^2 = 13.89$
Number of Incorrect Responses	14	32	46	df = 1
	42	42	84	$p < .001$

6 Discussion

INTERPRETATION OF RESULTS

Introduction

In chapter 1, Givón's (1979) communicative continuum and Draizar's (1982) application of it to remediation in aphasia were discussed. The similarity of this approach to that of Brown (1977, 1979, 1980, 1982); Lamendella (1976, 1977a, 1977b, 1979); Goldstein (1933, 1948, 1959); and Lebrun and Buyssens (1982) was noted. The basic claim of the present study is that aphasia[1] represents a regression in linguistic processing and/or representation in the direction of the pragmatic mode. This claim will entail (a) that aphasics will tend to perform better on tasks that can be mediated by pragmatic-mode processes or strategies, and (b) that aphasics will tend to perform tasks that require syntactic-mode processes for their successful completion by using strategies characteristic of the pragmatic mode.

---

[1]The use of the term *aphasia* in this way is not meant to imply that there are no other types of linguistic deficit caused by neuropathology (e.g., anomia, apraxia of speech, pure word deafness and other modality-specific disorders, so-called *conduction aphasia,* which is probably not an aphasia in the sense being used here, but may represent a short-term memory disorder (Caramazza et al., 1981, but see Green & Howes, 1977, for a cogent survey of interpretations), *transcortical motor aphasia,* which may represent a cognitive, nonlinguistic problem (Luria, 1970, Rubens, 1976)). Justification for this use of the term comes from evidence to be adduced in this chapter and the next that the syndromes traditionally called "aphasia" (in particular Broca's and Wernicke's) share this reduction to a presyntactic communicative mode. Phonological disorders, which are beyond the scope of the present work, will require additional analysis (see, for example, Berndt & Caramazza, 1980).

The distinction between the pragmatic and the syntactic modes of linguistic processing is not representable by a sharp dichotomy, but rather by a continuum of gradations between the two. Hence, certain syntactic-mode functions may be thought of as "higher level" or more "computational" (for example, the use of the subjunctive–indicative distinction in Spanish or anaphoric pronouns in English), whereas others may be considered "low level" or more "automatic" (for example, gender agreement in Spanish or the morphophonemics of regular past tense forms in English). As a corollary of the basic claim, it was hypothesized that the more automatic, less computational functions of the syntactic mode would tend to be better preserved among aphasics than would the higher level more computational functions. See footnote 4 in chapter 1.

Overall Trends

As noted in chapter 5, there was a distinct tendency for subjects to answer more correctly in the speaking than in the writing modality. This was significant for all tests in Spanish. Because speaking mediates pragmatic as well as syntactic-mode behavior, whereas writing is a function of the syntactic mode, this is to be expected.

In English, the tendency was significant only in the most "pragmatic" test of all, Sentence Comprehension. The other tests were all more metalinguistic, requiring specific attention to linguistic form. This fact is of importance in view of the fact that none of the patients (with the possible exception of Patient 10, who was unable to take any test in English) had acquired English at home as a child. Thus it is reasonable that the more metalinguistic tasks of the remaining tests in English would be affected in speech as well as in writing, because speaking English for most of these bilingual patients was not as natural an activity as speaking Spanish.

Sentence Comprehension

These tests are the most natural, least metalinguistic of all the tests. They most closely reproduce a natural communicative situation, in that subjects are instructed to attend to the meaning rather than the morphosyntactic form of the test sentences and questions concerning them. Nonetheless, many of the questions were formulated specifically in order to require sensitivity to syntactic form for their correct response. Chapter 5, "Hypotheses," discusses a post hoc categorization of the items in these tests in terms of five dichotomous parameters that were hypothesized to make items easier or harder, depending on whether an item received the more "pragmatic" or less "pragmatic" value of the category.

Thus, items that were classified as syntacially transparent (not requiring syntactic or lexical recording or transformation) were hypothesized to be easier than those classified as opaque (those that could not be answered by following the word order and/or vocabulary of the original sentence).

Items that were classified as pragmatically odd (by virtue of violating communicative or sociocultural norms) were hypothesized to be more difficult than items that were classified as pragmatically normal.

Similarly, for certain items there was no reasonable alternative to the correct answer, based on the test sentence. It was hypothesized that because these could generally be answered without recourse to morphosyntactic analysis because no choice needed to be made, they should be easier to answer than questions for which there were reasonable alternative answers.

Short locutions are characteristic of the pragmatic mode. It was hypothesized that questions that required short answers (as defined in "Short Answer versus Long Answer" in chapter 5) would be easier than those requiring long answers.

Finally, because "Where" ("¿Dónde?") questions were generally syntactically transparent, pragmatically normal, required a short answer, and had no apparent alternative, it was hypothesized that these questions were particularly susceptible to correct pragmatic-mode mediation and that they would therefore prove to be easier than "non-where" questions.

As shown in chapter 5, "Sentence Comprehension," there were significant effects for the first three characteristics in both languages in at least the listening–speaking modality combination and for all modalities combined.

For "Where" questions there was a significant effect in each language, only for all modalities combined (perhaps because of the relatively small number of "Where" questions). The effect of long versus short answer was significant only when the results of all tests in both languages were combined.

Thus, the basic claim, that aphasics tend to revert to a pragmatic-mode level of linguistic function is supported by the results of the sentence comprehension tests in both English and Spanish. For each of the five dichotomies, there were more correct answers to items that were classified as more "pragmatic" than to items that would require greater participation of the syntactic mode.

Syntax Correction

Under ordinary communicative circumstances, ungrammatical sentences occur relatively rarely (Chomsky's statements concerning the degenerate nature of the input for language acquisition notwithstanding. See Labov, 1972, pp. 221–222). To recognize the correctness of a perfectly grammatical sentence is thus a more natural, less metalinguistic task than to judge an ungrammatical sentence as wrong. As shown in "Syntax Correction" in chapter 5, in both languages patients scored significantly better in their judgments of grammatically correct sentences than grammatically incorrect ones. (It was necessary to combine the results of the four tests, because there were only two grammatically correct items per test.)

It might be objected that *correcting* an ungrammatical sentence is inherently more difficult than judging a grammatical one as correct (apart from pragmatic vs. syntactic-mode considerations), that comparisons should in fact be made between grammaticality *judgments* alone. But the patients in fact almost never responded that an item was incorrect without offering an attempt at correction, and frequently responses consisted of the corrections without prior statements of judgments of ungrammaticalness. This tendency to make corrections without first stating a grammaticality judgment occurred with items that were grammatically correct as well as ungrammatical ones.

Furthermore, these results are consistent with data presented by Linebarger, Schwartz, & Saffran (1983), in which four anglophone agrammatic aphasics were presented 451 sentences (of which 221 were ill-formed) and instructed to judge their grammaticalness. In this study (conducted exclusively in the listening–pointing modality combination), in which patients were *not* instructed to correct the ungrammatical sentences, the subjects tended overwhelmingly to perform better on correct items than on incorrect ones, as can be seen by the following chi-square table.

	Grammatical	Ungrammatical		
Number of Correct Responses	828	651	1479	$\chi^2 = 80.56$
Number of Incorrect Responses	92	233	325	df = 1
	920	884	1804	$p < .0005$

Thus one may conclude that the Syntax Correction Tests tend to support the basic claim.

English Verb Morphology

As noted in chapter 5, the frame in which the past participles were elicited was of a purely syntactic nature: "{I, you, he, she, we, they} have ____," whereas the past tenses were elicited in a more pragmatic, real-world frame: "Yesterday, {I, you, he, she, we, they} ____."

The better performance on the past tenses than on the past participles thus supports the basic claim: Patients operating at the level of the pragmatic mode are more likely to interpret a past tense conversationally than a past participle. In these test frames, the past participle can be approached only metalinguistically.[2]

Apart from the point about test frames, the results may suggest something about past tenses versus past participles in themselves: The past tense may be an inherently more pragmatic form, being used to refer to remote points in real time. The past participle is, on the other hand, tightly interwoven with the syntactic system of the language.

Spanish Verb Morphology

Analysis of Responses

The six tense-aspects that were used in the Spanish Verb Morphology Tests were the preterite, imperfect, present perfect, present, conditional, and future (all in the indicative mode). The frames consisted of two short phrases in which two different personal pronouns were used with the appropriate form of the same verb in the same tense-aspect. The patient was to provide the correct verb form for a third personal pronoun. Although any of these tenses can be used perfectly correctly in single-clause sentences, some tenses are more commonly used than others.

The present indicative is typically used in single-clause declaratives, as is the preterite. On the other hand, the conditional is most frequently used in main clauses of sentences with an apparent or implied *si* (''if'') clause to express counterfactual conditionals, or in complement clauses of root sentences in the preterite or imperfect. The future tense is rarely used conversationally in Puerto Rican Spanish to refer to future time. For the latter function, the construction ''ir a'' (''to be going to'') plus infinitive form of verb are generally used. The future tense is most commonly used to refer to the present time when one wishes to express uncertainty or probability: ''Ya estará ahí'' (''[S]he is probably there already,'' literally ''Already [s]he will be there''). Present perfect forms are typically used in discourse in construction with qualifiers or complement clauses, but rarely in isolation, as in the test items.

Thus the observed poor performance on items that used future, conditional, and present perfect is predicted by the basic claim, because these tense-aspects are not likely to be used in ordinary communication in the (isolated) context (or lack of context) in which they were presented in these tests.[3]

---

[2]See Boller et al. (1979) for evidence of the facilitating effect on aphasic performance of natural as opposed to artificial presentation of stimuli.

[3]It is thus certainly conceivable that frequency could have played a role in the results of these tests. However, frequency in itself is not an explanation of anything; interpretation of frequency effects awaits further research incorporating the notion of frequency in an overall theory of language dissolution. From the perspective of the present work, I would suggest that perhaps more frequent forms are either more likely to be mediated successfully by pragmatic–mode stategies, or else more likely to become automatized in the syntactic mode and thus be more resistant to Givonian regression.

But the present indicative is likely to be used for basic communication even in the pragmatic mode, and hence, is likely to be well preserved even among aphasics, especially in the short, single-clause locutions of these tests. The observed superior performance on present-tense items is consistent with the basic claim.

Analysis of Errors

The analysis of the types of errors made in the Spanish Verb Morphology Tests is also revealing in light of the basic claim derived from Givón's theory.

Person Errors

In the *speaking* modality there was a clear pattern of (a) a high proportion of incorrect responses to items requiring a second-person response[4] (see Table 6.1), and (b) a low proportion of erroneous responses in second-person form (see Table 6.2). Both these patterns follow from the basic claim, if one takes into account the nature of the testing procedure. With respect to the large number of incorrect second-person responses, it is plausible that the patients were responding to the second-person pronoun, "tú," in a conversational way, understanding the pronoun as refering to themselves. This interpretation is supported by the fact that the great majority of erroneous responses to the second-person items were in the form of first person rather than third person (4.7 first person to 2.0 third person for the listening–speaking modality combination; 3.3. first person to 2.0 third person for the reading–speaking combination).

The second pattern (b), the low proportion of erroneous responses in the form of second person can also be related to the testing procedure. In Puerto Rican Spanish, the only form that requires inflection for second person is "tú" (you familiar singular nominative).[5] Given the formal circumstances of the testing situation, and the lack of familiarity with the examiner, if the patient were responding to the test item in a conversational way, it would be extremely unlikely that (s)he would use this familiar form of address.

Thus the types of errors that were made with respect to person in the speaking modality indicate the plausibility of imputing to the patients a conversational, rather than formal-linguistic interpretation of the testing situation. The former

[4]This is in spite of counting elided (i.e., ø) variants of Spanish /s/ as correct, when used as second-person ending. See López Morales (1983), Poplack (1977), Terrell (1976, 1978a, 1978b), Uber (1981), Hammond (1982), and Hochberg (1986, 1987), for discussion of the variability of postnuclear /s/ in Puerto Rican Spanish.

[5]*Vosotros* (second person plural) is not used anywhere in the New World. *Usted* and *ustedes*, the polite forms for *you* (singular) and *you* (plural), respectively, require verbal conjugation in the third person, along with *él* (*he*) and *ella* (*she*) in the singular, and *ellos* (*they*) and *ellas* (*they* [feminine]) in the plural.

TABLE 6.1
Number of Incorrect Responses Made *per Item* to Items Requiring First, Second, and Third-Person Responses

Errors per Item in	*Listening–Speaking*	*Reading–Speaking*	*Listening–Writing*	*Reading–Writing*
First Person	2.0	2.8	0.5	1.4
Second Person	6.7	5.3	0.5	—
Third Person	1.8	2.0	0.2	1.0

TABLE 6.2
Nature of Incorrect Responses Made:
Errors in Form of First, Second, and Third Person

Incorrect Responses in Form of	*Listening–Speaking*	*Reading–Speaking*	*Listening–Writing*	*Reading–Writing*
First Person	3.4	2.4	0.3	0.3
Second Person	0.1	0	0.2	0.7
Third Person	2.0	2.6	0.2	0.7

but not the latter is consistent with processing at the level of the pragmatic mode. The failure of these two trends to manifest themselves in the writing modality lends further (albeit weak) support to the assumption that the patients were reacting conversationally to these tests in the speaking modality.

Tense–Aspect Errors

Tables 5.13 through 5.16 summarize the error patterns for tense-aspect in the four modality combinations. From these tables, three facts emerge, all of which support the basic claim: (a) Erroneous present-indicative and (b) erroneous preterite-indicative forms occur more frequently than other errors, and (c) erroneous forms in the future indicative tend to occur more frequently in the speaking modality. If we assume that patients reacted to the items of these tests as though they were (admittedly artificial) conversations, it is not surprising that preterite and present tenses predominated, because these tenses would predominate in single-clause sentences in conversation. Furthermore, because erroneous responses in preterite form were by far the most frequent, it is important to note that of the six tense-aspects tested, four are used to refer to past events. But preterite (+ past, + perfective, + indicative) is generally the only one used in single-clause sentences unless there is context conditioning the use of another tense-aspect form. Hence, in a conversational interpretation (which would be consistent with pragmatic-mode processing) of these morphology tests, it would be expected that mistakes in the form of preterite would predominate, replacing the more syntactically implanted imperfect, present perfect, and conditional forms used to refer to past time. If is also worth noting that conditional forms rarely occur in single-clause sentences, and present perfect and imperfect do so much less than preterites (See footnote 3).

The fact that erroneous future-tense forms in the speaking modality also tend to predominate, supports the conversational (and pragmatic-mode) interpretation I have been suggesting regarding these tests: As noted previously, in Puerto Rican Spanish, the morphological future tense is most often used to indicate doubt or wonder concerning present (time) events. The high proportion in the speaking modality of future-tense responses suggests a guessing strategy ("I wonder if it's . . ."). Given a conversational interpretation of the test items on the part of the patient, and given a lack of certainty as to the correct form, the use of the future tense-aspect may indicate that the patient is guessing. Under this interpretation, the excessive use of the future indicative in the speaking modality tests would indicate a correct use of pragmatic strategies rather than a mere lack of sensitivity to the fine points of Spanish verb morphology.

Spanish Number and Gender Agreement

As already noted, it is expected that in aphasia certain automatic, early acquired, and overlearned forms of the syntactic mode will be resistant to dissolution due to brain damage. Spanish number and gender agreement would be included in this category. The fact that performance was better in speaking (a more automatic modality than writing for most people) than in writing supports this claim. More persuasive evidence comes from the fact that patients were much more likely to be correct in *both* article and adjective (rather than in just one or the other) in the speaking modality than in the writing modality (see Table 5.19). This result presents a picture of the patient automatically saying full noun phrases with appropriate agreement: once the number and gender of the noun are retrieved (or in some way decided), the agreements are quite automatic. On the other hand, in the writing modality, the choices with respect to the agreement of article and adjective are apparently more conscious, more independent of each other in this less natural modality.

English Plural Formation

The morphophonemic alternation of English regular plural formation is an early acquired phenomenon (see Krashen, 1981) and one that is extremely well learned, since the same alternations apply to third person singular present formation and to the possessive form of nouns. It is thus no surprise that the regular plural in English would be among those forms of the syntactic mode highly resistent to aphasic dissolution (see "English Plural Formation" in chapter 5).

On the other hand, the irregular forms are unrelated to other morphemes and follow no single pattern. They are for the most part suppletive and therefore, not surprisingly, more susceptible to aphasic impairment than the regular forms.

Summary

Recent approaches to aphasia have emphasized localization of function (see Kean (1984) for discussion) despite disclaimers often paid to the illegitimacy of claiming localization of function on the basis of localization of symptom(s) (cf. Caplan, 1981, 1982; Geschwind, 1984; Wood, 1982). Recent less-than-strict localizationist approaches (e.g., Brown, 1977; Lamendella, 1976, 1977a; Luria, 1970) as well as others (e.g., Cappa & Vignolo, 1979; Darley, Brown, & Swenson, 1975; Mohr, Walters, & Duncan, 1975; Naeser, 1983; Naeser et al., 1983; Ojemann, 1975, 1976) have stressed subcortical as well as cortical-level correspondences between brain and language.

In this study, I have adopted a Givonian framework and have observed that aphasia tends to reduce linguistic performance to a pragmatic-mode level. This observation comes from a variety of tests in two languages and four modality combinations. Some tests are more "natural," more amenable to a pragmatic-mode approach than others. Certain items within tests are more pragmatic-mode oriented and less syntactic- mode oriented than others. That aphasia tends to reduce linguistic processing and/or structure to the pragmatic mode is what I have called the "Basic Claim."

In particular, it was found that sentence-comprehension questions classified as syntactically transparent, pragmatically normal, lacking in reasonable alternative answers to the correct one, and requiring a short response were more likely to be answered correctly by aphasics than questions lacking these properties. It was found that the testing procedures for both Spanish and English verbal morphologies engendered a tendency to respond in a conversational (i.e., pragmatic as opposed to metalinguistic) mode.

In addition, a second claim based on the results of this study is that certain syntactic-mode forms are more automatic, less "computational,"[6] and hence, more resistant to dissolution due to aphasia than others. Results indicated that Spanish number and gender agreement and English regular plurals tend to be among those syntactic-mode elements resistant to dissolution in aphasia.

---

[6]The distinction between the pragmatic and syntactic modes appears to be similar in some ways to Chomsky's distinction between the "conceptual" and the "computational" aspects of language, in which only the latter is strictly linguistic (Chomsky, 1980, p. 55).

EVIDENCE FROM OTHER STUDIES

Agrammatism

The Syntactic Approach

In recent years, much research has focused attention on analysis of the phenomenon known as agrammatism. This pattern of speech, characteristic of aphasics with anterior lesions, which is generally characterized by a "telegrammatic" style in which functors and inflections tend to be omitted (Caplan, 1985; Kean, 1978) or misselected (Grodzinsky, 1984; Grodzinsky, Swinney, & Zurif, 1985), and in which normal rate and prosody are disrupted (Benson & Geschwind, 1976; Goodglass, 1968), and utterance length reduced (Goodglass & Kaplan, 1972), has long been a central theme in neurolinguistic literature.

This speech pattern, combined with distorted articulation and phonemic paraphasias characteristic of infero-posterior left frontal cortical lessions constitutes the oral-expressive aspect of a syndrome most often referred to by the name of "Broca's aphasia," after the discoverer of the lesion locus associated with the syndrome, but also frequently referred to as "motor aphasia" or "expressive aphasia," due to the apparent superiority demonstrated by these patients in comprehension, as compared to production, both in speech and writing (Alajouanine, 1968).

Although in the early part of this century, Bonhoeffer (1902) and Salomon (1914) had noted receptive components to this syndrome, in most of the aphasia literature of this century, Broca's aphasics have been referred to variously as having (in addition to "motor" and "expressive" aphasia), "aphemia" (Broca's term was "aphémie"), "verbal aphasia," "verbal apraxia," "cortical dysarthria," "efferent motor aphasia," "syntactic aphasia," "apraxic dysarthria," and other more and less colorful labels, many of which have imputed to these patients a purely expressive disorder (Bay, 1962; Lenneberg, 1973; Pick, 1913; Weisenburg & McBride, 1985).

Recent attention to the issue of the existence and nature of a possible receptive aspect of agrammatism began with the publication of a paper in which it was reported that agrammatic patients grouped closed-class lexical items (i.e., articles, pronouns, copulas, prepositions, etc.) in a bizarre fashion, when asked to arrange words from presented sentences in groups of two words (from sets of three words presented at a time) judged to be most closely related (Zurif, Caramazza, & Meyerson, 1972). Whereas the judgments of normal speakers resulted in a hierarchical clustering (Johnson, 1967) pattern very similar to correct surface syntactic phrase markers, the agrammatics' patterns portrayed an insensitivity to the role of the grammatical functors.

The receptive side of agrammatism has subsequently been assiduously probed in a wide variety of experimental paradigms such as comprehension of center-embedded clauses with and without the possibility of employing semantic or pragmatic cues (Caramazza & Zurif, 1976), paragraph- and sentence-interpretation tasks emphasizing "semantic, 'real-word' " versus "syntactic, relational" vocabulary (Samuels & Benson, 1979), sentence-comprehension tests in which the position of a determiner alone altered meaning (Caplan, Matthei, & Gigley, 1981; Heilman & Scholes, 1976), comprehension of embedded versus conjoined sentences (Goodglass et al., 1979), picture-pointing tests involving word order (Schwartz, Saffran, & Marin, 1980), arrangement of cards containing sentence fragments to test sensitivity to word order (Saffran, Schwartz, & Marin, 1980), ordering of constituents either to form sentences (Von Stockert, 1972), or to form either grammatically or lexically anomalous strings (Von Stockert & Bader, 1976), and others.

Although all these studies putatively demonstrated that agrammatic speech was not merely a production problem, the question remained as to how to interpret the phenomenon in terms of a model of language form and/or processing. Superficially, the deficit appears to be one of syntax, and many researchers have interpreted it in exactly such terms (Berndt & Caramazza 1980; Caplan 1985; Caramazza, Berndt, Basili, & Koller, 1981; Caramazza & Zurif 1976; Marshall 1977; Samuels & Benson 1979; Zurif et al. 1972; Zurif & Caramazza 1976; and others). Other research has shown the syntactic problem to go beyond the difficulties with closed-class items: Schwartz et al. (1980) and Saffran et al. (1980) claim to have shown the existence of word-order difficulties in agrammatics' production and comprehension (word order having been generally regarded as preserved among these patients [Goodglass & Kaplan 1972]), but see Caplan (1983) for an alternative analysis. Kolk (1978) reports that in a sorting task similar to that of Zurif et al. (1972), agrammatic patients had difficulty in grouping adjectives in addition to functors.

In spite of the strong evidence for a syntactic deficit in agrammatics, at least three types of nonsyntactic interpretations have recently appeared in the literature: semantic, lexical, and phonological.

The Semantic Approach

One claim for semantic involvement has come from Goodenough, Zurif, & Weintraub (1977), who found agrammatic aphasics to be insensitive to meaning distinctions conveyed by determiners, especially the definite–indefinite dimension. Furthermore, the relevance of semantics has been implicit in much of the research that has been used to support a syntactic interpretation. For example, Zurif and Caramazza (1976) note that the agrammatic aphasic's control over a functor be it in production, comprehension, or metalinguistic task "seems primarily determined by the typical usefulness of the functor in imparting meaning"

(p. 290; see also Schnitzer, 1974). Friederici (1982) found results congruent with this interpretation in acceptability-judgment and production tasks involving syntactic (i.e., obligatory) and semantic (i.e., lexical) aspects of prepositions. Schnitzer (1982, 1986), employing a stratificational-grammar framework (Lockwood, 1972) argues that Broca's aphasia affects the morpholexotactics of a language, leaving the sememic stratum intact; this approach would distinguish between those functors with sememic mapping and those without (i.e., purely morpholexemic). Heilman and Scholes (1976), however, found an insensitivity to determiners among Broca's (and conduction) aphasics even when the determiners were used critically to determine a sentence's meaning.

The Lexical Approach

Bradley, Garrett, and Zurif (1980) report a difference between the performance of Broca's (agrammatic) aphasics and that of normal subjects on two types of lexical decision task. Essentially, in tasks requiring one to decide if a presented string of letters was a word or not, normal subjects showed a reaction-time difference related to the word's frequency of occurrence in the language (Bradley, 1978). The time needed to determine that a string was a real word correlated inversely with its frequency of occurrence. For normals, this difference was found for open-class ("content") words only. But for Broca's aphasics, there was no difference found between their reaction-time behavior on closed-class items and open-class items: The Broca's aphasics reacted to the closed-class items as though they were open-class items. In a similar lexical-decision experiment, Bradley et al. (1980) found that although for normal subjects, nonsense words containing initial sequences that formed real words (e.g., "**toastle*," which contains *toast*) tended to delay reaction time, this phenomenon occurred only when the initial sequences represented open-class vocabulary. For Broca's aphasics, the difference between open- and closed-class sequences did not appear: The delayed reaction time occurred for closed-class items as well.

Bradley et al. (1980) used these results to argue for the existence of different word-retrieval strategies for open- and closed-class vocabulary, and for the impairment of the closed-class access routine in Broca's aphasia. Thus, although they characterize the Broca's deficit as "syntactic," in fact their model involves the impairment of a particular sort of lexical retrieval.

Recently, Gordon and Caramazza (1982) failed to replicate the word-frequency results with normals and argue against Bradley's (1978) interpretation on theoretical grounds. In a subsequent study of frequency sensitivity to closed-class items among agrammatic and nonagrammatic aphasics, Gordon and Caramazza (1983) found that reactions were similar whether or not the patient was agrammatic.

Phonological Approaches

Due in part to the dysprosody and phonemic paraphasias commonly noted in the speech of agrammatics and the relatively good comprehension of these patients, phonological interpretations of the syndrome have had a long history. Many investigators have taken the articulatory disorder to be the essence of the problem and have argued for an interpretation in which a verbal apraxia or phonological disintegration is considered to be the central problem of these patients (e.g., Alajouanine, Ombredane, & Durand, 1939; Bay 1962, 1964, 1967; De Jong 1958; Denny-Brown 1965; Foix, 1928; Hécaen 1972; Nathan, 1947; Shankweiler & Harris 1966).

Goodglass (1968) concluded that the underlying deficit in agrammatic aphasia was "an increased threshold for initiating and maintaining the flow of speech" (p. 204). He accounted for the problem of functors by noting the importance of phonological stress and prominence for initiation of speech in agrammatism, and the tendency for functors to occur in unstressed positions (see also Goodlass, Fodor, & Schulhoff; 1967). In a metalinguistic (sentence completion) task, Gleason et al. (1975) found results that paralleled Goodglass's production interpretation, i.e., function words were most frequently lost in initial position except when stressed. Patients sometimes reworded sentences in order to begin with a stressed word. However, in another (receptive) task, Swinney, Zurif, & Cutler (1980) found that although all speakers could identify a stressed "target word" in a presented sentence more quickly than an unstressed one, Broca's aphasics responded more quickly to open-class than to closed-class words, whereas normals showed no word-class effect.

Kean (1977, 1978, 1979, 1980) has recently proposed a phonologically based interpretation of agrammatism with a much more abstract basis in phonology. Accepting the open-versus closed-class interpretation of the disorder (and including inflectional morphemes with closed-class items), she argues that in current linguistic theory the only place in which the two classes are nonarbitrarily distinguishable is the phonological component, where they are divided into those formatives that are and those that are not phonological words. She interprets agrammatism as a tendency to "reduce the structure of a sentence to the minimal string of elements that can be lexically construed as phonological words in the patient's language" (1978, p. 88).

Lapointe (1983) points out, however, that in a "unified theory of morphology," both derivational morphology (traditionally handled in the lexicon) and inflectional morphology (traditionally handled in the readjustment component of the phonology) can be carried out in the same component. With the assumption of this model, the (presumably) appropriate word-class distinction can be made in terms of "those stemlevel items (of major categories) that are inserted into morphosyntactic structures during lexical insertion" (p. 24) as being those elements "relatively retained" in agrammatism.

Grodzinsky (1984, cf. Grodzinsky, Swinney, & Zurif 1985) has challenged Kean's analysis on empirical grounds, with data from languages in which (some) major-class lexical items cannot occur uninflected for phonetic, phonological or morphological reasons. Grodzinsky (1984) defines "the agrammatic condition" as follows: (a) "if a terminal element at S-structure" (Chomsky 1980, 1981, 1982) "is not lexically specified, then it will be unspecified at this level" in agrammatism, and (b) "every preposition at S-structure will be deleted unless it is a head of a prepositional phrase attached to S" (p. 112).

Although condition b seems to be a hard-core example of a syntactic condition, Rizzi (1985) has shown it possible to divide the class of prepositions appropriately in terms of their participation in the assignment of thematic roles (Jackendoff, 1972). Specifically, Rizzi notes that theta assigners and assignees are more likely to be preserved in agrammatism; in other words, those elements from the class of phonological clitics (i.e., elements not classified as phonological words) which are more likely to be preserved in agrammatism, are those affected by thematic-role structure, either as assigners (prepositions) or assignees (pronouns).

Grodzinsky (1986a) has recently made his proposal more explicit in terms of GB theory (Chomsky, 1981, 1982). He claims that agrammatism is describable in terms of a failure to represent traces with their indices in S-structure representation and proposes a "default principle" to permit the assignment of theta roles to NP that have not been assigned them: A universal list would assign default values to syntactic *positions*. See Caplan and Hildebrandt (1986), Sproat (1986), and Grodzinsky (1986b) for discussion.

Multiple-Deficit Approaches

Berndt and Caramazza (1980), after an extensive review of the literature on Broca's aphasia, conclude that it cannot be accounted for as a single neuropsychological phenomenon. They cite the history of approaches to the production problem, which was once thought of as representing an economy of effort (Isserlin, 1922; Pick, 1913), and later as one related to stress and "saliency" (Goodglass, 1968). The latter might be useful for explaining the speech of agrammatics but hardly for the agrammatic comprehension and metalinguistic dysfunction found in the various studies cited (and cited earlier herein). These studies, which indicate a receptive component, when considered along with the speech output and evidence of reading deficits in these patients (Benson, 1977) argue for a central linguistic deficit in what Berndt and Caramazza interpret as a "syntactic parser" (cf. Clark & Clark, 1977). But the central-parser deficit does not account for the halting, dysprosodic sometimes paraphasic speech behavior typically co-occurring with agrammatism; hence, they posit the disruption of a second mechanism, one that is specifically responsible for motor speech production. These two systems are theoretically independent. Berndt and Caramazza explain the frequent co-occurence of the two syndromes on the basis of postulated proximity of the neuroanatomical loci of the two neuropsychological systems.

More recently, Caramazza and Berndt (1985) have refined this approach to take into account the phenomena of (a) asyntactic comprehension without agrammatic speech (as in conduction aphasia), (b) agrammatism without asyntactic comprehension (Miceli, Mazzucchi, Menn, & Goodglass, 1983), and (c) agrammatism with spared grammaticality judgments (Linebarger et al., 1983). Although their conclusions are extremely tentative and liberally sprinkled with caveats, the authors (Caramazza & Berndt, 1985) conclude that the current evidence "strongly implies the existence of independent production and comprehension mechanisms at the level of computation of grammatical features" (p. 45). They conclude by proposing a "syntactic mapping deficit" for expression and a "semantic mapping deficit" for comprehension, once again attributing frequent co-occurrence of the input and output disorders to neuroanatomical proximity.

Paragrammatism

Lecours et al. (1981) define "paragrammatic deviation" as one that "causes the clause, phrase or sentence in which it occurs to transgress one rule or another of normative grammar" (p. 10). This phenomenon is most frequently associated with superior left temporal lesions and a host of other symptoms including hyperfluency of speech, word-finding difficulty, anomia, circumlocutions, verbal and phonemic paraphasias, and marked comprehension problems, which represent a syndrome known as "Wernicke's aphasia." In extreme cases characterized by unrecognizable speech forms, it has been referred to as "neologistic jargon aphasia" (Buckingham & Kertesz, 1976).

The speech output of paragrammatics appears to be complementary to that of agrammatics, that is, closed-class items tend to be used correctly, whereas major-class items are affected by retrieval problems, circumlocution, and verbal and phonemic paraphasia. Hence the names: the agrammatic speaker without grammar; the paragrammatic with a distorted grammar with incorrect use of grammatical relations. The term *paragrammatism,* coined by Kleist (1916) highlights this putative distinction.

Many of the investigations mentioned in the previous discussion of agrammatism were also performed using Wernicke's aphasics as subjects. Von Stockert (1972), reporting the results of an ordering-of-constituents task, found Wernicke's aphasics to be better than Broca's aphasics at forming simple declaratives. Von Stockert and Bader (1976), in an extension of this test designed to force a choice between lexical and grammatical anomaly, found that whereas Broca's aphasics tended to prefer ungrammaticalness, Wernicke's aphasics tended to preserve syntactic structure at the expense of lexico-semantic anomaly.

Friederici (1982) found a difference between Broca's and Wernicke's aphasics in a production task and an acceptability-judgment task. Wernicke's patients more accurately determined the acceptability of prepositions in their syntactic (i.e., obligatory) role than in their semantic role—e.g., Peter steht *auf* dem Stuhl (Peter stood *on* the chair) versus Peter achtet *auf* das Feuer (Peter watched the fire). In production, Wernicke's aphasics were more likely to produce prepositions in primarily syntactic roles than were Broca's aphasics.

Luria (1975) reports on two sets of experiments designed to probe Jakobson's (1963, 1964; Jakobson & Halle, 1956) division of the aphasics along the paradigmatic-syntagmatic dimension. He found that aphasics with posterior lesions "could deal with the task of discovering syntactical inaccuracies and mistakes in simple sentences . . . and easily correct wrongly constructed sentences" (Luria, 1975, p. 50). Patients with anterior lesions "experienced great difficulty" or entirely failed to notice syntactic errors" (p. 50). He found opposite trends between these two groups of patients in tasks involving logical relationships (e.g., "summer before spring" vs. "spring before summer").

Jones and Wepman (1965) did a factor analysis on aphasic speech and found a factor that distinguished agrammatics from paragrammatic subjects. Positive scores on this factor denote a higher incidence of nouns and adjectives than auxiliary verbs and pronouns (Goodglass, 1976). Agrammatics tended to have high scores on this factor. Paragrammatics tended to have low scores. (Also see Jones and Wepman, 1961 for discussion of their analytic technique.)

Consistent with these findings of Wernicke's aphasics' tendency to preserve "grammatical" words in their speech, Lavorel (1982) reports that a computerized immediate-constituent parser (AMEDE, Lavorel, 1979, 1982) accepted 96% of Wernicke's aphasics' language as grammatical! Heeschen (1985) has challenged these findings, claiming that they were due to focusing on English and French, languages that are relatively "impoverished" morphologically. He states, "in morphologically less impoverished languages the speech of Wernicke patients is full of morphological errors, syntagmatic as well as paradigmatic" (p. 212).

A Unified Approach

Kertesz (1982) states that "the striking difference between the nonfluent patient with an effortful speech who comprehends rather well and the patient with fluent jargon output but without comprehension is powerful evidence against the unitary concept of aphasia" (p. 43). Indeed. Nonetheless, the theory of a unitary phenomenon has had a number of proponents, most prominently Schuell and Jenkins (1961; Jenkins & Shaw, 1975; Schuell, Jenkins, & Carroll, 1962; Schuell, Jenkins, & Jiménez-Pabón, 1964).

Recent research in favor of a unified-phenomenon approach include Goodglass's (1968) findings in a variety of structured production tasks (such as repetitions and sentence completions), that grammatical tasks arranged themselves in a hierarchy of difficulty, which were invariant across aphasic type. Parisi and Pizzamiglio (1970) concur, having found a constant hierarchy of difficulty across Broca's and Wernicke's aphasics in a sentence comprehension task that probed a variety of syntactic contrasts (many of which involved functors). In a similar vein, Shewan and Canter (1971) in a study of auditory comprehension of sentences in which test items were varied systematically with respect to length, difficulty of vocabulary, and syntactic complexity, found no qualitative differences among Broca's, Wernicke's, and amnestic aphasics, and a fourth group of normal subjects. Although aphasics performed worse than normals, and Wernicke's patients performed worst of all, there was no difference in the ordering of the parameters among the four groups. In each group, syntactic complexity caused the most difficulty.

Goodglass and Menn (1985) argue against the agrammatism–paragrammatism distinction on a number of grounds, most relevant of which to the present discussion being their claim that grammatical comprehension studies have failed to distinguish the two syndromes. In particular, they cite Kurowski (1981) who found, on submitting Zurif's sorting task to Wernicke's aphasics, that the same kind of patterns in hierarchical clustering analysis arose as with the Broca's aphasics. They also cite Goodglass et al. (1979) who found no difference between Broca's and Wernicke's aphasics in a variety of grammatical tasks, and Blumstein, Goodglass, Statlender, & Biber (1983), who found that all aphasics tend to approach reflexive-pronoun anaphora with a "minimal distance principle" (between the reflexive and the closest preceding noun) regardless of diagnostic classification. Finally, Goodglass and Menn take issue with Von Stockert and Bader's (1976) differentiation of Broca's and Wernicke's aphasics based on the former's preference for lexical correctness at the expense of grammatical incorrectness (and the opposite tendency for the Wernicke's patients) in the forced choice task cited previously. They claim that another possible (and "more conservative") interpretation would be that Broca's aphasics had superior lexical comprehension to Wernicke's patients and could thus use a lexical strategy to select the combination of cards that yielded a plausible message; the Wernicke's aphasics, however, because of their grave comprehension problems were forced to rely on their grammatical knowledge.

Heeschen (1985) also rejects the agrammatism–paragrammatism distinction, arguing that the underlying deficit is the same (although paragrammatics have a more severe lexical problem). His claim is based on the lack of clear evidence for differences between the two groups in comprehension, or on any receptive task. This position is consistent with that of Kolk, Grunsven, and Keyser (1985). Heeschen and Kolk et al. also agree that the marked differences observed in speech production between Broca's and Wernicke's aphasics are not due to differences in the deficit but to different strategies for dealing with the deficit.

The position of Kolk and his colleagues is that the basic deficit is a delay in processes that underlie language production. To serve his/her communicative needs, the agrammatic *chooses* to adapt by eliminating grammatical morphemes in an attempt to maintain a normal speech rate. Although Kolk et al. do not discuss paragrammatism, one would assume that under this interpretation it would somehow represent either a failure to adapt, or else a different kind of adaptation.

Heeschen (1985), on the other hand, believes that syntax per se is disrupted in aphasia. He accounts for agrammatic production in terms of an avoidance strategy, "avoiding any potential source of syntactic trouble in . . . spontaneous speech" (p. 234). Paragrammatic patients "do not try to circumvent the danger points" (p. 234), in part because they tend to be unaware of the nature of their problem. Heeschen adduces evidence for this position from an experiment in which agrammatics were forced to use case marking (in German) in order to distinguish between two pictures. Under this condition, the speech of the agrammatics closely resembled that of paragrammatics in spontaneous speech, i.e., with greater presence of incorrectly used case markings and other closed-class elements. On the other hand, in spontaneous speech, the agrammatics produced no incorrect obligatory case markings (as compared to 23% for paragrammatics) and only 2% incorrect usage of other obligatory closed-class elements (as compared to 17% for paragrammatics).

The Basic Claim

Accepting the views expressed by Goodglass and Menn (1985), Kolk et al. (1985), and Heeschen (1985) as to what the data *are* regarding the interpretation of agrammatism and paragrammatism, it is immediately clear that these data are consistent with the Basic Claim stated at the beginning of this chapter, and its corollary. Agrammatic speech represents a regression in the direction of the pragmatic mode. Kolk et al. object to all-or-nothing, presence-or-absence interpretations of agrammatism; because the pragmatic-mode syntactic-mode axis defines a continuum, one would naturally expect cases of more and less regression. The Basic Claim is consistent with data adduced by Goodglass (1968), Parisi and Pizzamiglio (1970), and Shewan and Canter (1971), demonstrating a constant hierarchy of difficulty across Broca's and Wernicke's aphasics, and with those of Gordon and Caramazza (1983), showing a closed-class frequency effect in a lexical decision task for fluent as well as agrammatic aphasics. Both syndromes represent a regression along the Givonian continuum. The Basic Claim's corollary, viz. that more automatic, less computational functions of the syntactic mode will tend to be better preserved among aphasics than higher level more computational functions is illustrated by the preservation of grammatical elements and low-level grammatical functions in paragrammatism in the absence of overall morphosyntactic coherence. The relative preservation of functors, agreement relations, etc., in the absence of control over the lexicon and propositions among paragrammatics signals a more drastic regression in Givonian terms than does the essentially communicatively coherent performance of agrammatics. In other words, paragrammatics have a more severe aphasia (in the sense defined previously) than agrammatics. In extreme cases, the former are not functioning even at the lower limits of the pragmatic mode: Attempts at communication will then result in the "liberation" of the overlearned automatic units in an incoherent fashion (often while the patient vainly searches for the major-class lexical items [s]he needs to communicate). Agrammatics, with less severe aphasia, are able to function at least in pragmatic-mode terms: They are able to suppress those overlearned automatic units, when they are a hindrance because they can no longer be used computationally.

Evidence for this position can be found in Blumstein et al. (1983), in a study in which comprehension of reference as reflected in reflexivization was studied with a group of Broca's, conduction, and Wernicke's aphasics in a sentence-to-picture matching paradigm. The use of various types of cues in the test sentences (syntactic only, syntactic + lexical, syntactic + morphological, and syntactic + morphological + lexical) resulted in the following: All groups tended to use the minimal distance principle mentioned earlier to relate reflexives with possible antecedents. The minimal distance principle is a nonsyntactic strategy (because it operates over strings rather than constitutents) and would be usable in pragmatic-mode processing. In addition, Blumstein et al. found that performance was impaired among all groups when only syntactic cues were provided, and that *all groups* showed slight improvement with the addition of morphological cues. Lexical cues, although aiding the Broca's and conduction patients' comprehension, resulted in *poorer* performance among the Wernicke's, which illustrates the extent to which these patients have lost communicative function. Heilman and Scholes (1976), in the syntactic-relationships study mentioned previously, note that although their results suggest that Wernicke's aphasics have worse syntactic comprehension than Broca's, "a closer analysis of this data suggests that our Wernicke's aphasics' comprehension of major lexical items was so poor that we were not testing syntax but rather eliciting random choices" (p. 262). This observation that Wernicke's aphasics have such poor lexical comprehension also sheds light (as noted by Goodglass & Menn 1985) on Von Stockert and Bader's (1976) reported results of the forced-choice card-arranging task in which Broca's aphasics grouped lexically at the expense of grammar whereas Wernicke's patients chose the opposite course: According to this interpretation, in fact the Wernicke's aphasics had no choice because their lexical and computational capabilities were so limited that they could only rely on the disconnected grammatical functions that remained. The Broca's aphasics, who were not so communicatively deprived, were able to form plausible propositions using a pragmatic-mode strategy. Further evidence for the disruption of lexical knowledge among paragrammatics ("posterior aphasics") comes from a study of semantics reported by Grober, Perecman, Kellar, and Brown (1980) in which posterior aphasics were found to base their decisions of category membership of nouns on the basis of "characteristic features," which resulted in errors on atypical members of various categories. Knowledge of the semantic properties of major-class lexical items is essential for propositional language. Anterior aphasics' performance was indistinguishable from that of normal controls.

Other evidence for the Basic Claim comes from Goodglass et al. (1979), in which it was found that recoding of sentences with subordinate clauses into ones with coordinate structure enhanced the auditory comprehension of aphasics. This concurs with Givon's claim that pragmatic-mode phrase structure tends to conjoined rather than embedded clauses, if one interprets aphasia as regression along a continuum in the direction of the pragmatic mode.

Linebarger et al. (1983) report evidence of the ability of Broca's aphasics to judge correctly the grammaticality of sentences. These data, although not consistent with ones I have presented herein, were derived from a sufficiently different sort of study to call into question the position I have been advocating. Therefore, it is important to consider that the types of rule violation on which the subjects performed most successfully tended to be violations of the automatic, less computational functions that I have been claiming tend to be relatively preserved in aphasia, or ungrammatical forms that were also ill formed in semantic structure (basic propositional form). The Basic Claim predicts that the latter would not be especially problematical for agrammatic aphasics, because pragmatic-mode strategies should detect anomalies of that sort. Linebarger et al.'s results indicate that subjects tended to perform worst on subject copying and aux copying in tag questions, the two most computational functions in the study, because both require syntactic subcategorical information that is encoded on a form in one part of the sentence to be reproduced on a form in another part of the sentence. The aphasics also performed poorly on reflexives, which require person, number, and gender computation, and, as found by Blumstein et al. (1983), which tend to be processed by aphasics by means of a nonsyntactic strategy of minimal distance. The subjects performed relatively well on the seven other types of violation considered in the Linebarger et al. paper. Let us examine them in turn.

1. Strict Subcategorization

This phenomenon is very likely lexical rather than computational. Thus, if transitivity (vs. intransitivity) for example, is stored as a property of each verb, it is not surprising that the aphasics would recognize the anomaly in a sentence in which this subcategorization feature was violated.

2. Particle Movement

In fact the phenomenon tested was the particle-preposition distinction. As in the case of strict subcategorization, if particles are stored lexically as part of the verb with which they are associated, then the recognition of them as movable and of prepositions as immovable comes as no surprise either, because the latter are presumably stored lexically as independent closed-class elements not associated with any particular open-class elements.

3. Empty Elements

In some cases at least, this phenomenon of phonologically unrealized NP in subject or object position in tensed or infinitival clauses, although manifestly syntactically computational may have been handled with a lexical or propositional strategy. For example, Linebarger et al.'s sentence 21 (*Who did you think [_____ would invite _____]?) is ill formed, in that no matter which blank the word "who" is taken to refer to, there is a missing argument for the two-place predicate "invite."

4. Left Branch Condition

Violations of this condition (Ross, 1967) can also be viewed as having lexical or propositional distortions, which could be dealt with by a pragmatic-mode strategy. For example, sentence 26 (*Which old did you invite men to your party?) might seem incorrect to an aphasic reduced to the pragmatic mode if (s)he interpreted "old" as direct object and found it unacceptable because "old" is not a noun.

5. Gapless Relative Clauses

These are relative clauses with a fully specified (and noncoreferential) NP in the position of the relative pronoun. These are quite clear examples of sentences that are ill formed propositionally, even assuming a pragmatic-mode interpretation. They are uninterpretable.

6. Phrase Structure Rules

Two of the three sentences presented in this group can be interpreted as having strict-subcategorization rather than phrase-structure violations: (30) *The paper was full mistakes, and (31) *The gift my mother is very nice. The comments made previously concerning strict-subcategorization apply to these examples. The third sentence, (32) *The man his car is washing, might be interpreted using pragmatic-mode strategies as an NP with a relative clause in which the subject is "his car" (with "the man" as (implied) direct object). Such a sentence might then be rejected for its selectional (or pragmatic) anomaly: Cars cannot wash.

7. Subject-Aux Inversion

I have no explanation for why the subjects performed well on sentences with this type of violation. This is a highly computational nonlexical syntactic function that the communicative-continuum-regression hpyothesis predicts should be relatively impaired.

It is important to note, however, that the Basic Claim and its corollary in particular, and the regression hypothesis in general do not make any claim about any elements being destroyed, deleted, or omitted, which is an advantage over interpretations such as Kean's or Grodzinsky's. There is a regression along a continuum, and it can be a slight regression, a moderate regression, or a profound regression. The claim does entail that any omissions, distortions, misinterpretations, or other errors that are made will be in the direction of the pragmatic mode of communicative function (or in severe cases, approaching the monopropositional mode).[7]

SUMMARY

The results of the present study and of recent research in aphasiology are consistent with an interpretation of aphasia as a unitary disorder involving a regression in communicative capacity along Givón's communicative continuum. The radically different speech patterns of agrammatics and paragrammatics can be explained by assuming that with regression to the pragmatic mode, much or most of the automatic grammatical functions, elements, and relations become useless. The agrammatic, whose regression is relatively mild, is able to function communicatively in pragmatic-mode terms and successfully suppress these now largely useless elements. Still, the present study shows that aphasics *can* make use of some of these elements and relations when called upon to do so in metalinguistic tasks: those that are best preserved are the most automatic ones, the ones least

[7]It is interesting to note at this point that in a study (Caplan et al., 1981) of 11 Broca's aphasics in a sentence-comprehension task involving gerunds and participles, younger patients were better able to utilize grammatical structures. Obler, Albert, Goodglass, & Benson (1978) found that Broca's aphasia tends to affect younger patients, whereas Wernicke's aphasia tends to affect older patients. These results have been replicated (for males at least) in 11 populations (Obler & Albert, 1981). It is at least conceivable that the poorer performance by paragrammatics than by agrammatics on virtually all tasks may be due not to the severity of the aphasia itself, but to a reduced adaptability to the deficit among older patients.

requiring computation for their integration. Paragrammatism represents a more severe regression along the Givonian continuum. The paragrammatic has effectively lost communicative ability, functioning linguistically at the monopropositional level, or not at all. His/her output is full of nonintegrated grammatical forms (that are released because the patient is too communicatively disrupted to know that they must be suppressed), circumlocutions (that indicate the disruption of the lexicon, on which the propositional structure of language depends), and in very severe cases, neologistic jargon in which even the phonological integrity of the lexicon is destroyed, reaching the level of undifferentiated jargon in the most extreme cases. The paragrammatic has regressed to the point at which (s)he cannot function communicatively except in the most primitive way.

The conceptual framework of Talmy Givón does not account for everything and at best provides a conceptual *framework* for looking at aphasia, one that needs to be filled in by detailed study of aphasic phenomena in which the framework is used as a guide to research. For example, the type of analysis that Lapointe (1985) has done for verb-form use in agrammatic speech (using another model, Garrett [1975]) could perhaps be incorporated. His two-dimensional matrices, ordered according to hierarchies of markedness, clearly represent a continuum. On the surface, some of the facts of aphasia are at odds with Givón's picture of the pragmatic mode. For example, in the pragmatic mode, one should find a lower noun-to-verb ratio than in the syntactic mode. Yet agrammatic aphasics are notorious for their excessive use of nouns relative to verbs. But agrammatics do not use nouns in a normal way; they use them to express propositions in the absence of normal access to a verbal system, and frequently nominalizations of verbs (i.e., gerunds, infinitives, participles, etc.) are used for purposes of predication. So perhaps Givón's N : V ratio criterion needs to be amended, or reinterpreted in terms of the number of arguments lexical items take in logical form. Although verbs tend to be polyadic predicates whereas nouns tend to be monadic, there are a great many exceptions. It should be instructive to examine agrammatic output in these terms to see what proportion of lexical items used by agrammatics and paragrammatics are interpretatble as having monadic and polyadic structures.

A second example is the hyperfluency commonly observed among paragrammatics, which violates the pragmatic-mode condition of slow delivery with multiple intonation contours. Agrammatics do fit this description nicely; clearly some explanation is required for the paragrammatics' rate and intonation.

Overall, however, the hypotheses based on the Givón framework seem to fit the data both of this study and of recent aphasiological literature at least as well as any other interpretation to date. What I think argues most strongly for the acceptance of the Givón (cum Draizar) approach over other interpretations is its applicability to fields of linguistic investigation other than neurolinguistics. A brief exploration of a few such related areas in terms of the Givonian continuum constitutes the remainder of this book.

7 Relevance to Related Fields

INTRODUCTION

Whether or not one is persuaded by the arguments adduced by Givón (1979) concerning morphosyntactic theory, it is clear that one of the book's greatest strengths is the applicability that the author shows his framework to have for the study of language change, language acquisition, creolization, and the origins of language. In this chapter I review some recent literature in the fields of first and second language acquisition, pidgins and creoles, language death, and attempts to teach human language to pongids, for two principal purposes: (a) to show that these fields of investigation support Givón's conception of a communicative continuum, and (b) to show how in several cases, acceptance of the Givonian conception of language could resolve disputes within these fields. In conclusion, some implications for the study of linguistics are discussed.

FIRST LANGUAGE ACQUISITION

Givón's communicative continuum provides an appropriate framework for an accurate description of first language acquisition. The properties of the mono-propositional mode (which Givón attributes to communication among canines and among pongids) correctly describe the level of the earliest stage of human infant language, the preverbal stage through Brown's (1973) Stage I. In this mode, communication is invariably about the ''here and now,'' ''the immediate, perceptually accessible situation and environment'' (Givón, 1979, p. 278). There is no reference to past events or to objects outside the immediate environment. There is a concept of (physical) ''object'' (although object permanence may not be fully developed) and perhaps one of animacy (i.e., some things move without being moved). The only participants are *you* and *I* (which are not coded), never a third person unless considered as ''object.'' Illocutionary force is overwhelmingly manipulative or ''proto-imperative'' (Halliday, 1975a), with some affectives and some declaratives (i.e., naming). Bates, Camaioni, & Volterra (1975) found proto-imperatives prior to 9 months of age and proto–declaratives somewhat later. In the one-word stage, topic-comment-goal-object are ''all rolled into one'' (Givón, 1979, p. 293). Subsequently coding of patient-object and location-goal takes place, but the participants (which in fact are largely predictable) and verb tend to remain unexpressed.

As the child progresses to the two-word stage (and to Brown's Stage II), (s)he moves into the presyntactic *pragmatic mode*. At this point we begin to find the characteristics of this mode in the verbalizations of children, e.g., topic-comment word order, concatenation rather than subordination, a low noun-to-verb ratio, a lack of grammatical morphology and pronouns, and pragmatic intonation (higher intonation contours for new information and lower for presupposed elements).

Under this interpretation, the child's subsequent morphosyntactic development as (s)he passes into the syntactic mode, can be viewed as the superimposition of the more sophisticated system on the more primitive pragmatic-mode system, as neocortical control is superimposed on a limbic-based system (Lamendella, 1976, 1977a, 1977b) or as lateralized neocortical control is superimposed on a more primitive bilateral system (Brown, 1977; Lamendella, 1976).

First-language acquisition literature is replete with evidence supportive of this general interpretation. The telegraphic nature of early child speech, reminiscent of (although not identical to) the speech of agrammatics (see Dennis & Wiegel-Crump, 1979), is hard to ignore (Bloom, 1970; Braine, 1971; Schlesinger, 1975). In addition, it appears that pragmatic or semantic aspects of language are invariably acquired before purely formal morphosyntactic aspects, and that communication that is critically dependent on the latter is therefore manifested late. The following presentation is not intended to be an exhaustive survey of the literature relevant to this issue, but merely an illustrative sample of findings. I have found no research relevant to the issue that is inconsistent with Givón's position.

Miller (1975), cited by Greenfield (1978), found that children in transition from one-word to two-word utterances tend to use a single word when all situational elements are redundant but tend to use two-word utterances when there is less contextual redundancy. This is consistent with Givón's observation that in the monopropositional mode, all communication refers to the immediate setting, and that therefore this information (i.e., time, place, participants, illocutionary force, etc.) goes uncoded, because it is redundant.

Givón maintains that the pragmatic mode is dominated by topic-comment word order. Bates and MacWhinney (1979) have found evidence that suggests that children have the topic-comment function established even at the one word stage. There is evidence that for some languages, children first use topic-comment order in their 2–3 word utterances, and with other languages, an agent-action order (Braine, 1976; Braine & Wells, 1978; Brown, 1973).

Givón maintains that the most primitive kind of speech act is the imperative, or manipulative. (As evidence, he cites Bates et al., 1975.) Griffiths and Atkinson (1978) found that in the speech of seven children, *on, off, open,* and *door* were used first as requests (imperatives) and only later as statements. Carter (1974), in a study of one child (aged 11–16 months) categorized his communicative acts into nine schemata, eight of which were requests for some kind of transformation of his environment. Bruner (1983), in a study of two children from age 8 to 24 months, found that (in addition to "reference" in play situations) *requests* (or demands) of various types constituted the bulk of the children's communicative behavior. Interestingly, in the early stages (8–12 months), there were no instances of requests for remote or absent objects, which is congruent with Givón's "here-and-now" position regarding the primitive stages of communication. Halliday (1975a, 1975b), in a study of one child's development, postulates a phase that he calls "proto-language" (from about 9 to 15 months). He found that during this phase the child used words exclusively for the purpose of regulating social interaction (manipulative). It is worth noting that young children tend to interpret the speech acts of others as imperatives as well. Shatz (1978) found that five children (1;7 to 2;4) responded to direct and indirect requests by their mothers as requests no matter how subtly they were coded morphosyntactically, including "interrogative requests" (Ervin-Tripp, 1977, e.g., "Is the door shut?, Are there any more suitcases?"). Shatz does not attribute high-level morphosyntactic and illocutionary knowledge to these children, in part because they frequently responded to genuine requests for information as though they were directives as well (e.g., "Can you jump?").

Givón attributes to pragmatic-mode communication a tendency to use coordinate structure rather than the embeddings characteristic of the syntactic mode. It is therefore significant to note that Wing and Scholnick (1981, Scholnick & Wing, 1982) found that even older children (9- and 11-year-olds) do not have full comprehension of sentences with subordinate clauses introduced by *because, although, unless,* and *if.* Although Limber (1973) found many instances of complex sentences among 2- and 3-year-olds, they all involved verbs that take NP complements ("true object-complements"). Conjoined clauses tended to predominate in the speech of these children. Furthermore, Limber (1973) states that he would be "chary of assuming that an utterance such as *I want car* differs syntactically from *I want see* or even *I want up* as far as the child's language processes are concerned" (p. 177).

In a related vein, Johnson (1985) found that use and comprehension of the present perfect is not well established even among children aged 4;5 to 5;11. In this study, their behavior was influenced by pragmatic and semantic factors such as whether the construction referred to a single event or an habituality, and whether the verb was lexically continuative or momentary. This finding is consonant with results of the study presented herein in the first six chapters, in particular chapter 6, in which the aphasics' better performance on English past tenses than on past participles was attributed to the simple past's being interpretable conversationally, using a pragmatic-mode strategy; however, the past participle (which was tested in a present-perfect syntactic frame) is tightly interwoven with the syntactic system of English. Late acquisition of the present perfect has been found in a number of studies. Fletcher (1979) cites Cromer (1974) and Nussbaum and Naremore (1975), who found that this form had not generally stabilized by 5 or 6 years of age (but see Wells, 1979, for contrasting evidence).

Another source of support for the Givón framework comes from first language acquisition studies of the use of extralinguistic and pragmatic strategies for interpreting syntactic constructions. For example, de Villiers and Flusberg (1975) found that 2- to 4-year-old children understood plausible negations before implausible ones. One of the 2-year-olds made errors on five sixths of the implausible negatives but answered correctly on all plausible ones. This performance is consistent with a pragmatic-mode strategy. So are the data reported in two papers dealing with comprehension of passives, one by Bridges (1980) and one by Sudhalter and Braine (1985). Bridges (1980) tested children aged 2;6 to 5;0 on reversible active and passive sentences and found that up to age 4;0, the most common type of response (in two tasks that involved acting out of events described) was "situational," i.e., extralinguistic (from a formal perspective), and consistent with pragmatic-mode processing. Bridges interprets the study as supporting "the suggestion that even children who might be expected to know their language well (i.e., three-year-olds) frequently fail to attend to the grammatical form of an utterance when they are trying to understand/respond to what has been said to them" (p. 100). He cites Cromer (1976), who states that "a child uses an extra-linguistic strategy when he does not know how to make use of the grammatical structure in the adult manner" (p. 313). Sudhalter and Braine's study involved "younger" (3–4 year old) and "older" (5–6 year old) preschoolers, and first, third, and sixth graders in a test that required them to identify actors and experiencers in active and passive sentences. Subjects performed better on active than on passive sentences and better on passives with actional verbs (*push, cut, kick, call*) than experiential verbs (*see, hear, believe, understand*). Since a topic-comment word-order strategy is often more successful for interpreting active than passive sentences, which are generally more "syntacticized," these results support Givón's model. Furthermore, Sudhalter and Braine did not find a bimodal distribution of children who did know and who did not know the passive, but rather a unimodal distribution indicative of a gradual acquisition. This result is consonant with Givón's idea of a *continuum,* as is Suppes's (1976) finding that children's grammatical development, as traced by grammatical descriptions based on corpora from three languages, is better described by a "continuous incremental" model than by an "all-or-none stage model" (p. 229).

A further kind of (indirect) support for Givón's approach comes from studies that show that children acquire knowledge of grammatical functions pragmatically before they gain control of the precise morphosyntactic instantiations of those functions in their language. Klima and Bellugi's (1966) data suggest that Stage I children form negatives by preposing or postposing "no" or "not" to an utterance, thus using a nonsyntactic string analysis consistent with pragmatic-mode processing. Golinkoff and Martessini (1980), in a study of five groups of six children (with MLU's from 1.00 to 4.5 and ages from 1;7 to 5;5) who were tested by their own mothers for comprehension of two-noun possessive phrases, found that even the youngest children (all but three) had clear notions of possessors and possessions, but that word order was not used to comprehend possessive phrases, except in the post-Stage-IV group (MLU > 4). Mulford (1985) found that a group of 16 Icelandic children (aged 4 to 8) were better at identifying the referents of pronouns when the referents were familiar to them and/or there was natural gender information available than when they had to rely on purely formal factors. These results, although consistent with Givón's framework, are in contrast with Böhme and Levelt's (1979) data on natural and grammatical gender in German possessive pronouns (with 3–6 year olds) and Karmiloff-Smith's (1979) report on French gender development (among 3–12 year olds). Mulford accounts for the discrepancy in terms of the relatively greater availability of phonological (and other formal) cues to gender in the latter two languages as compared with Icelandic. Steffensen (1978) found that although two children (1;5 to 2;3 and 1;8 to 2;2) recognized adults questions as questions, they did not understand and relationship between the syntactic form of questions and their meaning, or the semantics of the negative and affirmative particles. She concludes that each child developed his own system, which she refers to as "pragmatic variation."

Perhaps the strongest evidence of all from first language acquisition research in favor of Givón's model comes from the study of Genie (Curtiss, 1977), a person who acquired her first language after the so-called "critical period" (Lenneberg, 1967). After 5 years of concentrated language experience, Genie still showed numerous features of the pragmatic mode in her linguistic behavior. In comprehension, she did not process reversible passives with a level of accuracy above chance. Her comprehension of S-V-O actives was only 75% correct. She was not able to decode structures in which an embedded clause ended in a N followed by the VP of the matrix sentence; she consistently interpreted the N + VP sequence as subject-verb; that is, sentences such as "The boy who is looking at the girl is sitting" were interpreted by Genie as meaning "The boy is looking at the girl and the girl is sitting," thus reflecting the pragmatic-mode preference for concatenation over subordination.

Although Genie had a good deal of trouble understanding various means for expression of the future (*will, going to*), and regular past tenses,[1] she comprehended utterances in which past time was marked by 'finish' rather well. This very form "finish ([pinis])" is in fact the marker of past time in Melanesian Pidgin English (Hall, 1943), aka Neo-Melanesian, Tok Pisin, a pragmatic-mode system. Temporal relations in general are expressed in pidgins by clause external adverbials (Bickerton, 1981). Genie showed clear evidence here of comprehending a form consistent with pragmatic-mode processing better than a morphological marker (syntactic mode).

Finally, Genie could not understand sentences containing the preposition "before" in which the order of the clauses was opposite to the order of events in real time (i.e., "Before you touch X, touch Y" [Curtiss, 1977, p. 119]), and thus displayed an extragrammatical, pragmatically-based strategy for their interpretation. Clark (1971) observed the same phenomenon among normal children before they acquired the adult grammar.

On the production side, Genie produced no relative pronouns, no modals, no indefinites, no WH forms, coordination only in conjoined NP, and almost no embedding. She did, however, use serial verbs characteristic of pidgins. She never produced a third-person-singular-present morpheme (one of the last to be acquired by second-language learners, and rare in agrammatic speech). Efforts to "teach" Genie WH questions resulted in uninterpretable asyntactic strings of words that included a WH word. Most revealing is the fact that the only subject pronouns Genie ever used were "I" and "you."

The evidence in favor of Givón's approach from Genie's data is particularly strong in view of the fact that she was found to be using exclusively her right hemisphere for linguistic tasks. Having failed to acquire language during the critical period, when under normal circumstances, the limbic mediation presumably gives way to neocortical control of the left hemisphere, resulting in the acquisition of syntactic-mode structures, Genie seemed to be using a different sort of system for language mediation, one that prevented her full development in the syntactic mode (although Albert and Obler, 1978 show evidence that there may be a primary role played by the right hemisphere in language acquisition). Evidence from neonates (Molfese, 1972; Molfese, Freeman, & Palermo, 1975) and hemidecorticates (Dennis & Kohn, 1975; Dennis & Whitaker, 1976) indicates the likelihood of early specialization of the left hemisphere for language and the necessity of its participation (in most people) for normal language development to take place.

Thus, there is much evidence from first-language acquisition that is consonant with Givoń's model. Even more importantly, adoption of such an approach can put an end to a rather heated and sterile debate in this field that has been raging

---

[1]It is significant that Genie performed better with irregular than regular past tenses, in view of second-language acquisition data reviewed by Krashen (1981) to be addressed in the next section.

for some time. I refer to the so-called holophrastic hypothesis, to the debate between "rich" and "lean" interpretation of early child language forms.

In its modern (i.e., transformational) form, the holophrastic hypothesis was first proposed by McNeill (1970). although essentially the same claim was made by Stevenson (1893) cited by Barrett (1982; also see McCarthy, 1954; Lenneberg, 1967). McNeill proposed that the single-word utterances of children were the structural equivalents of whole sentences of adult language, because the relations of the latter were implicit in the former (although they could not be so expressed since children lack the ability to express these relationships formally). Perhaps the most extreme version of this hypothesis is that of van der Geest (1975), who imputes complex underlying phrase markers to the child with MLU of 1, along with an output constraint that deletes everything except the rightmost element. For the two-word stage, he proposes a second output condition, one that eliminates everything except the "two rightmost elements of the specification in such a way that the rightmost of these elements is the primarily stressed one" (p. 213).

Lois Bloom, once a proponent of rich interpretation (Bloom, 1970), reversed herself (Bloom, 1973), rejecting the term *holophrase* as incorrectly imputing knowledge of syntactic structure to the child. Van der Geest challenges Bloom primarily over what he takes to be her concept of what a sentence is.

Others have taken more moderate positions, attributing underlying structures that are semantic rather than syntactic (Bowerman. 1973a,b; Brown, 1973; Greenfield & Smith, 1976; Schlesinger, 1971) to these early language users. Still others have proposed a "functional" rather than "structural" version of the hypothesis, attributing various communicative functions (speech acts) to the one and two-word utterance, but no complex deep structure (Barrett, 1982; Dore, 1975). Greenfield (1978) takes issue with Dore (1975) for his Fillmorian (Fillmore 1968) interpretation of Greenfield and Smith's (1976) view of linguistic structure at the earliest stages, claiming that she and Smith view perceptual and action schemata "as the basis for but not identical with later linguistic structure" (Greenfield, 1978, p. 348).

It should be obvious that if one were to recast the data in Givón's terms, the dispute about the nature of the underlying structure of early child language would dissolve; recall that in the monopropositional mode, communication is restricted to *you* and *I* as subject-agents, to the here-and-now in space and time, and to concrete, currently perceivable objects as referents. Instead of arguing about whether the nature of the underlying form of one- and two-word utterances were syntactic, semantic, or functional, or nonexistent, one could view this early language development from the perspective of a phylogenetic and ontogenetic interpretation of linguistic communication progressing from the monopropositional mode (in which the features claimed by some to be encoded in underlying trees are taken as "given," and therefore left uncoded) to the pragmatic mode (in which significant relationships begin to be explicitly coded, although not in the way adults do it). At each stage, the linguistic forms controlled by the child at a normal stage of neurological development and with normal linguistic input would be viewed as representing a linguistic communicative competence (functional, *and* semantic, *and* syntactic, *and* phonological) congruent with the child's neurological maturation (Brown, 1977; Lamendella, 1976).

SECOND/FOREIGN LANGUAGE ACQUISITION/LEARNING

The slash notation in the title of this section represents a dichotomy that has been given (at least) two names. For over a decade Stephen Krashen and his colleagues have been developing and implementing an approach to second and foreign language instruction that makes critical use of a distinction between "language acquisition" and "language learning" (Dulay, Burt, & Krashen, 1982; Krashen, 1981, 1982, 1985a, 1985b; Krashen & Terrell, 1983). "Acquisition" refers to an unconscious process "identical in all important ways to the process children utilize in acquiring their first language." "Learning" refers to a "conscious process that results in 'knowing about' language" (Krashen, 1985a, p. 1). Essentially the same distinction is made by Lamendella (1977b), who distinguishes "second language learning" (akin to Krashen's "acquisition"), which takes place in a natural setting, from "foreign language learning" (akin to Krashen's "learning"), which takes place by means of formal (grammatically based) instruction, typically in a classroom setting.

One who has "acquired" a language can function in it as a speaker–hearer and has a "feel" for correctness of utterances. One who has "learned" a language can state what the rules of grammar are (Krashen, 1982). Central to Krashen's model is the view that acquisition is necessary for one to be able to *use* a language, to function as a speaker–hearer; learning, no matter how intensive or extensive can never be sufficient for this purpose in the absence of acquisition. In addition to the acquisition-learning distinction, the theory contains four related hypotheses: the input hypothesis, the affective-filter hypotheses, the monitor hypothesis, and the natural-order hypothesis.

The input hypothesis entails that we acquire language in only one way: "by understanding messages in the second language that utilize structures we have not yet acquired" (Krashen, 1985b, p. 39). We acquire by means of comprehensible input, not by speaking. For evidence for this hypothesis, see Krashen (1985a, pp. 4–19).

The "affective filter," first proposed by Dulay and Burt (1977), is a mental obstacle that "prevents acquirers from fully utilizing the comprehensible input they receive for language acquisition" (Krashen, 1985a, p. 3). The filter may include factors such as anxiety, poor motivation, or lack of self-confidence

(Krashen, 1982), and is least obstructive when the acquirer identifies with the target-language-speaking group, has an "outgoing personality," and/or is extremely involved in the content of what (s)he is hearing (Chastain, 1975; Stevick, 1976; see Krashen, 1981, Chapter 2 for a review of the relevant research).

The monitor hypothesis states that although acquisition is essential to knowing a language as a functional speaker–hearer, learning may nonetheless be useful in certain situations, in that material that has been consciously learned can be used for editing the output of the (imperfectly) acquired system. This retrieval of consciously known linguistic information for the purpose of output editing is called a "monitor." According to Krashen (1981, 1985a), the optimal use of the monitor is for writing and for previously prepared speech, because time is required for its implementation. Two additional conditions are required as well: that the speaker know the rules (consciously) and that (s)he be concerned about correctness.

In a study of adult ESL (English as a Second Language) students, Bailey, Madden, & Krashen (1974) found that adult second-language acquirers showed a characteristic order of acquisition of certain grammatical morphemes. Although the order was not identical to the first-language acquisition order discovered by Brown (1973) and de Villiers and de Villiers (1973), it was quite close to the order found in several child second-language acquisition studies (Burt, Dulay, & Hernandez, 1975; Dulay & Burt, 1973, 1974; Rosansky, 1976). The natural order seems to appear only under test conditions in which the monitor is unlikely to be usable (so that *learned* knowledge cannot be used, Krashen, 1981). Krashen summarizes the results of several studies of the natural order of morpheme acquisition for English as follows: *-ing*, plural, and copula precede aux and article, which precede irregular past, which precedes regular past, possessive and third person singular present (Krashen, 1981, p. 59). These results are interesting in that they conform in the main to the data obtained from Genie (cited earlier) and also to data obtained by de Villiers (1974) from agrammatic aphasics. (See also Lapointe (1985) regarding use of the verbal inflections *-ing, -ed, -s* among agrammatics.)

These grammatical morphemes that have been looked at in acquisition-order studies represent syntactic-mode phenomena in Givonian terms. That they should be acquired in a given sequence in second language acquisition suggests that acquirers pass through a pragmatic-mode stage before these morphemes begin to be acquired, and that the acquisition sequence is governed by a dynamic continuum with native adult grammar at the end point. Extreme cases exist: There are many fluent nonnative speakers of English who have never had any formal instruction in the language (and hence have no monitor). Many of these speakers (frequently illiterate in both native language and English) never progress beyond a pragmatic-mode communicative level, having never acquired most of the grammatical morphemes. They speak what is commonly called "broken English" and misunderstand complicated structures. The fact that the morpheme order in acquisition studies parallels the control of these grammatical morphemes shown by agrammatics lends further support to the hypothesis that aphasics regress in the direction of the pragmatic mode, and ipso facto, to Givón's framework in general.

PIDGINS AND CREOLES

Derek Bickerton (1977) has claimed that "pidginization is second-language learning with restricted input, and creolization is first-language learning with restricted input" (p. 49). The kind of pidginization and creolization to which he refers is one in which there is minimal contact with superstrate speakers and in which there is no parallel cultural life in which speakers habitually continue to use another language. The first criterion eliminates such languages as Réunion Creole, in which speakers had extensive early contact with French; the second eliminates those such as Tok Pisin, in which speakers continued and in most cases continue today to use other languages (Woolford, 1979). Sankoff (1979) has claimed that true pidgins have developed only in the context of the colonial plantation system, which employed slaves (Atlantic plantations) or indentured laborers (Pacific plantations).

Bickerton's position (1981, 1984) is that there is a "bioprogram" for language acquisition in human genetic structure that unfolds to allow for language acquisition to occur at a characteristic rate and in a characteristic pattern, given *any* sort of linguistic input (cf. Lamendella, 1976; Slobin, 1973). Creolization results from the application of this human endowment to inadequate (i.e., pidginized) linguistic input. Pidginization results from adults' application of it in the absence (or extreme paucity) of input. Adults are beyond the stages at which the bioprogram is scheduled to unfold. Hence, it is inadequate to the task of language acquisition, and pidgins are therefore characteristically lacking in the grammatical characteristics which Bickerton attributes to creoles. Besides, adult pidginizers have already acquired a native language: first-language characteristics frequently intrude into the speech of pidgin speakers (Bickerton, 1981).

In support of his position, Bickerton (1981) adduces evidence (a) that major features common to all creoles (in the limited set that he defines as relevant) are among the easiest (i.e., earliest acquired by children acquiring their first language) features of non-creole languages that manifest them; and (b) that aspects of non-creole natural languages that are incompatible with features of the bioprogram as evidenced in the creoles, are late acquired and show evidence of the bioprogram at work in the kinds of errors made by children en route to acquisition of the correct form.

As an example of the bioprogram, Bickerton presents four distinctions that he claims are found universally in (the appropriate type of) creoles. He presents evidence for their early acquisition in non-creoles, which mark them overtly, as well as evidence that strategies based on these distinctions appear in acquisition data for languages that do not directly manifest them. The distinctions are *specific–nonspecific, state–process, punctual–nonpunctual,* and *causative–noncausative.*

In Givón's model, the pidgin is represented by the pragmatic mode. Bickerton's putative innate linguistic distinctions would not be expected to appear in pidgins because pidgins are acquired too late for the bioprogram to play a significant role in their formation. And as Bickerton clearly shows, they do not. Creoles are represented by the syntactic mode in Givón's model. All the features of the syntactic mode lacking in pidgins (e.g., subordination, grammatical morphology, high N : V ration) are found in creoles, which frequently develop in a single generation. The normal human being is "hard wired" for syntactic-mode representation and function. It takes brain damage (aphasia) or profound deprivation (Genie) to reduce him/her (exclusively) to the pragmatic mode. It is interesting to note that English-speaking agrammatics tend to preserve *-ing* forms (Goodglass & Geschwind, 1976; Lapointe, 1985), and Spanish-speaking agrammatics, forms in *-ndo.* For Bickerton, the existence of *-ing* forms is a manifestation of his state-process distinction. Also frequently preserved in agrammatism is the Spanish particle *se,* one of whose uses is for the causative–noncausative distinction ("Cerró la puerta" ("[Somebody] closed the door") (causative) vs. "Se cerró la puerta" (The door closed) (noncausative)). Nonetheless, the distinction between the preterite and the imperfect in Spanish, which clearly marks the punctual–nonpunctual distinction, is not generally preserved in agrammatism (author's clinical impressions). A study specifically directed toward this issue would be of interest.

LANGUAGE DEATH

Nancy Dorian (1973, 1977, 1978, 1982, 1983) has for the past 2 decades been studying the progress of the dying dialect known as East Sutherland Gaelic (ESG), spoken in three coastal villages on the northeastern side of Highland Scotland, in the county of Sutherland. Dorian introduces the notion of "semi-speaker," technically a member of the speech community, but one who is perfectly proficient in another language (in this specific case, English) and who speaks a distorted "simplified" version of the language in question, although (s)he may consider the latter to be his/her "mother tongue." ESG, being a dying language, shows numerous grammatical discrepancies between older and younger fluent speakers in both its nominal and verbal systems. Significantly, among fluent speakers, this difference between older and younger speakers is noted in the nominal system in gender and case but not in number, and in the verbal system in number only, but not in tense or voice. Semispeakers, on the other hand, show reduction of all these distinctions in their speech. Nonetheless, Dorian notes (in connection with one aspect of ESG grammar known as "mutation'') that not one change has involved ''a serious loss of information'' (1973, p. 436), and that the simplification shown in the speech of semispeakers does not approach that shown in '' 'classical' pidginization'' (1978, p. 607). Most impressive is the semispeaker's receptive ability, which exceeds that of the fluent nonnative speaker, in spite of the latter's superior control of the grammar in speech.

Using Givón's framework, the linguistic behavior of semispeakers can perhaps be viewed as a regression (in their nondominant language, of course) in the direction of the pragmatic mode.[2] They show a milder regression in most cases than Broca's aphasics, although Dorian cites two members of the speech community who have regressed to the point at which they can no longer be called ''semispeakers'' but are rather ''passive bilinguals,'' because they cannot be called ''speakers'' at all. Broca's aphasics have ''relatively good'' comprehension. Semispeakers have ''perfect'' comprehension. Both show morphosyntactic reduction in their speech. Semispeakers (and adult second-language acquirers who have not had formal instruction in the language) should be subjected to the same kinds of comprehension and metalinguistic tests that have been given to aphasics. It would be interesting to see if some of these ''perfect'' comprehenders showed deficits similar in kind (although presumably milder in degree) to those of agrammatic aphasics, when forced to attend to morphosyntactic distinctions critically required for interpretation. Presumably, further study of this dying language, ESG, in this living speech community, will shed further light on the nature of the communicative continuum, as will the study of other dying languages.

TALKING APES: FROM PIGEONS TO PIDGINS

Introduction

Since David Premack and Arthur Schwartz first announced their preparations for discussing behaviorism with a chimpanzee (Premack & Schwartz, 1966), a number of attempts have been made to impart language or language-like systems to nonhuman primates. Although differing markedly in methodology and theoretical basis, all these projects have shared the basic premise that in order to discover what linguistic abilities apes had, it would be necessary to bypass the oral-vocal modality. Kellogg's (Kellogg & Kellogg, 1933) and Hayes's (1951) attempts to teach speech-mediated language to home-raised chimpanzees attest to the lack of motor capacity for speech in this species (pan troglodytes).

---

[2]The term *regression* is used here to refer to the result, not the process, although some of Dorian's informants had in fact been fluent speakers during childhood and had regressed in a literal sense.

The three principal media used in the nonspeech-modulated studies have been:

1. Plastic tokens (Premack, 1971, 1983; Premack & Premack, 1972, 1983).
2. "Lexigrams" (word symbols) printed on a keyboard connected to a display panel and to a computer (Rumbaugh, 1977; Rumbaugh & Gill, 1976; Rumbaugh, Gill, & von Glaserfeld, 1973; Savage-Rumbaugh, Rumbaugh, & Boysen, 1978, 1980; von Glaserfeld, 1976).
3. Gestural signing (Fouts, 1973, 1977; Fouts, Chown, & Goodin, 1976; Fouts, Chown, Kimball, & Couch, 1976; Gardner & Gardner, 1969, 1971, 1975, 1978; Miles, 1983; Patterson, 1978; Patterson & Linden, 1981).

The key question is of course, "Is what the animals do properly characterizable as language?" (J. H. Hill, 1978, p. 90). As Jane Hill (1978) notes in her excellent review, these studies offer "the extraordinary opportunity of a truly marginal and deviant case of what is at least very like language, and would probably be assumed to be the beginning of language should the same manifestations appear in the behavior of a human infant" (p. 90). In this section I review these studies and attempt to relate them to the principal theme of this volume; in particular, I hope to show that a Givonian perspective can eliminate some of the confusion manifested in this field's polemics.

Artificial Systems

The system developed by Premack (1971; Premack & Premack, 1972) involves plastic tokens of different shapes and colors, which represent nouns, verbs, adjectives, and "concepts" (SAME, DIFFERENT, NEGATION, NAME-OF, IF-THEN, and INTERROGATION). Initially success was achieved with Sarah, a chimpanzee who learned to use this code; (a) to follow instructions, (b) to behave in such a way (given statements by her trainer) as to receive rewards, and (c) to answer questions, using the tokens. Three other chimpanzees subsequently received instruction in this system and were successful in learning it. A fifth chimp raised with Sarah was totally unsuccessful.

As to whether Sarah actually acquired a language, Premack (1971) replies that apes constitute "the unclear middle case" (p. 808). Although many of the tasks performed successfully depended on word order and involved "displacement" (Hockett, 1958; Hockett & Altman, 1968), Premack and Premack (1983) emphasize that "a sentence is not merely a thought expressed in words; it is a thought expressed in words arranged in a sequence chosen from indefinitely many other possible sequences" (p. 118). None of Premack's chimpanzees had more than one way of conveying any message. In this system, the animals did not ask questions, although they were quite capable of answering them. Significantly, Premack found that language training enhanced certain cognitive abilities (when compared to performance by chimpanzees not trained in the token system): in particular, analogical reasoning, matching propositions, and selection of instruments used to causally relate a prior and subsequent state (Premack & Premack, 1983). This led him to conclude that primates have, in addition to an *imaginal* system common to most higher animals (such as rats and pidgeons), a *representational* system that is capable of utilizing symbols.

The approach to ape language training developed by Rumbaugh (1977) and his colleagues, inspired by both the Gardners' sign-language studies and Premack's works, involves an artificial language, "Yerkish" (von Glaserfeld, 1977), which has a "correlational grammar" such that any string that is interpretable (i.e., semantically well formed) is grammatical. The basic unit of the language, the "lexigram." consists of nine basic "design elements" (somewhat analogous to the basic strokes of Chinese characters) that are combined in various patterns, and represented in different colors. A chimpanzee named Lana (followed by two others, Austin and Sherman) had access to a keyboard on which these lexigrams were represented, along with a lighted display panel that represented the lexigram sequence indicated (by chimpanzee or trainer). This methodology yielded several advantages: The system could be connected to a computer, which would automatically record a complete protocol; and the artificial language could be constructed to provide a complete isomorphism between syntactic and semantic representation, while being translatable "easily and without major structural changes into comprehensible English" (von Glaserfeld, 1977, p. 114).

Results of the Lana project showed her to be aware of well-formedness (Rumbaugh & Gill, 1977): She used the *period* key as an eraser function for ill-formed sequences. She also displayed ability and predisposition to engage in conversation and a tendency to extend vocabulary to novel situations (e.g., DRINK [beverage] to DRINK [activity]). Most significantly, Savage-Rumbaugh et al. (1978, 1980) found that two chimpanzees trained in Yerkish used the system in the absence of human experimenters to request tools from each other that were required to obtain food. They performed at a joint accuracy rate of 92%, but when their keyboards were disconnected, this joint accuracy dropped to 10%. Thus animals made critical use of the Yerkish "language" for communication with each other.

Sign Language

Before discussing any projects involving the teaching of manual or gestural signing to pongids, it is necessary to say a few words about sign languages because there has been so much confusion concerning them. As recently as 1974,

Robert Scholes claimed that signing is communicatively inadequate because it lacks relational conventions, i.e., syntax (Scholes, 1974). Before responding to this assessment, it is necessary to distinguish among (at least) three distinct phenomena, all of which are popularly referred to as "sign language." The first phenomenon is the "natural" signing that one finds in use among deaf people who have been deprived of training in and/or exposure to any formal sign system. These signs are *sui generis* but when used for very general needs may be understandable because of the coherent nature of the nonlinguistic world in which human beings live and the experiences that people have in common. These gestures are not unlike those used by hearing people trying to communicate with someone who speaks another language. When highly developed, such gestures approach the art form known as pantomime. Clearly, such signing behavior is not governed by any syntactic or morphological system.

The second phenomenon is signed versions of spoken languages. These systems are frequently taught in schools for the deaf and are intended to be gestural representations of the language spoken in the hearing community. Thus "signed English" refers to a number of systems in which standard English is represented by gestural signs. Each morpheme of standard English is represented by a sign in signed English (or else is "fingered spelled"—indicated by a series of manual signs representing letters of the alphabet). The word order and morpheme order of spoken or written English is maintained. The same point applies to signed French, signed Spanish, etc. These systems are not anyone's native language, and in practice one finds a tendency for signers to eliminate some of the inflectional and derivational morphology in order to conserve time.

The third phenomenon is the native sign language. This is a natural language acquired as a native language during childhood by hearing and deaf children of signing parents. Among those sign languages that have been the object of linguistic description are French, British, Italian, Chinese, and most extensively, American Sign Language (Ameslan or ASL). These fully formed natural languages (Klima & Bellugi, 1979; Wilbur, 1979) are mutually unintelligible (Frishberg, 1975), (Bellugi & Klima, 1975; Deuchar, 1981). Because Ameslan has been the basis of all studies of ape language mediated by gestural signs, I focus the present section on a discussion of some of its properties that are relevant to the ape studies.

Although Ameslan is alleged to have a hierarchical structure (Bellugi & Klima, 1975), it is likely that it does not have the type of configurational hierarchy that a language such as English has. Nonetheless, as Rizzi (1985) has noted, many spoken languages, such as Japanese, have a linear rather than highly configurational (hierarchical) structure.[3] Clearly, Ameslan has rather strict well-formedness conditions, because for example, only certain hand configurations,

[3]Rizzi's position is not uncontroversial. For relevant discussion see Kiss (1981), Kuroda (1983), Saito and Hoji (1983), Farmer (1984), Horvath (1985), and Sproat (1985).

types of movements, manual orientations, and physical areas in which signs are made are permitted (Bellugi & Klima, 1975; Klima & Bellugi, 1979; Stokoe, 1960). For some time it was believed that Ameslan lacked embedded sentences (Stokoe, 1980), but Liddell (1978) in an analysis of ASL relative clauses found that whereas embedded and main clauses are signed identically *manually,* there are characteristic head positions and facial expressions that identify dependent clauses. (Hence the use of the term *gestural* rather than *manual* signs.) Coulter (1983) has, however, more recently argued that Ameslan relative clauses are correctly analyzed as conjuncts rather than as subordinates.

Whatever the status of clausal relations, it is obvious that ASL has a rich and complicated system of morphology, which makes use of recursion (Bellugi, Poizner, & Zurif, 1982). Klima and Bellugi (1979) describe *root level* and *word level* derivational processes, the former classified as idiomatic because of a lack of any consistent correlation between changes in form and changes in meaning; the relationship is idiosyncratic (Bellugi & Newkirk, 1981). The latter, word level processes, are correlated with consistent changes in meaning, in particular, change in lexical category (Supulla & Newport, 1978). Inflectional morphology is ubiquitous, involving eight different categories of modification (Klima & Bellugi, 1979): manner, degree, number, aspect, termporal focus, "distributional aspect" (e.g., "to each one" "to any one"), reciprocity, and referential indexing. Klima and Bellugi (1979) have also found that inflections can be applied recursively. For example, the "durational" morpheme can be embedded in the "exhaustive" morpheme to yield the sense of *action done continuously to each one in turn.* Conversely, "exhaustive" can be embedded in "durational" to yield *action done to each one, with the action recurring over time.* A double embedding of "durational" within "exhaustive" within "durational" would then have the sense of *action done continuously to each one in turn, that whole action recurring over time.* Compounding is also an important morphological process of ASL. Kegl and Wilbur (1976) have also discovered a gender system based on physical properties, which they refer to as a system of "classifiers."

Most importantly, it has been shown that deaf children acquire ASL signs in terms of morphological components rather than holistically (Newport, 1984), and that adult native signers decompose signs into their morphemic structure during comprehension and remember meanings rather than the structure of the signs (Hanson & Bellugi, 1982). These latter results are consistent with those of Bransford and Franks (1971); Bransford, Barclay, & Franks (1972) for (hearing) English speakers. Both sets of results are significant in that they are indicative of a psychological reality of the morphological system for the signer.

Before returning to our discussion of ape studies, it is important to clarify the status of word order in American Sign Language. As we have seen, Ameslan is a highly inflected language, and as noted by Van Cantfort and Rimpau (1982), order of constituents plays a less important role in such languages than in languages with less developed inflectional systems. In addition, the mesotic

(Schnitzer, 1976) of ASL allows for *temporal* freedom in subject-object-verb order because ASL *spatial* ordering is iconic with real-world order, both spatial and temporal (Stokoe, 1980). Stokoe refers to as "agglutinative" (in a sense obviously different from the way the term is applied to languages such as Turkish and Swahili, in which constituent order is very rigid) the capacity of Ameslan to restructure a three part transitive proposition into a single sign (Stokoe, 1980). Bellugi and Fischer (1972) state that because some signs require the use of only one hand, the signing-visual mesotic permits the formation of two signs simultaneously, thereby obviating the need for strict linear ordering. Finally, Patterson and Linden (1981) cite Louis Fant's observation that in short sentences of three or four signs, there are few constraints on word order, although in longer sentences, signs are arranged according to the sequence of events, iconically.

Sign Language Studies with Pongids

From the perspective of this volume and its attempt to relate various linguistic phenomena within a coherent framework, ape language projects that make critical use of ASL are important, because ASL is thus far the only natural nonspoken language to which pongids have been systematically exposed. J. H. Hill (1978) finds it superior to the artificial systems discussed previously because the animals' control over usage allows one to see many kinds of cognitive and communicative behaviors at work: "constructing" the world, regulating the behavior of others, obtaining desirables, etc. Hill finds the grammar of Yerkish too strict because the system does not tolerate grammatical errors, however minor. "Premackese" is even more restricted in terms of vocabulary available, and reliance on tasks that involve selection by the animal from a display of two choices (Gardner & Gardner, 1978).

In Gardner and Gardner's first report (1969), they describe Project Washoe, in which a chimpanzee was instructed in ASL over a period that began when the ape was 11 months old and was to continue for 50 months. They report that Washoe had acquired 30 signs (using an extremely strict criterion for claiming that a sign was acquired) by the end of her 22nd month of training, and that by the time she had acquired 8 to 10 signs, she began to use them in two or three-word combinations. They also note that Washoe invented combinations (e.g., 'OPEN FOOD DRINK' as a request to open the refrigerator, which the trainer had referred to as 'COLD BOX'), and transferred signs spontaneously to new (appropriate) referents. Fouts (1973) had similar results with four chimpanzees, thus showing Washoe not to be unique. He did find that there was individual variation in acquisition rate however, and that some signs were inherently more difficult to acquire than others.

Although they did not speak while they signed (as did Fouts), the Gardners feared that because they were not native signers, Washoe was not getting "real"

Ameslan, but rather some pidginized version. And they considered the possibility that 11 months of age might be too old to begin exposure to language. Thus, in a sequel to Project Washoe, Gardner and Gardner (1975, 1978) describe the teaching of ASL by native signers to four chimpanzees acquired shortly after birth (one of whom died before age 2). They found that the chimpanzees acquired a 10-sign vocabulary by the age of 5 to 6 months (as compared to 25 months for Washoe). They also found that as of 1978, two of the chimps had acquired vocabularies of 50 signs by age 21 to 23 months (as compared to Washoe, who achieved this level at age 37 months). Human children generally acquire a 10-word vocabulary from 13 to 19 months (with a mean of 15), and a 50-word vocabulary from 14 to 24 months (with a mean of 20) (Gardner & Gardner, 1978). Furthermore, Brown (1970) notes that Washoe displayed the same repertoire of relations as a Stage I human child: *recurrence* (''more''), *agent-action, action-object, action-location, agent-action-object, agent-action-location,* and *instrument.*

Fouts et al. (1976a) report evidence of a chimpanzee who could translate. More precisely, after being taught English words and their referents, followed by the sign that corresponded to the English word (in the absence of the referent) the chimpanzee could give the correct sign when shown the referent. Fouts et al. (1976b reported in Fouts, 1977) describe this same chimpanzee as able to use prepositions (''ON, IN, UNDER'') correctly even with novel relata. Significantly, the chimpanzee *never* made any errors in sign order. These results are consistent with those of Muncer and Ettlinger (1981), who found that a chimpanzee used word order correctly when relationships depended on the prepositions ''BEHIND'' and ''IN.''

Similar results regarding structure and productivity (and a vocabulary of over 600 signs) have been reported for a gorilla (Patterson, 1978; Patterson & Linden, 1981). Miles (1983) reports on a 3-year-old orangutan who had a MLU of 1.93 at age 26 months, with a maximum utterance length of six signs, and notes that the orangutan seemed to show more deliberate delivery in sign production than chimpanzees do.

In contrast to the positive results reported in the references thus far cited, the results of Project Nim (Terrace, 1979, 1983; Terrace, Petitto, Sanders, & Bever, 1979) have shown it to be unlikely that this chimpanzee acquired the rudiments of ASL. Terrace and his colleagues observed the following characteristics in Nim's signing:

1. Much of Nim's signing was imitative of the sign or signs made by the trainer. Whereas the imitation rate of children decreases from 20% at 21 months to near zero at 3 years of age, Nim's rate increased from 38% at 26 months to 54% at 44 months. According to Bloom, Lightbrown, & Hood (1975), children tend to imitate primarily when learning new words and/or syntactic structures; this was not the case with Nim. Furthermore, whereas children tend to ''expand'' on their imitations, Nim rarely did so.

2. Long utterances were often redundant and repetitive, rather than increasing information or complexity by means of increased length.
3. In children, the MLU and maximum utterance length increase together. Nim's did not. Nor did his MLU increase with age in spite of an increase in vocabulary.
4. Nearly all beneficiaries in *object-beneficiary* constructions were 'NIM' and 'ME.' Three quarters of the agents in *agent-object* constructions were 'YOU.'
5. Nim tended to interrupt trainers' signing frequently (which is rare in children), seldom contributed information in conversation, and showed no evidence of turn-taking skills.
6. Nim produced a high proportion of routine combinations, and when he did produce novel utterances, they tended to be redundant and repetitious "run-on" sentences.

Terrace and his colleagues take issue with the claims made by the other researchers cited. Although they admit that studies have shown apes to be capable of learning a vocabulary of visual symbols, they reject the claim that these creatures can use them to create new meanings (Terrace et al. 1979), and deny (Terrace, 1983) that apes sign in order to exchange information.

Criticisms of Ape Language Studies

There have been many criticisms of methodology and interpretation of these studies, including several by some of the principal investigators, who take issue with the work of other researchers (Gardner & Gardner, 1978; Petitto & Seidenberg, 1979; Savage-Rumbaugh et al., 1978; Seidenberg & Petitto, 1979; Terrace et al., 1979). Thus, for example, Savage-Rumbaugh et al. (1978) reject the results of manual sign studies as being merely "anecdotal," because it is impossible to record complete protocols of the animals' behavior in this paradigm (as compared to the lexigram console, which automatically records all interactions).

Gardner and Gardner (1978) in turn criticize Rumbaugh's group's focus on grammar. Because Lana was rewarded for making new requests if and only if they were in accord with the rules of Yerkish, and since to get a reward, it was necessary only to produce one of a small number of lexigram sequences, the Gardners see no reason to suppose that Lana's production had any semantic content. The fact that two chimpanzees used the console to communicate information about tools (as noted earlier), presumably would be sufficient reason.

In the same paper, the Gardners criticize Premack as well, for his use of caged subjects, strict reinforcement schedules, and the use of forced-choice testing in which the chimpanzee was required to select from a display of two tokens. They argue that "since Sarah's [Premack's chimpanzee] program of training and testing concentrated on each 'linguistic concept' for days and weeks at a time, she could have solved Premack's entire battery of problems by rote memory alone," and that a "learning-set sophisticated rhesus monkey could have passed all of Premack's transfer tests at the average level he required" (Gardner and Gardner, 1978, p. 61).

But the most profound sort of criticism has come from those who would deny even the attribution of knowledge of visual symbols to apes. Sebeok and Umiker-Sebeok (1980, Umiker-Sebeok & Sebeok, 1981) amass arguments that there is really no sort of communication going on in the ape experiments except for a kind of subliminal and unintentional cueing on the part of the experimenter, which signals the correct response to the animal, the so-called "Clever Hans" phenomenon (Rosenthal, 1965). As noted by de Luce and Wilder (1983), the Sebeoks' point is not that there is an obvious system of cues at work, but rather that cues must be there whether anyone can detect them or not, because these studies require close social interaction. Although this may be true during instruction, all three experimental paradigms have made use of double-blind procedures and/or absence of experimenters (or experimenters knowledgeable in the system) during the apes' performance. Thus Premack (1971) used a trainer unfamiliar with his "language" of plastic tokens; Rumbaugh and his colleagues describe pongid interactions with the keyboard in the absence of humans (Rumbaugh, 1977; Savage-Rumbaugh et al., 1978), and the Gardners (1978) describe an elaborate double-blind procedure in which the human who sees the chimpanzee sign does not see the referent of the sign and vice versa.

Other critics have focused on the system being taught. Stokoe (1983) for example has pointed out that what most of the apes in the sign-language studies have been exposed to has not been truly ASL, because the great majority of trainers were not native signers. What frequently has been used is therefore a kind of "pidginized" Ameslan on which an English order of constitutents is imposed. Petitto and Seidenberg (1979) criticize Patterson (1978) in these terms. In all fairness, let us note again that the Gardners took pains to eliminate this limitation by using native signers.

Thompson and Church (1980) showed the most of Lana's linguistic behavior in Yerkish could be simulated by a computer program in which one of six stock sentences with largely fixed elements (containing fixed slots for the insertion of variable vocabulary) is selected. In fairness to Rumbaugh's group, it should be noted that stock sentences were used intentionally as a way of showing the animals that they could ask for a reward; thus, it is not surprising that utterances using stock sentences would make up the bulk of the animals' communicative behavior. The question is, of course, is there anything else?

Not content with presenting their evidence that a chimpanzee failed to acquire sign language (Terrace, 1979), Terrace and his colleagues have argued that none of the other investigators have shown nonhumans to be capable of using language, and that all their data can be explained by "simpler interpretations"

(Petitto & Seidenberg, 1979; Seidenberg & Petitto, 1979; Terrace et al., 1979). Terrace et al. (1979) analysed two films (Gardner & Gardner, 1973, 1976) of Washoe, Ally (Fouts's translating chimp, who also happens to be Nim's brother), and Koko (Patterson's gorilla) and claim that these animals merely imitated what their trainers signed immediately before. As noted earlier, they conclude that apes do not use signs to exchange information and cannot combine signs to create new meanings (Terrace, 1983; Terrace et al., 1979).

Seidenberg and Petitto (1979; Petitto & Seidenberg, 1979) have written two lengthy critiques of the major studies of sign language among pongids, the former focusing primarily on the Gardners' work, the latter on Patterson (1978). In both papers, there are criticisms of two principal types: (a) *procedural,* in terms of both the experiments themselves and the way they have been reported, and (b) *interpretative,* the legitimacy of attributing linguistic knowledge to these animals and of considering the signs used by them as representing American Sign Language. Among the main procedural criticisms are: that these investigators do not publish full corpora of the apes' utterances; that they instead publish anecdotal evidence to support the claims they are making; that the published data have been highly *edited,* with many repetitions and functors eliminated from the reported data (in the case of the Gardners); and that criteria for determining what has been signed are subjective or nonexistent (in the case of Patterson).

Seidenberg and Petitto reject claims that the Gardners' and Fouts's chimpanzees and Patterson's gorilla are involved in linguistic communication, for the following reasons:

1. Because only anecdotes are reported, many of the interesting examples of creative use of language, for example, WATER BIRD (= 'duck') and COOKIE ROCK (= 'stale sweet-roll'), may be nothing more than chance combinations. In the absence of a statistical analysis of frequency of occurrence of signs in combination, no claims can be made, because combinations of signs might have been made randomly, as observed in the case of Nim.
2. In order to attribute syntactic structure to an ape's utterance, it is necessary to show that signs combined in different linear orders have different meanings, *and* that "each regular ordering [is] not specific to a unique combination of lexical items" (Seidenberg & Petitto, 1979, p. 187). This has not been shown.
3. The Gardners' program of requiring the chimpanzee to learn simple associations between individual behaviors and individual objects (as tested in their double-blind naming task) can be accomplished by many animals, including pigeons (Herrnstein, Loveland, & Cable, 1977).
4. To claim that apes are using "reduced forms of human language rests upon demonstrating that signs have similar meanings for both ape and

experimenter'' (Petitto & Seidenberg, 1979, p. 165). This demonstration was not provided in the studies being critiqued.

5. Apes do not use ''loci'' for purposes of deictic and anaphoric reference, nor do they use facial expressions to modulate sign meanings, as do human signers.
6. ''Overgeneralization'' (attributed by Patterson, 1978. to her gorilla) could be likened to the overgeneralizations made by human children only in a detailed study that showed exactly which signs (or words) were and were not used to refer to incorrect referents.

Petitto and Seidenberg also reject the identification of apes' gestures with Ameslan signs: Apes' signs resemble human ones in hand configuration, but not in orientation, movement, or location; Patterson counted as vocabulary items a number of signs that Koko invented; many ''signs'' counted as part of these animals' vocabulary are used by apes in the wild (Goodall, 1968, 1971). The fact that apes' signs physically resemble ASL signs is in itself irrelevant; and as noted previously, Washoe and Koko were probably not taught ASL at all, but rather some form of signed English. In addition, ape signing is highly imitative and extremely redundant and repetitive, to the point of logorrhea. By editing out redundant forms (as well as others considered to be irrelevant) and failing to indicate complete context in which all signs were emitted, the Gardners, Fouts, and Patterson are distorting data.

In both critiques, Seidenberg and Petitto conclude that the fragmentary data that are reported are overinterpreted (and can be explained by simpler, more conservative hypotheses), that apes sign because they are rewarded for signing, and that in the absence of consideration of what a language is and how it may differ from other communication systems, attributing language to apes is unwarranted.

Answers to Criticisms

The Clever Hans brand of criticism appears to be successfully answered by the use of double-blind studies (Fouts, 1973; Gardner & Gardner, 1978; Premack & Premack, 1983) or use of trainers ignorant of the system (Premack, 1971). Most telling of all is the Premacks' report (1983) that the chimpanzee, Sarah, insisted on using problem-solving strategies rather than social cues even when the latter were readily available; Sarah consistently failed tests that were too difficult for her even when she could have made use of social cues to help her pass. Apes apparently do not ''cheat'' on tests.

Claims that apes cannot make communicative use of word order can be laid to rest by the experiments reported in Fouts (1977) and Muncer and Ettlinger (1981) cited earlier, although word order is not as critical in highly inflected languages such as classical Latin or modern Lithuanian or American Sign Language as it is in more analytic languages. Furthermore, as Nelson (1980, cited by Van Cantfort & Rimpau, 1982) has noted, if apes do not produce completely grammatical sentences, neither can one say that children at the 2–3-word stage do, if one judges both according to the same criteria.

Why, we might then ask, did Terrace and his colleagues fail to find evidence of linguistically mediated communication in Project Nim? Fouts (1983) has considered this question in detail and has attributed this result to Terrace's training procedures. Fouts's point is that Terrace's main goal was to train Nim to produce a sentence. To accomplish this aim, he used highly structured drilling procedures that focused on structural aspects of language at the expense of social aspects. Nim was trained in a bare cell to sign names for referents in the absence of those referents. The social aspects of language that Terrace ignored in his training program, and that Nim did not demonstrate, were the very things Terrace chose to use to argue that Nim had not acquired language (e.g., turn-taking behaviors not acquired by Nim, Nim's propensity to interrupt).

Fouts likens Project Nim to a deprivation experiment: if a behavior does not develop under deprivation of certain stimuli, then those stimuli are necessary for the development of that behavior. What is remarkable, according to Fouts, is that even under conditions of deprivation, Nim did succeed in learning certain *structural* aspects of language. Evidence indicating that Nim may have developed more social aspects of language than observed by Terrace and his associates comes from a paper by Yaeger, O'Sullivan, & Autry (1981, cited by Fouts, 1983), who examined Nim's conversational abilities under two distinct conditions. The first was modeled after Terrace's training sessions; the other was an informal "conversational interaction" in which Nim was allowed to sign whatever he wanted to talk about. Under the first condition, Yaeger and colleagues observed behaviors similar to those observed by Terrace. Under the second condition, spontaneous and novel utterances increased, and imitations and interruptions were minimal.

Van Cantford and Rimpau (1982) have responded in some detail to criticisms by Terrace, Seidenberg, and Petitto of other invertigators involved in ape sign-language research. They concur with Fouts's estimate of Project Nim, noting that because Nim was raised as a pet rather than a child, pet-like behaviors would be expected. They note that repetitions by Nim would not be unexpected because his training involved withholding of desired objects *even if signed for appropriately,* unless the sign being taught at the moment was used; Nim would offer his hand to be molded in the form of the sign being taught. It is hardly surprising that Nim would repeat signs to obtain rewards, given the obvious (to Nim) concerns of his trainers.

Let us now consider five main points of defense by Van Cantfort and Rimpau.

1. In response to criticisms by Seidenberg and Petitto regarding (a) the counting of signs which occur among feral apes as part of these captive animals' ASL vocabularies, and (b) the considering of formal similarity of an ape gesture to an Ameslan sign as evidence for acquisition of the sign, Van Cantfort and Rimpau reply that, in the case of the Gardners, the signs had to resemble ASL signs *and* be used in appropriate contexts. Form *alone* was never criterial. The onus is placed on Seidenberg and Petitto to show the similarity of these signs to those of apes in the wild.

2. To the criticism that these apes were not instructed in pure ASL, the Gardners responded by using native signers as trainers, as already noted. Furthermore, as Van Cantfort and Rimpau point out, Maestas y Moores (1980) observed that ASL-signing parents tend to use a kind of "motherese" with their children that includes, besides normal sign formation, signed English and finger spelling; they also tend to hold signs in location longer than normal and repeat frequently when signing to children. The native signers in the Gardners' study tended to use infant-adapted Ameslan.

3. To the charge that pongids have failed to produce proper eye-gaze behavior and establishment of "loci"—essential elements of correct ASL—Van Cantfort and Rimpau respond that control of both of these functions is late acquired among human signers, the former not being perfected until adulthood. It would be truly astonishing if juvenile chimpanzees were to perform at a level expected only of adult humans. The authors point out, however, that five chimpanzees and one gorilla have exploited the *juvenile* form (by human standards) of locus establishment, facial expression, eye gaze, and use of repetition for purpose of modulation in Ameslan.

4. In response to the charge that in the films cited earlier, Washoe tended to interrupt just as Nim had done, Van Cantfort and Rimpau state that Terrace and Petitto misread normal conversational overlap as interruption. They take Terrace et al. (1979) to task for the use of individual frames taken from the films, as evidence to prove their point: In the static display of stop-motion prints, the dynamic interaction of communication is inevitably lost.

5. To the charge concerning anecdotal reporting, Van Cantfort and Rimpau offer in essence the rather feeble retort that it is American Psychological Association policy not to publish raw data, and that nobody else publishes any more detailed descriptions of data than the researchers attacked by Petitto and Seidenberg.

Whatever APA policy may be, given the intensity of debate and the acerbity of discussion in this field, I think it behooves all researchers in ape language studies to publish complete, detailed protocols (a) of all interactions used as a basis for claims and (b) of all experimental situations whether they provide evidence for or against positions of the investigator(s). In fairness, one must note that not all anecdotes have been self-serving. For example, as noted by Van Cantfort and Rimpau, the Gardners (1978) state that a young chimpanzee overgeneralized the sign "DRINK," not only to food but to noncomestibles.

Miles (1983) has described a study of ASL in an organgutan and compared the results with those of Project Nim. Unlike Nim, who did most of his learning in a prison-like environment, Chantek learned signs in the presence of referents, took trips on which more signs could be learned, and had a small number of trainer-caretakers (as opposed to a very large number for Nim), who spent 15 hours a week or more with Chantek. Although Terrace found that Nim's MLU did not increase with length of maximum utterance or with age, Miles found that Chantek had a MLU of 1.93 at 26 months of age (with a maximum utterance length of 6) and had shown a steady MLU increase from 1.00 to 1.91 from January 1979 to May 1980. Chantek did not string signs together in repetitious sequences. Chantek spontaneously initiated 37% of her signed conversations (as compared to Nim's 8%) and imitated signs previously produced by a caretaker only 3% of the time (as compared to Nim's 38%). Miles notes that Stage I children have shown a 22% to 47% imitation rate. Chantek tended not to interrupt: Miles counted 391 utterances by Chantek compared to 418 by the caregiver during conversation; in 2½ hours, Miles found that 8% of Chantek's and 9% of the caregiver's utterances were interruptions (vs. 38% for Nim).

Thus Miles, in accord with Fouts, concludes that the failure of Project Nim (in light of the success of Project Chantek) was due to the failure of the training method used by Terrace and his colleagues.

In conclusion, let us consider Terrace's (1983) and Seidenberg and Petitto's (1979) claim that apes' signing behavior is *basically* imitative and therefore should not be credited with being under linguistic control. First of all, Fouts, Shapiro, & O'Neil (1978) found that a chimpanzee named Lucy initiated 77.9% of 267 conversations sampled, and participated actively in these communicative interactions. Similar observations have been made by the Gardners (1978), Patterson and Linden (1981), and Miles (1983) with other chimpanzees, a gorilla, and an orangutan. As already noted, Miles (1983) found that Chantek did not tend to imitate signs emitted by humans. In fact, Chantek signed even when the caregiver intentionally did not. Nelson (1980), on the other hand, notes that hearing children *do* repeat, citing a sequence repeated 11 times in a row by a 2-year-old girl. And Hoffmeister, Moore, & Ellenberger (1975) have found that children acquiring sign language frequently repeat signs "without apparent significance" (p. 123). Van Cantfort and Rimpau claim that the reason children's speech seems to be relatively free of repetitions is that repetitions are frequently edited out of reported corpora.

Marx (1980), in an insightful review of the controversy, states that Allen Gardner has shown that imitative behavior can be turned on and off, in an unpublished videotape in which two thirds of the tape is virtually free of imitation. The last third shows approximately 70% imitative behavior; in this final third, operant conditioning techniques are used to elicit signing. Gardner concluded that Terrace observed a great deal of imitation because he used largely operant conditioning techniques.

As a final word on "imitation," let us note that Terrace et al. (1979) use the term to refer to the use of the same sign as the trainer used, in order to refer, in a response, to the same topic of conversation (Van Cantfort & Rimpau, 1982). In a study of child language, such "imitations" would be considered as expansions "that added information about the topic of a prior utterance" (Bloom, Rocissano, & Hood, 1976, p. 530). If the criterion for "imitation" were the use of a locution in a response, that was identical to one previously used by the interlocutor, perhaps the great majority of human conversation would have to be considered "mere imitation."

Conclusion

> There is no universally accepted definition of language against which to measure the ape experiments, and that is precisely why they are so valuable. (J. H. Hill, 1978, p. 90)

> From time to time we have been asked . . . "Do you think that Washoe has language?" . . . imply[ing] a distinction between one class of communicative behavior that can be called language and another that cannot. This in turn implies a well-established theory that could provide the distinction. (Gardner & Gardner, 1969, p. 672)

> The ape . . . emerges as the unclear middle case: Neither wholly comparable to man (the clear positive case) nor to parrot (the clear negative), the "talking" ape puts the question of language to its first severe test. (Premack, 1971, p. 808)

> Rather than showing similarities to human language use, many aspects of the apes' behavior . . . show similarities to the pre- and early-linguistic behaviors of very young children. (Seidenberg & Petitto, 1979, p. 200)

> A chimpanzee's cognitive linguistic ability allows it to construct a linguistic proposition to convey a conceptual content at approximately a human two-year-old level. (Miles, 1976, p. 592)

> The ability of apes or even [human] 2-year-olds to communicate and use simple names is not sufficient reason to attribute the use of human language to them. The creative . . . aspect of language cannot be overlooked. (Limber, 1977, p. 280)

As can be readily seen from the quotations, much of the discussion concerning the evaluation of ape language studies has been fueled by the nonexistence of universally accepted criteria for what is to count as knowing a language. Although, as Marx (1980) points out, nearly all researchers would agree to the following two criteria as *necessary* conditions for language: (a) that "the words or signs be symbols for something and be recognized as such by the user," and, (b) that "the words be combined with one another to form novel phrases or sentences that are nonetheless understandable by others" (p. 1331), it is clear that for many investigators these are not at all *sufficient* conditions. Limber (1977), for example, would include as *sine qua non* for crediting a behavior as linguistic, word order or inflections, hierarchical constituent structure, and recursivity in nominalization, complementation, and relativization. If Coulter (1983) is correct in his coordinate analysis of ASL relatives, Limber's last criterion would eliminate Ameslan. His hierarchical structural requirement would eliminate Japanese, because in single clauses, this language displays no hierarchical configuration (Rizzi, 1985). In response to Brown's (1970) observation that Washoe had the same repertoire of semantic relations as children did, Limber suggests that these relations might be inherent in any system using concatenation. The Penn Central Railroad can be used to falsify Limber's claim, because all railroads use concatenation (of rails as well as railway cars). Furthermore, railroads are *communicative* systems.

It should be obvious that the source of much of the sterile and pointless debate on the issue of ape language could be eliminated with the adoption of a Givonian perspective on these studies. It is clear that the pongids studied in these projects are utilizing communicative systems far more advanced than the monopropositional mode (the mode characterized by Givón as representative of feral pongid communication), and equally clear that no ape has achieved the same kind of syntactic-mode linguistic complexity as found on these pages. These animals seem to be functioning at various points in the pragmatic-mode domain of the communicative continuum, using a kind of pidgin-like approach to communication. To deny this is to play the role of the skeptic who can always reject a description of an event and substitute his own description of "what really happened" (Simon, 1983). Simon notes that a behaviorist critique regarding the ascription of internal states to animals could be equally used against ascribing them to children or even adult humans. Noting that signing apes are able consistently to construct meaningful structures, Simon argues that to claim "in ad hoc fashion" that this stage of development does not qualify as syntactic language (in ape *or* child) places one on "the skeptic's endless track" (Simon, 1983, p. 100).

Simon's assessment of the skeptic's critique is emulated by Miles's (1983) characterization of the "yes but" game: To the demonstration that apes use signs spontaneously, one could respond, "Yes, but in combinations?" Upon demonstration of the latter, one could always respond, "Yes, but are the sequences governed by grammatical rules?" To evidence of this last, one could respond, "Yes, but do they use dependent clauses?," ad infinitum (Miles, 1983, p. 45).

The insistence upon all-or-nothing (as opposed to continuous) characterizations has plagued aphasiology with attempts to describe aphasic syndromes in terms of elements preserved and lost (chapter 6, this volume), and child-language-acquisition studies with attempts to determine at what state a child "has" language ("First Language Acquisition", this chapter). But it would not plague ape language studies any more than it would these other fields, if a continuous framework were generally adopted. Premack and Premack (1983) have found that whereas a pigeon or a rat has only one representational system, a chimpanzee has two. Thus a rat and a chimp can both be trained, but only the chimp can be instructed. Once an ape is taught a bit of language (s)he can be instructed, i.e., told what to do. Although apes can be taught either by training (e.g., operant conditioning) or by instruction (via communicative media), human beings will automatically convert training into instruction. This situation may be indicative of three cognitive levels that one might call the imaginal (the rat, ape, and human), the representational (the ape and human), and the symbolic (Brown, 1976), or computational, or syntactic, or linguistic (human only), in which the rat's behavior is limbically mediated only, the ape's behavior may be neocortically motivated (suppressing limbic mediation), and the human's behavior susceptible to hemispherically lateralized cortical mediation (Brown, 1976, 1977).

The idea of a continuum gives one the freedom necessary to observe a great number of phenomena without blinders. Archibald Hill's (1978) observation that animals taught Ameslan tend to invent and use swear words and phrases is consonant with the fact that such words and phrases are frequently preserved in the speech of aphasics, even when no other forms of speech are spared. These forms, which occur in aphasic speech as ictal speech automatisms (Chase, 1967; Whitaker, 1971), are most likely limbically mediated and hence, originate from the most primitive kind of connection between meaning and expression. There is of course no reason to believe the pongid limbic system to be any more primitive than that of humans.

Hughes (1975) describes the successful use of Premack's symbol system with four children aged 8 to 13, diagnosed as having "developmental aphasia." These children did not acquire language, despite normal hearing and nonverbal IQ. All of them scored at or below the level of a 2-year-old on formal language comprehension and expression tests. Following training in Premack's system, the 70% success rate of the children on tests of identifying objects named by tokens, of identifying class concepts, of following commands, of completing sentences describing actions performed by the instructor, of ordering constituents using "ON," and of answering yes-no questions, strongly suggests that although these children lack the normal neurophysiological system required to acquire syntactic-mode language, they may nonetheless be able to function successfully with a system based on functions and relations which can be mediated at the level of the pragmatic mode. "Premackese" may represent just such a system, as may Yerkish.

IMPLICATIONS FOR LINGUISTICS

Knowing a language is something like knowing the rules of a game (Schnitzer, 1973). One can learn how to play chess in a few minutes, if by "learning how to play chess" one means learning the rules—which moves are legal and which are illegal. Playing chess presupposes this knowledge, and complete adherence to the rules is required in order for what is being done to qualify as a game of chess. *Skill* at playing chess, what move one makes at any particular point in a game, is something very different indeed, something not governed in any obvious way by rules.

Similarly, communicative skill in a language presupposes knowing the (grammatical) rules of the language. But there are obvious differences between games (such as chess or bridge) and languages (such as Spanish or English). First, players' knowledge of the rules of chess is explicit: They are known consciously by all chess players. Speakers' knowledge of the rules of Spanish is in large part unconscious. The chess player can state all the rules of chess on demand. The Spanish speaker cannot do so for more than a few of the rules of Spanish grammar.

Second, chess permits no rule violations. (Other games recognize rule violations and establish penalties for them; the established penalties are, of course part of the rules of the game.) Any illegal move made in chess would be immediately noted by the opponent and nullified. But rule violations do occur in the linguistic behavior of native speakers, and they are tolerated.[4]

There is one further difference between the rules of Spanish and the rules of chess: The latter are well defined; every move in chess is either legal or illegal. But it is not the case that every string of Spanish formatives either is or is not a grammatical sentence of Spanish.

In a study reported by Schnitzer (1978b, 1981), 31 native speakers of Spanish were asked to judge the grammaticality of 96 sentences formed from the following two collections of constituents,

1. *Pedro - mató - a Juan - con un martillo*
   (Peter killed John with a hammer)
2. *Pedro - rompió - el espejo - con un martillo*
   (Peter broke the mirror with a hammer)

[4]Note that bad moves, stupid moves, and the like are all *legal* moves and do not reflect on the player's knowledge of the rules of the game, only on his/her skill at playing it. Similarly, unsuccessful attempts at communication of information, misinterpretation of messages, etc., do not necessarily reflect on speakers' knowledge of the language.

in all possible permutations of constituent order and with the direct object pronoun *lo* present/absent immediately before the verb. Subjects were asked to judge each sentence as grammatical or ungrammatical or to indicate if they were unsure. They were also instructed to use their own intuitions and not any knowledge of the grammar approved by the Spanish Royal Academy and to consider the sentences as transcriptions of spoken Spanish, not to be judged by literary criteria. Results are summarized in Table 7.1.

The most salient result is that there was unanimous agreement on only 3 of the 96 sentences (1 grammatical, 2 ungrammatical) and 90% agreement on only 24 (25%) of the sentences (with about a 1 : 5 ratio of grammatical to ungrammatical).

There was a strong tendency to reject the presence of the direct object pronoun in sentences in which the lexical direct object followed the verb (e.g., *Pedro lo mató a Juan con un martillo*). Every "−III" sentence had this violation, four fifths of the "−II" sentences had this violation, and no sentence judged to be +III, +II, +I, 0, or −I had this violation. There was also a weak tendency to prefer the presence of the object pronoun in sentences in which the lexical D.O. preceded the verb. Except for sentences with the prepositional phrase in the initial position, all sentences with O-V order that did not contain the pronoun were classified as −II, −I, or 0.

There was a strong preference for S-V-O order. Seven eighths of the +III sentences had this order. And except for sentences beginning with the prepositional phrase, seven eighths of all sentences with this word order were judged as +III; the eighth was judged as +II. There was also a weak tendency to reject verb-final order.

Perhaps the most interesting result is that the greatest number of sentences (more than a quarter) are found in the 0 category, i.e., approximately equal numbers of acceptances and rejections among the judges. Apparently Spanish speakers do not have intersubjectively consistent judgments about word order—the "hallmark" of syntax. Several years ago, Lakoff (1971a) proposed the

TABLE 7.1
Results of Grammatical-Acceptability Study

Category	*Definition*	*Number of Sentences*
+III	3 rejections or fewer	8
+II	4 to 8 rejections	5
+I	9 to 13 rejections	5
0	14, 15, 16, or 17 acceptances or rejections	25
−I	9 to 13 acceptances	18
−II	4 to 8 acceptances	15
−III	3 acceptances or fewer	20
	Total	96

grammaticality could be judged only in relation to a set of presuppositions associated with a given sentence (''relative grammaticality''). McCawley (1982) has argued along similar lines that it is simply wrong to consider a language to be a set of sentences, akin to considering an automobile to be a set of trips taken in it. But the results of this study (Schnitzer 1978b, 1981) are not explicable along the lines that Lakoff and McCawley suggest, because the lexical content, overall meaning, and main constituents of the sentences remain unchanged; only the order of the constituents varies, so it seems unlikely that the lack of intersubject agreement could be due to different assumed presuppositions among the judges.

In an informal study I have been conducting in linguistics classes at the University of Puerto Rico for about 10 years, I ask bilingual students to translate the following sentences into Spanish:

3. My mother and my father are respectively tall and short.[5]
4. I taste like ketchup.

I invariably receive responses to sentence 3 which include all of the following:
Mi mamá (madre) y mi papá (padre) son respectivamente

3a. alto y bajo.
3b. altos y bajos.
3c. alta y bajo.
3d. Mi mamá es alta y mi papá es bajo.

No student has ever claimed that (s)he would actually use any of these sentences other than 3d, nor has any native speaker I have encountered so claimed on being told of these results.

For sentence 4, I generally receive the following responses:

4a. Sepo a ketchup.
4b. Sé a ketchup.
4c. Tengo sabor a ketchup.

Of these, no one would ever actually use 4a or 4b, and all informants agree that 4c does not mean the same as 4a or 4b.

What is revealed by these exercises is that speakers do not have intuitions concerning these sentences in Spanish. For sentence 3, those who answer with 3a

[5]See Lakoff (1969), Chomsky (1972), Sánchez de Zavala (1974), and McCawley (1982) for differing gramaticality judgments and interpretations of them. (The relevant section is deleted from Lakoff, 1971b.) I cite these references only to give credit for these and some related sentences, originally attributed to David Perlmutter, which raise the issue discussed here.

are consciously using the rule that says that adjectives must be masculine when they modify NP referring to groups consisting of males and females. Speakers who answer with 3b are consciously using the Spanish number agreement rule (plural copula and adjective required with conjoined subject). Speakers who answer with 3c are following logical form; their intuitions do not automatically provide this structure. The only natural response is 3d, which all subjects agree is the only one they would ever use to convey the meaning of sentence 3 in Spanish, except in a formal exercise such as this.

For sentence 4, the situation is a bit more complex. The verb *saber* means "to know" when used transitively, and "to taste (like)" when followed by the preposition *a*. *Saber* is morphologically irregular in that (among other things) the first person singular present indicative form is *sé* (rather than **sabo*), and present subjunctive is *sepa-* (instead of **saba-*). There is a strong constraint in Spanish against the use of first person singular present indicative forms ending in *-abo*. Every verb that would have this form is irregular, and thus avoids it (e.g., **habo* → *he*, **cabo* → *quepo*) although there would be no violation of Spanish phonotactics (The form *cabo* in fact exists as a noun.).[6]

Speakers who respond with 4a are using a nonexistent verb form **sepo* (presumably by analogy with *sepa*) rather than an impossible form **sabo*. Those who respond with 4b are using a form that nearly all speakers agree only can be used for *saber* in the sense of "to know," not "to taste like." Although 4c presents no linguistic problem, it does not quite mean the same as 4a or 4b, because these (but not 4c) entail that the speaker has been tasted.

It is important to note that virtually no one translates either of these sentences quickly, the typical time taken for a class of 20 students to do either of the translation exercises exceeding 10 minutes. The excessive time needed may represent attempts to access formal grammatical rules in the absence of native-speaker intuitions.

There are some obvious conclusions to be drawn from these results. One is that a language is not a set of sentences (McCawley, 1980, 1982), and native speakers therefore do not have intuitions regarding the grammaticality of any arbitrary string constructed from the formatives of their language (such as those of 1 and 2). Secondly, it appears that when speakers are confronted with a

---

[6]There is, I believe. a functional explanation for this restriction. Is Spanish, the present subjunctive and first person singular present indicative *always* share the same stem. The present subjunctive can be formed by dropping the final *o* of the present indicative form and adding *-e-* to first conjugation verbs (*hablo* → *hable*) and *-a-* to second and third conjugation verbs (*como* → *coma*, *vivo* → *viva*) plus person-number endings (*Ø*, *-s*, *Ø*, *-mos*, *-n*).

If first person singular present indicative forms ending in *-abo* were permitted, this would result in the existence of present subjunctive forms ending in *-aba*. But since *-aba* is the characteristic ending of the imperfect indicative for first conjugation verbs, these forms could lead to confusion between present subjunctive and imperfect indicative.

metalinguistic task for which their grammatical knowledge does not prepare them (such as translation of sentences 3 and 4), they try to somehow objectify their unconscious rules in order to formulate an *ad hoc* algorithm for dealing with the presented string. What I am claiming is not merely that grammatical knowledge is squishy (Ross, 1972, 1973a, 1973b) or inherently variable (Labov, 1972), but rather *intrinsically incomplete,* if by "grammatical knowledge" we understand a system that assigns structural descriptions to all and only the sentences of a language. The notion of "all and only the sentences of a language" is incoherent if we are speaking of natural languages.

In an important and thought-provoking anthology, Moravcsik and Wirth (1980) have compiled position statements with examples of analysis by representatives of 12 current schools of thought on syntax. This book, based on a conference on current approaches to syntax held at the University of Wisconsin-Milwaukee in 1979 is most revealing in that it at the same time demonstrates how entrenched the concept of a language as a set of sentences generable by a grammar is, and how discontent with this vision is emerging from several corners. Of the 12 school-of-thought papers, two thirds accept this vision. However, Dik's "functional grammar," Van Valin and Foley's "role and reference grammar," tagmemics (presented herein by Linda Jones), and McCawley's nameless approach represent departures from this conception: These latter four assume an essentially communicative basis to language.

I would like to go a step further than these papers and argue that the evidence adduced in the present volume suggests that linguistic communication (including linguistically mediated thought) at the syntactic-mode level represents an immense and largely inaccessible hierarchy—linguistically, phylogenetically, and cognitively. Attempts to describe languages with grammars will inevitably fail if the language is taken to be a coherent single system. The formal operations, functions, and relations characteristic of syntactic-mode linguistic behavior cannot be considered as forming a system. They are the mere tip of a cognitive-communicative iceberg, analogous to Jason Brown's neurological iceberg (Brown, 1977, 1980). The tip of the iceberg is perhaps describable. Clearly there are certain morphosyntactic forms that are required and certain others that are absolutely disallowed in natural languages (as shown, for example in the study cited previously, by the strong rejection of direct object pronouns in Spanish sentences in which the lexical direct object follows the verb). But in cases in which no clear syntactic-mode rule is violated, there will inevitably be widespread disagreement about "grammatical" acceptability, because in a sense, speakers are being asked to judge a whole rosebush when they have access only to a single flower.[7]

---

[7]Or a book on seeing only the cover, or a cake on tasting only the frosting. These synechdochic images of iceberg tips and roses can be called forth virtually without limit. I shall resist the temptation.

Human linguistic communication is founded on a hierarchy that includes a limbic (monopropositional mode) basis on which a pragmatic-mode representation is superimposed. Normal adult linguistic performance has yet another system superimposed—the syntactic mode, which serves as a kind of system of output constraints. It is only to this last, most phylogenetically recent, most physically and cognitively superficial system (its complexity notwithstanding) that native speakers have access, and it is only concerning this system that native speakers have clear intuitions. But when asked for their intuitions, speakers have no way of telling what it is they are judging. Perhaps a given sentence presented to an informant may reflect a pragmatic-mode presupposition or judgment with which the informant unconsciously disagrees. This reaction could be reflected as a judgment of ungrammaticality.

What I am suggesting is that attempts to view languages as organic wholes are essentially wrong-headed. Linguistic phenomena represent an evolutionary hierarchy in human cognition, and the "truly linguistic" (i.e., syntactic mode) part of these phenomena cannot be looked at as though it were a separate system. The goal of writing a descriptively adequate grammar is inherently unreachable. What then, should linguists be doing?

The answer to this is of course that it is a matter of taste. Linguists could be observing syntactic-mode phenomena that make structural impositions on communicated messages in absolute or relative ways. They could be studying what types of such phenomena exist and search for evidence of different means of effecting the same constraints in different languages of the world. They could be studying language in communicational context, and the creative use of language as it interacts with nonlinguistic aspects of context (Harris, 1981). In short, they could be doing very many of the things they are doing now but without the unrealizable goal of someday putting it all together into a full-fledged coherent grammatical description.

Traditional pedagogical grammars have never pretended to be exhaustive. They provide just enough information for the student to be able to correctly use the required syntactic-mode structures of the target language. There is no way that any book could prevent a nonnative speaker from formulating messages in ways that natives speakers would not, because many of these differences go well beyond and stem from far below the (superimposed syntactic-mode) linguistic system.

Roy Harris (1981) has argued along similar lines that linguistic theory has neglected a distinction that he draws between "grammar" and "usage." Usage is determined by many (nonformal) factors that are unrelated to the formal grammar. What, for example, could be the grammatical basis for the fact that speakers of British English refer to persons who operate newsstands as "newsagents" rather than as "newspaper dealers"? Harris views trying to include grammar and usage in a single system as misguided, because they are distinct. As he puts it, "The grammatical properties of an arbitrary string of words are believed [erroneously] to constitute a subset which forms the basis of speakers' judgments, independently of any other properties the example may have, and even though no one is clear about which the grammatical properties are'' (Harris, 1981, pp. 84–5).

A FEW FINAL WORDS

In this volume I have tried to show that results from a number of linguistic tests administered to aphasics tend to support a framework for language study espoused by Talmy Givón (1979). I have argued that viewing aphasia phenomenally as a regression along the communicative continuum, and neurologically as a regression along the phylogenetic hierarchy, allows one to make sense of the data discussed herein, as well many other aphasiological data presented and discussed in recent neurolinguistic literature. In this chapter, I have tried to show that this conception helps to clarify issues in other related fields as well, in particular, language acquisition by humans and apes, and general linguistic theory.

It is hoped that this book will stimulate discussion in these areas.

Afterword

''Pragmatic-mode'' need for speak.

First talk primitive. Baby. Animal. Bad aphasic. Call ''monopropositional.'' Use limbic brain.

''Pragmatic-mode'' use for child, aphasic, pidgin. Language die. For learn language. Teach ape. ''Pragmatic-mode'' good. Say what like. Everybody understand. No problem. Use cortex brain.

''Syntactic-mode'' for grownup. For creole. For develop child and aphasic. For learn more language. You say *more*. Say more what like. Everybody understand more. Use lateralized cortex brain. No problem.

No good try explain language only ''syntactic-mode.'' No work. Language hierarchy. Brain hierarchy. Species hierarchy.

Book finish.

References

Alajouanine, T. (1968). *L'aphasie et le langage pathologique* [Aphasia and pathological language]. Paris: J. B. Balliere.

Alajouanine, T., Ombredane, A., & Durand, M. (1939). *Le syndrome de désintegration phonétique dans l'aphasie* [The syndrome of phonetic disintegration in aphasia]. Paris: Masson.

Albert, M. L., & Obler, L. K. (1978). *The bilingual brain.* New York: Academic Press.

Bailey, N., Madden, C., & Krashen, S. (1974). Is there a 'natural sequence' in adult second language learning? *Language Learning, 21,* 235–243.

Barrett, M. D. (1982). The holophrastic hypothesis: Conceptual and empirical issues. *Cognition, 11,* 47–76.

Bates, E., Camaioni, L., & Volterra, V. (1975). The acquisition of performatives prior to speech. *Merrill-Palmer Quarterly, 21,* 205–226.

Bates, E., & MacWhinney, B. (1979). The functionalist approach to the acquisition of grammar. In E. Ochs & B. Schieffelin (Eds.), *Developmental pragmatics.* New York: Academic Press.

Bay, E. (1962). Aphasia and non-verbal disorders of language. *Brain, 85,* 412–426.

Bay, E. (1964). Principles of classification and their influence on our concepts of aphasia. In A. V. S. de Reuck & M. O'Conner (Eds.), *Disorders of language.* Boston: Little, Brown.

Bay, E. (1967). The classification of disorders of speech. *Cortex, 3,* 26–37.

Bellugi, U., & Fischer, S. (1972). A comparison of sign language and spoken language. *Cognition, 1,* 173–200.

Bellugi, U., & Kilma, E. S. (1975). Aspects of sign language and its structure. In J. F. Kavanagh & J. E. Cutting (Eds.), *The role of speech in language.* Cambridge, MA: MIT Press.

Bellugi, U., & Newkirk, D. (1981). Formal devices for creating new signs in American Sign Language. *Sign Language Studies, 30,* 1–35.

Bellugi, U., Poizner, H., & Zurif, E. B. (1982). Aphasia in a visual-gestural language. In M. A. Arbib, D. Caplan, & J. C. Marshall (Eds.), *Neural Models of language processes.* New York: Academic Press.

Benson, D. F. (1977). The third alexia. *Archives of Neurology, 34,* 327–31.

Benson, D. F., & Geschwind, N. (1976). The aphasias and related disturbances. In A. Baker & H. Baker (Eds.), *Clinical neurology.* New York: Harper and Row.

Berndt, R. S., & Caramazza, A. (1980). A redefinition of the syndrome of Broca's aphasia: Implications for a neuropsychological model of language. *Applied Psycholing., 1,* 225–278.

Bickerton, D. (1977). Language acquisition and language universals. In A. Valdman (Ed.), *Pidgin and creole linguistics.* Bloomington: Indiana University Press.

Bickerton, D. (1981). *The roots of language.* Ann Arbor: Karoma.

Bickerton, D. (1984). The language bioprogram hypothesis. *Behavioral and Brain Sciences, 7,* 173–188.

Bloom, L. (1970). *Language development: Form and function in emerging grammars.* Cambridge, MA: MIT Press.

Bloom, L. (1973). *One word at a time: The use of single word utterances before syntax.* The Hague: Mouton.

Bloom, L., Lightbrown, P., & Hood, L. (1975). Structure and variation in child language. *Monographs of the Society for Research in Child Development, 40* (Serial No. 160).

Bloom, L., Rocissano, L., & Hood, L. (1976). Adult–child discourse. *Cognitive Psychology, 8,* 521–552.

Blumstein, S. E., Goodglass, H., Statlender, S., & Biber, C. (1983). Comprehension strategies determine reference in aphasia: A study of reflexivization. *Brain and Language, 18,* 115–127.

Böhme, K., & Levelt, W. J. M. (1979). *Children's use and awareness of natural and syntactic gender in possessive pronouns.* Paper presented to the Conference on Linguistic Awareness and Learning to Read, Victoria, B.C.

Boller, F., Cole, M., Vrtunski, P. B., Patterson, M., & Kim, Y. (1979). Paralinguistic aspects of auditory comprehension in aphasia. *Brain and Language, 7,* 164–174.

Bonhoeffer, K. (1902). Zur Kenntnis der Rückbildung motorischer Aphasien [Towards an Understanding of the evolution of motor aphasias]. *Mitteilungen aus den Grenzgebieten der Medizen und Chirurgie, 10,* 203–224.

Bowerman, M. (1973a). *Early syntactic development: A cross-linguistic study with special reference to Finnish.* Cambridge: University Press.

Bowerman, M. (1973b). Structural relationships in children's utterances: Syntactic or semantic. In T. E. Moore (Ed.), *Cognitive development and the acquisition of language.* New York: Academic Press.

Bradley, D. C. (1978). *Computational distinctions of vocabulary type.* Unpublished doctoral dissertation, MIT, Cambridge, MA.

Bradley, D. C., Garrett, M. E., & Zurif, E. B. (1980). Syntactic deficits in Broca's aphasia. In D. Caplan (Ed.), *Biological studies of mental processes.* Cambridge, MA: MIT Press.

Braine, M. D. S. (1971). The acquisition of language in infant and child. In C. E. Reed (Ed.), *The learning of language.* New York: Appleton.

Braine, M. D. S. (1976). Children's first word combinations. *Monographs of the Society for Research in Child Development, 41.*

Braine, M. D. S., & Wells, R. S. (1978). Case-like categories in children: The actor and more related categories. *Cognitive Psychology, 10,* 100–122.

Bransford, J. D., Barclay, J., & Franks, J. J. (1972) Sentence memory: Constructive vs. interpretive approach. *Cognitive Psychology, 3,* 193–209.

Bransford, J. D., & Franks, J. J. (1971). The abstraction of linguistic ideas. *Cognitive Psychology, 2,* 331–350.

Bridges, A. (1980). SVO comprehension strategies reconsidered: The evidence of individual patterns of response. *Journal of Child Language, 7,* 89–104.

Brown, J. W. (1976). Consciousness and pathology of language. In R. W. Rieber (Ed.), *The neuropsychology of language.* New York: Plenum.

Brown, J. W. (1977). *Mind, brain, and consciousness.* New York: Academic Press.

Brown, J. W. (1979). *Neurobiology of social communication in primates.* New York: Academic Press.

Brown, J. W. (1980). Brain structure and language production: A dynamic view. In D. Caplan (Ed.), *Biological studies of mental processes*. Cambridge, MA: MIT Press.

Brown, J. W. (1982). Hierarchy and evolution in neurolinguistics. In M. A. Arbib, D. Caplan, & J. C. Marshall (Eds.), *Neural models of language process*. New York: Academic Press.

Brown, R. (1970). The first sentences of child and chimpanzee. In R. Brown (Ed.), *Psycholinguistics*. New York: Free Press. Reprinted in C. A. Ferguson & D. I. Slobin (Eds.). (1973). *Studies of child language development*. New York: Holt.

Brown, R. (1973). *A first language*. Cambridge, MA: Harvard University Press.

Bruner, J. (1983). *Child's talk: Learning to use language*. New York: Norton.

Buckingham, H. W., & Kertesz, A. (1976). *Neologistic jargon aphasia*. Amsterdam: Swets and Zeitlinger.

Burt, M., Dulay, H., & Hernández, E. (1975). *The bilingual syntax measure*. New York: Harcourt.

Caplan, D. (1981). On the cerebral localization of linguistic functions: Logical and empirical issues surrounding deficit analysis and functional localization. *Brain and Language, 14,* 120–137.

Caplan, D. (1982). Reconciling the categories: Representation in neurology and in linguistics. In M. A. Arbib, D. Caplan, & J. C. Marshall (Eds.), *Neural models of language process*. New York: Academic Press.

Caplan, D. (1983). A note on the "word-order problem" in agrammatism. *Brain and Language, 20,* 155–165.

Caplan, D. (1985). Syntactic and semantic structures in agrammatism. In M. -L. Kean (Ed.), *Agrammatism*. New York: Academic Press.

Caplan, D., & Hildebrandt, N. (1986). *Language deficits and the theory of syntax:* A reply to Grodzinsky. *Brain and Language, 27,* 168–177.

Caplan, D., Lecours, A. R., & Smith, A. (Eds.). (1984). *Biological perspectives on language*. Cambridge MA: MIT Press.

Caplan, D., Matthei, E., & Gigley, H. (1981). Comprehension of gerundive constructions by Broca's aphasics. *Brain and Language, 13,* 145–160.

Cappa, S., & Vignolo, L. A. (1979). Transcortical features of aphasia following left thalamic hemorrhage. *Cortex, 15,* 121–129.

Caramazza, A. (1984). The logic of neuropsychological research and the problem of patient classification in aphasia. *Brain and Language, 21,* 9–20.

Caramazza, A. (1986). On drawing inferences about the structure of normal cognitive systems from the analysis of patterns of impaired performance: The case for single patient studies. *Brain and Cognition, 5,* 41–66.

Caramazza, A., & Berndt, R. S. (1985). A multicomponent view of agrammatic Broca's aphasia. In M. -L. Kean (Ed.), *Agrammatism*. New York: Academic Press.

Caramazza, A., Berndt, R. S., Basili, A. G., & Koller, J. J. (1981). Syntactic processing deficits in aphasia. *Cortex, 17,* 333–348.

Caramazza, A., & Zurif, E. B. (1976). Dissociation of algorithmic and heuristic processes in language comprehension: Evidence from aphasia. *Brain and Language, 3,* 572–582.

Caramazza, A., & Zurif, E. (1978). Comprehension of complex sentences in children and aphasics: A test of the regression hypothesis. In A. Caramazza & E. Zurif (Eds.), *Language acquisition and language breakdown*. Baltimore: Johns Hopkins University Press.

Carter, A. (1974). *Communication in the sensory-motor period*. Unpublished doctoral dissertation, University of California, Berkeley.

Chase, R. A. (1967). Ictal speech automatisms and swearing. *Journal of Nervous and Mental Disease, 144,* 5.

Chastain, K. (1975). Affective and ability factors in second language learning. *Language Learning, 25,* 153–161.

Chomsky, N. (1972). Some empirical issues in the theory of transformational grammar. In S. Peters (Ed.), *Goals of linguistic theory*. Englewood Cliffs, NJ: Prentice–Hall.

Chomsky, N. (1980). *Rules and representations.* New York: Columbia University Press.

Chomsky, N. (1981). *Lectures on government and binding.* Dordrecht: Foris.

Chomsky, N. (1982). *Some concepts and consequences of the theory of government and binding.* Cambridge, MA: MIT Press.

Clark, E. V. (1971). On the acquisition of the meaning of *before* and *after*. *Journal of Verbal Learning and Verbal Behavior, 10,* 266–275.

Clark, H. H., & Clark, E. V. (1977). *Psychology and language.* New York: Harcourt.

Coulter, G. R. (1983). A conjoined analysis of American Sign Language relative clauses. *Discourse Processes, 6,* 305–318.

Cromer, R. F. (1974). The development of language and cognition: The cognition hypothesis. In B. Foss (Ed.), *New perspectives in child development.* Harmondsworth: Penguin.

Cromer, R. F. (1976). Development strategies for language. In V. Hamilton & M. D. Vernon (Eds.), *The development of cognitive processes.* New York: Academic Press.

Curtiss, S. (1971). *Genie: A psycholinguistic study of a modern day "wild child".* New York: Academic Press.

Darley, F. L., Brown, J. R., & Swenson, W. M. (1975). Language changes after neurosurgery for Parkinsonism. *Brain and Language, 2,* 45–64.

De Jong, R. N. (1958). *The neurologic examination.* New York: Hoeber.

de Luce, J., & Wilder, H. T. (Eds.). (1983). *Language in primates: Perspectives and implications.* New York: Springer-Verlag.

Dennis, M., & Kohn, B. (1975). Comprehension of syntax in infantile hemiplegics after cerebral hemidecortication: Left hemisphere superiority. *Brain and Language, 2,* 472–482.

Dennis, M., & Whitaker, H. A. (1976). Language acquisition following hemidecortication: Linguistic superiority of the left over the right hemisphere. *Brain and Language, 3,* 404–433.

Dennis, M., & Wiegel-Crump, C. A. (1979). Aphasic dissolution and language acquisition. In H. Whitaker & H. Whitaker (Eds.), *Studies in neurolinguistics,* (Vol. 4). New York: Academic Press.

Denny-Brown, D. (1965). Physiological apsects of disturbances of speech. *Australian Journal of Experimental Biology and Medical Science, 43,* 455–474.

Deuchar, M. (1981). *British Sign Language.* London: Routledge.

de Villiers, J. G. (1974). Quantitative aspects of agrammatism in aphasics. *Cortex, 10,* 36–54.

de Villiers, J. G., & de Villiers, P. (1973). A cross-sectional study of the acquisition of grammatical morphemes in child speech. *Journal of Psycholinguistic Research, 2,* 267–278.

de Villiers, J. G., & Flusberg, H. B. T. (1975). Some facts one simply cannot deny. *Journal of Child Language, 2,* 279–286.

Dik, S. C. (1980). Seventeen sentences: Basic principles and application of functional grammar. In E. A. Moravcsik & J. R. Wirth (Eds.), *Syntax and semantics* (Vol. 13). New York: Academic Press.

Dore, J. (1975). Holophrases, speech acts and language universals. *Journal of Child Language, 2,* 21–40.

Dorian, N. C. (1973). Grammatical change in a dying dialect. *Language, 49,* 413–438.

Dorian, N. C. (1977). The problem of the semispeaker in language death. *International Journal of the Sociology of Language, 12,* 23–32.

Dorian, N. C. (1978). The fate of morphological complexity in language death: Evidence from East Sutherland Gaelic. *Language, 54,* 590–609.

Dorian, N. C. (1982). Linguistic models and language death evidence. In L. K. Obler & L. Menn (Eds.), *Exceptional language and linguistics.* New York: Academic Press.

Dorian, N. C. (1983). Natural second language acquisition from the perspective of the study of language death. In R. Anderson (Ed.), *Pidginization and creolization as language acquisition.* Rowley, MA: Newbury.

Draizar, A. (1982). *Rapid linguistic recovery from aphasia.* Unpublished doctoral dissertation, Pennsylvania State University, University Park, PA.

Dulay, H., & Burt, M. (1973). Should we teach children syntax? *Language Learning, 23,* 245–258.

Dulay, H., & Burt, M. (1974). Natural sequences in child second language acquisition. *Language Learning, 24,* 37–53.

Dulay, H., & Burt, M. (1977). Remarks on creativity in language acquisition. In M. Burt, H. Dulay, & M. Finnochiaro (Eds.), *Viewpoints on English as a second language.* New York: Regents.

Dulay, H., Burt, M., & Krashen, S. D. (1982). *Language two.* New York: Oxford University Press.

Ervin-Tripp, S. (1977). Wait for me, roller skate! In S. Ervin-Tripp & C. Mitchel-Kernon (Eds.), *Child discourse.* New York: Academic Press.

Farmer, A. (1984). *Modularity in syntax.* Cambridge, MA: MIT Press.

Fillmore, C. J. (1968). The case for case. In E. Bach & R. T. Harms (Eds.), *Universals in linguistic theory.* New York: Holt.

Fletcher, P. (1979). The development of the verb phrase. In P. Fletcher & M. Garman (Eds.), *Language acquisition.* Cambridge: Cambridge University Press.

Fodor, J. A. (1983). *Modularity of mind: Faculty psychology.* Cambridge, MA: MIT Press.

Foix, C. (1928). Aphasies. In R. F. Widal & P. J. Teissier (Eds.), *Nouveau traté de médecine,* (Vol. 18). Paris: Masson.

Fouts, R. S. (1973). Acquisition and testing of gestural sign in four young chimpanzees. *Science, 180,* 978–980.

Fouts, R. S. (1977). Ameslan in Pan. In G. Bournes (Ed.), *Progress in ape research.* New York: Academic Press.

Fouts, R. (1983). Chimpanzee language and elephant tails: A theoretical synthesis. In J. de Luce & H. T. Wilder (Eds.), *Language in primates: Perspectives and implications.* New York: Springer-Verlag.

Fouts, R. S., Chown, W., & Goodin, L. (1976a). Transfer of signed responses in American Sign Language from vocal English stimuli to physical object stimuli by a chimpanzee (Pan). *Learning and Motivation, 7,* 458–75.

Fouts, R. S., Chown, W., Kimball, G., & Couch, J. (1976b). *Comprehension and production of American Sign Language by a chimpanzee (Pan).* Paper presented at the XXI Intl. Congress of Psychology, Paris.

Fouts, R. Shapiro, G., & O'Neil, C. (1978). Studies of linguistic behavior in apes and children. In P. Siple (Ed.), *Understanding language through sign language research.* New York: Academic Press.

Friederici, A. D. (1982). Syntactic and semantic processes in aphasic deficits: The availability of prepositions. *Brain and Language, 15,* 249–258.

Frishberg, N. (1975). Arbitrariness and iconicity: Historical change in American sign language. *Language, 51,* 696–719.

Galloway, L. (1983). Etudes cliniques et expérimentales sur la répartition hémisphérique du traitement cérébral du langage chez les bilingues: Modéles théoriques [Clinical and experimental studies on the hemispheric distribution of cerebral mediation of language among bilinguals: Theoretical models]. *Langages, 18,* 79–123.

Gardner, B. T., & Gardner, R. A. (1971). Two-way communication with an infant chimpanzee. In A. M. Schrier & F. Stollnitz (Eds.), *Behavior of nonhuman primates* (Vol. 4). New York: Academic Press.

Gardner, R. A., & Gardner, B. T. (1969). Teaching sign language to a chimpanzee. *Science, 165,* 664–672.

Gardner, R. A., & Gardner, B. T. (1973). *Teaching sign language to the chimpanzee Washoe.* University Park, PA: Psychological Cinema Register.

Gardner, R. A., & Gardner, B. T. (1975). Early signs of language in child and chimpanzee. *Science, 187,* 752–753.

Gardner, R. A., & Gardner, B. T. (1976). *The first signs of Washoe.* New York: Time–Life Films.
Gardner, R. A., & Gardner, B. T. (1978). Comparative psychology and language acquisition. *Annals of the New York Academy of Sciences, 309,* 37–76.
Garrett, M. E. (1975). The analysis of sentence production. In G. Bower (Ed.), *Psychology of learning and motivation* (Vol. 9). New York: Academic Press.
Garrett, M. E. (1976). Syntactic processes in sentence production. In R. Wales & E. Walker (Eds.), *New approaches to language mechanisms.* Amsterdam: North Holland.
Garrett, M. E. (1980). The limits of accommodation. In V. Fromkin (Ed.), *Errors in linguistic performance.* New York: Academic Press.
Garrett, M. E. (1984). The organization of processing structure for language production: Applications to aphasic speech. In D. Caplan, A. R. Lecours, & A. Smith (Eds.), *Biological perspectives on language.* Cambridge, MA: MIT Press.
Geschwind, N. (1984). Neural mechanisms, aphasia, and theories of language. In D. Caplan, A. R. Lecours, & A. Smith (Eds.), *Biological perspectives on language.* Cambridge, MA: MIT Press.
Givón, T. (1979). *On understanding grammar.* New York: Academic Press.
Givón, T. (in preparation). Modes of knowledge and modes of processing: The routinization of behavior and information. Chapter 7 of T. Givón, *Mind, code and context: Essays in pragmatics.*
Givón, T., Kellogg, W., Posner, M., & Yee, P. (1985) *The tracking of referents in discourse: Automated vs. attended processes* (Technical Report 85–3). Cognitive Science Program. University of Oregon.
Gleason, J. B., Goodglass, H., Green, E., Ackerman, N., & Hyde, M. R. (1975). The retrieval of syntax in Broca's aphasia. *Brain and Language, 2,* 451–471.
Goldin-Meadow, S. (1982). The resilience of recursion: A study of a communication system developed without a conventional language model. In E. Wanner & L. R. Gleitman *Language acquisition: The state of the art.* Cambridge, MA: Cambridge University Press.
Goldstein, K. (1933). L'analyse de l'aphasie et l'étude de l'essence du langage [The analysis of aphasia and the study of the essence of language]. *J. de Psychologie Normale et Pathologique, 30,* 430–496.
Goldstein, K. (1948). *Language and language disturbances.* New York: Grune and Stratton.
Goldstein, K. (1959). Notes on the development of my concepts. *Journal of Individual Psychology, 15,* 5–14.
Golinkoff, R. M., & Martessini, J. (1980). 'Mommy sock': The child's understanding of possessives as expressed in two-noun phrases. *Journal of Child Language, 7,* 119–135.
Goodall, J. V. L. (1968). A preliminary report on expressive movements and communication in the Gombe Stream chimpanzees. In P. Jay (Ed.), *Primates: Studies in adaptation and variability.* New York: Holt.
Goodall, J. V. L. (1971). *In the shadow of man.* Boston: Houghton–Mifflin.
Goodenough, C., Zurif, E. B., & Weintraub, E. J. (1977). Aphasics' attention to grammatical morphemes. *Language and Speech, 20,* 11–19.
Goodglass, H. (1968). Studies on the grammar of aphasics. In J. H. Koplin (Ed.), *Developments in applied psycholinguistic research.* New York: Macmillan. (Reprinted in Goodglass and Blumstein, 1973; page numbers refer to the latter.)
Goodglass, H. (1976). Agrammatism. In H. Whitaker & H. A. Whitaker (Eds.), *Studies in neurolinguistics* (Vol. 1). New York: Academic Press.
Goodglass, H., & Berko, J. (1960). Agrammatism and inflectional morphology in English. *Journal of Speech and Hearing Research, 3,* 257–267. (Reprinted in Sarno 1972.)
Goodglass, H., & Blumstein, S. (Eds.) (1973). *Psycholinguistics and aphasia.* Baltimore: Johns Hopkins University Press.
Goodglass, H., Blumstein, S. E., Gleason, J. B., Hyde, M. R., Green, E., & Statlender, S. (1979). The effect of syntactic encoding on sentence comprehension in aphasia. *Brain and Language, 7,* 201–209.

Goodglass, H., Fodor, I., & Schulhoff, C. (1967). Prosodic factors in grammar—Evidence from aphasia. *Journal of Speech and Hearing Research, 10,* 5–20.

Goodglass, H. & Geschwind, N. (1976). Language disorders (aphasia). In E. Carterette & M. Friedman (Eds.), *Handbook of perception* (Vol. 6). New York: Academic Press.

Goodglass, H., & Hunt, J. (1958). Grammatical complexity and aphasic speech. *Word, 14,* 197–207.

Goodglass, H., & Kaplan, E. (1972). *The assessment of aphasia and related disorders.* Philadelphia: Lea & Febiger.

Goodglass, H., & Menn, L. (1985). Is agrammatism a unitary phenomenon? In M. -L. Kean (Ed.), *Agrammatism.* New York: Academic Press.

Goodglass, H., Quadfasel, F. A., & Timberlake, W. H. (1964) Phrase length and the type and severity of aphasia. *Cortex, 1,* 133–153.

Gordon, B., & Caramazza, A. (1982). Lexical decision for open- and closed-class words: Failure to replicate differential frequency sensitivity. *Brain and Language, 15,* 143–160.

Gordon, B., & Caramazza, A. (1983). Closed- and open-class lexical access in agrammatic and fluent aphasics. *Brain and Language, 19,* 335–345.

Green, E., & Howes, D. H. (1977). The nature of conduction aphasia. In H. Whitaker & H. A. Whitaker (Eds.), *Studies in neurolinguistics* (Vol. 3). New York: Academic Press.

Greenfield, P. M. (1978). How much is one word? *Journal of Child Language, 5,* 347–352.

Greenfield, P. M., & Smith, J. (1976). *The structure of communication in early language development.* New York: Academic Press.

Grice, H. P. (1975). Logic and conversation. In P. Cole & J. L. Morgan (Eds.), *Syntax and semantics, Vol. 3, Speech acts.* New York: Academic Press.

Griffiths, P. D., & Atkinson, M. (1978). A '*door*' to verbs. In N. Waterson & C. E. Snow (Eds.), *The development of communication.* Chichester: Wiley.

Grober, E., Perecman, E., Kellar, L., & Brown, J. (1980). Lexical knowledge in anterior and posterior aphasics. *Brain and Language, 10,* 318–330.

Grodzinsky, Y. (1984). The syntactic characterization of agrammatism. *Cognition, 16,* 99–120.

Grodzinsky, Y. (1986a). Language deficits and the theory of syntax. *Brain and Language, 27,* 135–159.

Grodzinsky, Y. (1986b). Cognitive deficits, their proper description and its theoretical relevance. *Brain and Language, 27,* 178–191.

Grodzinsky, Y., Swinney, D., & Zurif, E. (1985). Agrammatism: Structural deficits and antecedent processing disruptions. In M. -L. Kean (Ed.), *Agrammatism.* New York: Academic Press.

Hall, R. A., Jr. (1943). *Melanesian Pidgin English: Grammar, texts, vocabulary.* Baltimore: Linguistic Society of America.

Halliday, M. A. K. (1975a). *Learning how to mean: Explorations in the development of language.* London: Arnold.

Halliday, M. A. K. (1975b). Learning how to mean. In E. H. Lenneberg & E. Lenneberg (Eds.), *Foundations of language development* (Vol. I). New York: Academic Press.

Hammond, R. (1982). El fonema /s/ en el español jíbaro. Cuestiones teóricas [The phoneme /s/ in "jíbaro" Spanish. Theoretical questions]. In O. Alba (Ed.), *El español del Caribe.* Santiago, República Dominicana: Universidad Católica Madre y Maestra.

Hanson, V. L., & Bellugi, U. (1982). On the role of sign order and morphological structures in memory for American Sign Language sentences. *Haskins Laboratories Status Report on Speech Research, 69,* 171–188.

Harris, R. (1981). *The language myth.* London: Duckworth.

Harris, Z. S. (1952). Discourse analysis. *Language, 28,* 1–30. Reprinted In J. A. Fodor & J. J. Katz (Eds.). *The Structure of language.* Englewood Cliffs, NJ: Prentice–Hall.

Harris, Z. S. (1957). Co-occurrence and transformation in linguistic structure. *Language, 33,* 283–340. Reprinted in J. A. Fodor & J. J. Katz (Eds.) *The Structure of language.* Englewood Cliffs, NJ: Prentice–Hall.

Hayek, F. A. (1952). *The sensory order.* Chicago: University of Chicago Press.
Hayes, C. (1951). *The ape in our house.* New York: Harper.
Hécaen, H. (1972). *Introduction à la neuropsychologie* [Introduction to neuropsychology]. Paris: Larousse.
Heeschen, C. (1985). Agrammatism versus paragrammatism: A fictitious opposition. In M. -L. Kean (Ed.), *Agrammatism.* New York: Academic Press.
Heilman, K. M., & Scholes, R. J. (1976). The nature of comprehension errors in Broca's, conduction, and Wernicke's aphasics. *Cortex, 16,* 5–19.
Herrnstein, R. J., Loveland, D. H. & Cable, C. (1976). Natural concepts in pidgeons. *Journal of Experimental Psychology: Animal behavior processes, 2,* 285–302.
Hill, A. A. (1978). On swearing apes. *Maledicta, 2,* 206–207.
Hill, J. H. (1978). Apes and language. *Annual review of anthropology, 7,* 89–112.
Hochberg, J. G. (1986). *Functional compensation for /s/ deletion in Puerto Rican Spanish. Language, 62,* 609–621.
Hochberg, J. G. (1987). /s/ deletion and pronoun usage in Puerto Rican Spanish. In D. Sankoff (Ed.), *Diversity and diachrony.* Philadelphia: John Benjamins North America.
Hockett, C. F. (1958). *A course in modern linguistics.* New York: Macmillan.
Hockett, C. F., & Altman, S. A. (1968). A note on design features. In T. A. Sebeok (Ed.), *Animal communication.* Bloomington: Indiana University Press.
Hoffmeister, R., Moores, D., & Ellenberger, R. (1975). Some procedural guidelines for the study of the acquisition of sign language. *Sign Language Studies, 7,* 121–132.
Horvath, J. (1985). *Focus in the theory of grammar and the syntax of Hungarian.* Dordrecht, Holland: Foris.
Hughes, J. (1975). Acquisition of a non-vocal 'language' by aphasic children. *Cognition, 3,* 41–55.
Isserlin, M. (1922). Über Agrammatismus [On agrammatism]. *Zeitschrift für die gesamte Neurologie und Psychiatrie, 75,* 332–416.
Jackendoff, R. S. (1972). *Semantic interpretation in generative grammar.* Cambridge, MA: MIT Press.
Jackson, J. H. (1958). *Selected writings of John Hughlings Jackson.* J. Taylor (Ed.). New York: Basic.
Jakobson, R. (1963). Linguistic types of aphasia. In E. Carterette (Ed.), *Brain function* (Vol. III). Los Angeles: University of California Press.
Jakobson, R. (1964). Towards a linguistic typology of aphasic impairments. In A. V. S. de Reuck & M. O'Conner (Eds.) *Disorders of Language.* Boston: Little, Brown.
Jakobson, R. (1968). *Child language, aphasia, and phonological universals* (A. R. Keiler, Trans.). The Hague: Mouton.
Jakobson, R., & Halle, M. (1956). *Fundamentals of language.* The Hague: Mouton.
Jenkins, J. J., & Shaw, R. E. (1975). On the interrelatedness of speech and language. In J. F. Kavanagh & J. E. Cutting (Eds.), *The role of speech in language.* Cambridge, MA: MIT Press.
Johnson, C. J. (1985). The emergence of present perfect verb forms: Semantic influences on selective imitation. *Journal of Child Language, 12,* 325–352.
Johnson, S. C. (1967). Hierarchical clustering schemes. *Psychometrika, 32,* 241–254.
Jones, L. K. (1980). A synopsis of tagmemics. In E. A. Moravcsik & J. R. Wirth (Eds.), *Syntax and Semantics* (Vol. 13). New York: Academic Press.
Jones, L. V., & Wepman, J. M. (1961). Dimensions of language performance in aphasia. *Journal of Speech and Hearing Research, 4,* 220–232.
Jones, L. V., & Wepman, J. M. (1965). *Grammatical indicants of speaking styles in normal and aphasic speakers.* Publication No. 46, Psychometric Laboratory. Chapel Hill: University N. Carolina.
Karmiloff-Smith, A. (1979). *A functional approach to child language.* Cambridge: Cambridge University Press.

Kean, M. -L. (1977). The linguistic interpretation of aphasic syndromes: Agrammatism in Broca's apasics, an example. *Cognition, 5,* 9–46.
Kean, M. -L. (1978). The linguistic interpretation of aphasic syndromes. In E. Walker (Ed.), *Explorations in the biology of language.* Montgomery, VT: Bradford.
Kean, M. -L. (1979). Agrammatism: A phonological deficit? *Cognition, 7,* 69–83.
Kean, M. -L. (1980). Grammatical representations and the description of language processes. In D. Caplan (Ed.), *Biological studies of mental processes.* Cambridge, MA: MIT Press.
Kean, M. -L. (1984). Linguistic analysis of aphasic syndromes: The doing and undoing of aphasia reaearch. In D. Caplan, A. R. Lecours, & A. Smith (Eds.), *Biological persectives on language.* Cambridge, MA: MIT Press.
Kegl, J., & Wilbur, R. B. (1976). Where does structure stop and style begin? Syntax, morphology, and phonology vs. stylistic variation in American Sign Language. In S. Mufwene, C. Walker, & S. Steever (Eds.), *Papers from the 12th Regional Meeting, Chicago Linguistic Society.* Chicago: CLS.
Kellogg, W. N., & Kellogg, L. A. (1933). *The ape and the child: A study of environmental influence upon early behavior.* New York: McGraw-Hill.
Kertesz, A. (1982). Two case studies: Broca's and Wernicke's aphasia. In M. A. Arbib, D. Caplan, & J. C. Marshall (Eds.), *Neural models of language processes.* New York: Academic Press.
Kiss, K. (1981). On the Japanese 'double subject' construction. *Linguistic Review, 1,* 155–170.
Kleist, K. (1916). Über Leitungsaphasie und grammatische Störungen [On conduction aphasia and grammatical disorders]. *Monatschrift für Psychiatrie und Neurologie, 40,* 118–199.
Klima, E. S., & Bellugi, U. (1966). Syntactic regularities in the speech of children. In J. Lyons & R. J. Wales (Eds.), *Psycholinguistics Papers.* Edinburgh: Edinburgh University Press.
Klima, E. S., & Bellugi, U. (1979). *The signs of language.* Cambridge, MA: Harvard University Press.
Kolk, H. H. J. (1978). Judgement of sentence structure in Broca's aphasia. *Neuropsychologia, 16,* 617–626.
Kolk, H. H. J., van Grunsven, M. J. F., & Keyser, A. (1985). On parallelism between production and comprehension in agrammatism. In M. -L. Kean (Ed.), *Agrammatism.* New York: Academic Press.
Krashen, S. D. (1981). *Second language acquisition and second language learning.* Oxford: Pergamon.
Krashen, S. D. (1982). *Principles and practice in second language acquisition.* Oxford: Pergamon.
Krashen, S. D. (1985a). *The input hypothesis.* New York: Longman.
Krashen, S. D. (1985b). *Inquiries and insights.* Hayward, CA: Alemany.
Krashen, S. D., & Terrell, T. D. (1983). *The natural approach.* Hayward, CA: Alemany.
Kuroda, S. -Y. (1983). What can Japanese say about government and binding? *Proceedings of the West Coast Conference on Formal Linguistics, 2,* 153–164.
Kurowski, K. (1981). *A constrastive analysis of the comprehension deficit in posterior and anterior aphasia.* Masters thesis, Brown University, Providence.
Labov, W. (1972). *Language in the inner city.* Philadelphia: Univeristy of Pennasylvania Press.
Lakoff, G. (1969). *On generative semantics.* Reproduced by the Indiana University Linguistics Club.
Lakoff, G. (1971a). Presupposition and relative well-formedness. In D. D. Steinberg & L. A. Jakobovits (Eds.), *Semantics: An interdisciplinary reader in philosophy, linguistics, and psychology.* Cambridge, MA: Cambridge University Press.
Lakoff, G. (1971b). On generative semantics. In D. D. Steinberg & L. A. Jakobovits (Eds.), *Semantics: An interdisciplinary reader in philosophy, linguistics, and psychology.* Cambridge, MA: Cambridge University Press.
Lamendella, J. T. (1976). Relations between the ontogeny and phylogeny of language: A neo-recapitulationist view. In S. R. Harnad, H. D. Steklis, & J. Lancaster (Eds.), *The origins and evolution of speech.* New York: New York Academy of Sciences.

Lamendella, J. T. (1977a). The limbic system in human communication. In H. Whitaker & H. A. Whitaker (Eds.), *Studies in neurolinguistics* (Vol. 3). New York: Academic Press.

Lamendella, J. T. (1977b). General principles of neuro-functional organization and their manifestation in primary and non-primary language acquisition. *Language Learning, 27,* 155–196.

Lamendella, J. T. (1979). Neurolinguistics. In B. Siegel (Ed.), *Annual review of anthropology.* Palo Alto, CA: Annual reviews.

Lapointe, S. G. (1983). Some issues in the linguistic description of agrammatism. *Cognition, 14,* 1–39.

Lapointe, S. G. (1985). A theory of verb form use in the speech of agrammatic aphasics. *Brain and Language, 24,* 100–155.

Lavorel, P. M. (1979). Grammaires pour les analyseurs morphosyntaxiques: Rappels théoriques et recettes prâtiques [Grammars for morphosyntactic analysers: Theoretical reflections and practical recommendations]. *T. A. Informations* (Vol. 1). Paris: Klinksieck.

Lavorel, P. M. (1982). Production strategies: A systems approach to Wernicke's aphasia. In M. A. Arbib, D. Caplan, and J. C. Marshall (Eds.), *Neural models of language processes.* New York: Academic Press.

Lebrun, Y., & Buyssens, E. (1982). Metalanguage and speech pathology. *British Journal of Disorders of Communication, 17,* 21–25.

Lecours, A. R., Osborn, E., Travis, L., Rouillon, F., & Lavallée-Huynh, G. (1981). Jargons. In J. W. Brown (Ed.), (1981). *Jargonaphasia.* New York: Academic Press.

Lenneberg, E. H. (1967). *Biological foundations of language.* New York: Wiley.

Lenneberg, E. H. (1973). The neurology of language. *Daedalus, 102,* 115–133.

Liddell, S. K. (1978). Non-manual signals and relative clauses in ASL. In P. Siple (Ed.), *Understanding language through sign language research.* New York: Academic Press.

Limber, J. (1973). The genesis of complex sentences. In T. E. Moore (Ed.), *Cognitive development and the acquisition of language.* New York: Academic Press.

Limber, J. (1977). Language in child and chimp? *American Psychologist, 32,* 280–295.

Linebarger, M., Schwartz, M. F., & Saffran, E. M. (1983). Sensitivity to grammatical structure in so-called agrammatic aphasics. *Cognition, 13,* 361–392.

Lockwood, D. G. (1972). *Introduction to stratificational linguistics.* New York: Harcourt Brace Jovanovich.

López Morales, H. (1983). *Estratificatión social del español de San Juan de Puerto Rico [Social stratification of the Spanish of San Juan, Puerto Rico].* México: Universidad Nacional Autónoma de México.

Luria, A. R. (1970). *Traumatic aphasia.* The Hague: Mouton.

Luria, A. R. (1975). Two kinds of disorders in the comprehension of grammatical constructions. *Linguistics, 154/155,* 47–56.

Maestas y Moores, J. (1980). Early linguistic environment: Interactions of deaf parents with their infants. *Sign Language Studies, 26,* 1–13.

Marshall, J. C. (1977). Disorders in the expression of language. In J. Morton & J. Marshall (Eds.), *Psycholinguistics: Developmental and Pathological.* Ithaca, New York: Cornell University Press.

Marx, J. L. (1980). Ape-language controversy flares up. *Science, 207,* 1330–1333.

McCarthy, D. (1954). Language development in children. In L. Carmichael (Ed.), *Manual of child psychology.* New York: Wiley.

McCawley, J. D. (1980). An un-syntax. In E. A. Moravcsik & J. R. Wirth (Eds.), *Syntax and semantics* (Vol. 13). New York: Academic Press.

McCawley, J. D. (1982). *Thirty million theories of grammar.* Chicago: Chicago University Press.

McNeill, D. (1970). *The acquisition of language: The study of developmental psycholinguistics.* New York: Harper and Row.

Miceli, G., Mazzucchi, A., Menn, L., & Goodglass, H. (1983) Contrasting cases of Italian agrammatic aphasia without comprehension disorder. *Brain and Language. 19,* 65–97.

Miles, L. W. (1976). Discussion paper: The communicative competence of child and chimpanzee. In S. R. Harnad, H. D. Steklis, and J. Lancaster (Eds.), *The origins and evolution of speech.* New York: New York Academy of Sciences.

Miles, H. L. (1983). Apes and language: The search for communicative competence. In J. de Luce & H. T. Wilder (Eds.), *Language in primates: Perspectives and implications.* New York: Springer-Verlag.

Miller, M. (1975). *Pragmatic constraints on the linguistic realization of 'semantic intentions' in early child language ('telegraphic speech').* Paper presented at the Third International Child Language Symposium, London.

Mohr, J. P., Walters, W. C., & Duncan, G. W. (1975). Thalamic hemorrhage and aphasia. *Brain and Language, 2,* 3–17.

Molfese, D. (1972). *Cerebral asymmetry in infants, children, and adults: Auditory evoked responses to speech and noise stimuli.* Unpublished doctoral dissertation, Pennsylvania State University, University Park, PA.

Molfese, D., Freeman, R. B., & Palermo, D. S. (1975). The ontogeny of brain lateralization for speech and nonspeech stimuli. *Brain and Language, 2,* 356–368.

Moravcsik, E. A., & Wirth, J. R. (Eds.) (1980). *Syntax and semantics. Vol. 13. Current approaches to syntax.* New York: Academic Press.

Mulford, R. (1985). Comprehension of Icelandic pronoun gender: Semantic versus formal factors. *Journal of Child Language, 12,* 443–453.

Muncer, S. J., & Ettlinger, G. (1981). Communication by a chimpanzee: First-trial mastery of word order that is critical for meaning, but failure to negate conjunctions. *Neuropsychologia, 19,* 73–78.

Naeser, M. A. (1983). CT scan lesion size and lesion locus in cortical and subcortical aphasias. In A. Kertesz (Ed.), *Localization in neuropsychology.* New York: Academic Press.

Naeser, M. A., Alexander, M. P., Helm-Estabrooks, N., Levine, H. L., Laughlin, S. A., & Geschwind, N. (1983). Aphasia with predominantly subcortical lesion sites: Description of three capsular/putaminal aphasia syndromes. *Archives of Neurology, 39,* 2–14.

Nathan, P. W. (1947). Facial apraxia and apraxic disarthria. *Brain, 70,* 449–478.

Nelson, K. (1980, March). *First words of chimp and child.* Paper presented at meeting of the Southeastern Psychological Association.

Newport, E. L. (1984). Constraints on learning: Studies in the acquisition of American Sign Language. *Papers and Reports on Child Language Development, 23,* 1–22.

Nussbaum, N., & Naremore, R. (1975). On the acquisition of the present prefect 'have' in normal children. *Language and Speech, 18,* 219–226.

Obler, L. K., & Albert, M. (1981). Language in the elderly aphasic and in the dementing patient. In M. T. Sarno (Ed.), *Acquired Aphasia.* New York: Academic Press.

Obler, L. K., Albert, M., Goodglass, H., & Benson, D. F. (1978). Aphasia type and aging. *Brain and Language, 6,* 316–322.

Ojemann, G. A. (1975). Language and the thalamus: Object naming and recall during and after thalamic stimulation. *Brain and Language, 2,* 101–120.

Ojemann, G. A. (1976). Subcortical language mechanisms. In H. Whitaker & H. A. Whitaker (Eds.), *Studies in neurolinguistics* (Vol. 1). New York: Academic Press.

Paradis, M. (1977). Bilingualism and aphasia. In H. Whitaker & H. A. Whitaker (Eds.), *Studies in neurolinguistics* (Vol. 3). New York: Academic Press.

Paradis, M. (Ed.) (1983). *Readings on aphasia in bilinguals and polyglots.* Quebec: Didier.

Paradis, M., Goldblum, M. -C., & Abidi, R. (1982). Alternate antagonism with paradoxical translation behavior in two bilingual aphasic patients. *Brain and Language, 15,* 55–69.

Parisi, D., & Pizzamiglio, L. (1970). Syntactic comprehension in aphasia. *Cortex, 6,* 204–215.

Patterson, F. (1978). The gestures of a gorilla. *Brain and Language, 5,* 72–97.

Patterson, F., & Linden, E. (1981). *The education of Koko.* New York: Holt Rinehart Winston.

Petitto, L. A., & Seidenberg, M. S. (1979). On the evidence for linguistic abilities in signing apes. *Brain and Language, 8,* 162–183.

Pick, A. (1913). *Die agrammatischen Sprachstörungen* [Agrammatic speech disorders]. Berlin: Springer-Verlag.

Poplack, S. (1977). The notion of the plural in Puerto Rican Spanish: Competing constraints on /s/ deletion. In W. Labov (Ed.), *Quantitative analysis of linguistic structure*. New York: Academic Press.

Posner, M. I., & Snyder, C. R. R. (1975). Attention and cognitive control. In R. L. Solso (Ed.), *Information processing and cognition* (chapter 3). Hillsdale, NJ: Lawrence Erlbaum Associates.

Premack, A. J. & Premack, D. (1972). Teaching language to an ape. *Scientific American, 227,* 92–99. Reprinted in W. S. Y. Wang (Ed.). 1982. *Human Communication*. San Fransisco: Freeman.

Premack, D. (1971). Language in chimpanzee? *Science, 172,* 808–22.

Premac, D. (1983). The codes of man and beasts. *Behavioral and Brain Sciences, 6,* 125–137.

Premack, D., & Premack, A. J. (1983). *The mind of an ape*. New York: Norton.

Premack, D., & Schwartz, A. (1966). Preparations for discussing behaviorism with chimpanzee. In F. Smith & G. A. Miller (Eds.), *The genesis of language*. Cambridge, MA: MIT Press.

Rizzi, L. (1985). Two notes on the linguistic interpretation of Broca's aphasia. In M. -L. Kean (Ed.), *Agrammatism*. New York: Academic Press.

Rosansky, E. (1976). Methods and morphemes in second language acquisition. *Language Learning, 26,* 409–425.

Rosenthal, R. (Ed.) (1965). *Clever Hans (The horse of Mr. von Osten)*, by Oskar Pfungst. New York: Holt, Rinehart, & Winston.

Ross. J. R. (1967). *Constraints on variables in syntax*. Unpublished doctoral dissertation, MIT, Cambridge, MA.

Ross, J. R. (1972). Endstation Hauptwort: The category squish. In P. M. Peranteau, J. N. Levi, & G. C. Phares (Eds.), *Papers from the Eighth Regional Meeting, Chicago Linguistic Society*. Chicago: CLS.

Ross, J. R. (1973a). A fake NP squish. In C. -J. N. Bailey & R. Shuy (Eds.), *New ways of analyzing variation in English*. Washington: Georgetown University Press.

Ross, J. R. (1973b). Nouniness, In O. Fujimura (Ed.), *Three dimensions of linguistic theory*. Tokyo: TEC.

Rubens, A. B. (1976). Transcortical motor aphasia. In H. Whitaker & H. A. Whitaker (Eds.), *Studies in neurolinguistics* (Vol. 1). New York: Academic Press.

Rumbaugh, D. M. (Ed.) 1977. *Language learning by a chimpanzee*. New York: Academic Press.

Rumbaugh, D. M., & Gill, T. V. (1976). Lana's mastery of language skills. In S. R. Harnad, H. D. Steklis, and J. Lancaster (Eds.), *The origins and evolution of speech*. New York: New York Academy of Sciences.

Rumbaugh, D. M., & Gill, T. V. (1977). Lana's acquisition of language skills. In D. M. Rumbaugh (Ed.), *Language learning by a chimpanzee*. New York: Academic Press.

Rumbaugh, D. M., Gill, T. V., & von Glaserfeld, E. C. (1973). Reading and sentence completion by a chimpanzee (pan). *Science, 182,* 731–733.

Saffran, E. M., Schwartz, M. F., & Marin, O. S. M. (1980). The word order problem in agrammatism: II. Production. *Brain and Language, 10,* 263–280.

Saito, M. & Hoji, H. (1983). Weak crossover and move alpha in Japanese. *Natural Language and Linguistic Theory, 1,* 245–260.

Salomon, E. (1914). Motorische Aphasie mit Agrammatismus und sensorisch-agrammatischen Störungen [Motor aphasia with agrammatism and sensory-agrammatic disorders]. *Monatsschrift für Psychiatrie und Neurologie, 35,* 181–275.

Samuels, J. A., & Benson, D. F. (1979). Some aspects of language comprehenson in anterior aphasia. *Brain and Language, 8,* 275–286.

Sánchez de Zavala, V. (Ed.). (1974). *Semántica y sintaxis en la lingüística transformatoria, I: Comienzos y centro de la polémica* [Semantics and syntax in transformational linguistics, I: Genesis and core of the polemics]. Madrid: Alianza Editorial.

Sankoff, G. (1979). The genesis of a language. In K. C. Hill (Ed.) *The genesis of language*. Ann Arbor: Karoma.

Savage-Rumbaugh, E. S., Rumbaugh, D. M., & Boysen, S. (1978) Linguisticaly mediated tool use and exchange by chimpanzees (Pan troglodytes). *Behavioral and Brain Sciences, 4,* 539–554.

Savage-Rumbaugh, E. S., Rumbaugh, D. M., & Boysen, S. (1980). Do apes use language? *American Scientist, 68,* 49–61.

Schlesinger, I. M. (1971). Production of utternaces and language acquisition. In D. I. Slobin (Ed.). (1971). *The ontogenesis of grammar*. New York: Academic Press.

Schlesinger, I. M. (1975). Grammatical development—the first steps. In E. H. Lenneberg & E. Lenneberg (Eds.), *Foundations of language development* (Vol. 1). New York: Academic Press.

Schneider, W. (1985). Toward a model of attention and the development of automatic processing. In M. I. Posner & O. S. M. Marin (Eds.), *Attention and performance XI*. Hillsdale, NJ: Lawrence Erlbaum Associates.

Schneider, W., & Shiffrin, R. M. (1977). Controlled and automatic human information processing, I: Detection, search and attention. *Psychological Review, 84,* 1–66.

Schnitzer, M. L. (1973). In search of an unproblematical notion of grammaticality. *Le langage et l'homme, 21,* 27–38.

Schnitzer, M. L. (1974). Aphasiological evidence for five linguistic hipotheses. *Language, 50,* 300–315.

Schnitzer, M. L. (1976). The role of phonology in linguistic communication. In H. Whitaker & H. A. Whitaker (Eds.), *Studies in neurolinguistics* (Vol. 1). New York: Academic Press.

Schnitzer, M. L. (1978a). Toward a neurolinguistic theory of language. *Brain and Language, 6,* 342–361.

Schnitzer, M. L. (1978b). *Spanish word order, context, and the intuitionist paradigm*. Paper presented at Annual Meeting of the Linguistic Society of America, Boston.

Schnitzer, M. L. (1981). A case-grammar approach to Spanish-English contrastive syntax. In R. Nash & D. Belaval (Eds.), 1981. *Readings in Spanish-English contrastive linguistics* (Vol. II). San Juan: Interamerican University Press.

Schnitzer, M. L. (1982). The translational hierarchy of language. In M. A. Arbib, D. Caplan, and J. C. Marshall (Eds.), *Neural models of language processes*. New York: Academic Press.

Schnitzer, M. L. (1986). A plea for neutral monism from aphasiology. In I. Gopnik & M. Gopnik (Eds.), *From models to modules*. Norwood, NJ: Ablex.

Scholes, R. J. (1974). Syntax, cerebral dominance, and the primary language system. *University of Florida Communication Sciences Laboratory Quarterly Report, 12*(1) 1–9.

Scholnick, E. K., & Wing, C. S. (1981). The pragmatics of subordinating conjunctions: A second look. *Journal of Child Language, 9,* 461–480.

Schuell, H. M., & Jenkins, J. J. (1961). Comment on "Dimensions of language performance in aphasia." *Journal of Speech and Hearing Research, 4,* 295–299.

Schuell, H. M., Jenkins, J. J., & Carroll, J. B. (1962). A factor analysis of the Minnesota test for differential diagnosis of aphasia. *Journal of Speech and Hearing Research, 5,* 349–369.

Schuell, H. M., Jenkins, J. J., & Jiménez-Pabón, E. (1964). *Aphasia in adults*. New York: Harper & Row.

Schwartz, M. F. (1984). What the classical aphasia categories can't do for us, and why. *Brain and Language, 21,* 3–8.

Schwartz, M. F., Saffran, E. M., & Marin, O. S. M. (1980). The word order problem in agrammatism: I. Comprehension. *Brain and Language, 10,* 249–262.

Sebeok, T. A., & Umiker-Sebeok, D. J. (Eds.). (1980). *Speaking of apes*. New York: Plenum.

Seidenberg, M. S., & Petitto, L. A. (1979). Signing behavior in apes: A critical review. *Cognition. 7,* 177–215.

Shankweiler, D., & Harris, K. S. (1966). An experimental approach to the problem of articulation in aphasia. *Cortex, 2,* 277–292. Reprinted in H. Goodglass & S. Blumstein (Eds.) *Psycholinguistics and aphasia*. Baltimore: John Hopkins University Press.

Shatz, M. (1978). Children's comprehension of their mother's question-directives. *Journal of Child Languages, 5,* 39–46.

Shewan, R. M., and Canter, G. (1971). Effects of vocabulary, syntax and sentence length on auditory comprehension in aphasic patients. *Cortex, 7,* 209–226.

Simon, T. W. (1983). Limits of primate talk. In J. de Luce & H. T. Wilder (Eds.), *Language in primates: Perspectives and implications.* New York: Springer-Verlag.

Slobin, D. I. (1973). Cognitive prerequisites for the development of grammar. In C. A. Ferguson & D. I. Slobin (Eds.), *Studies of Child language development.* New York: Holt, Rinehart, & Winston.

Sparks, R., Helm, N., & Albert, M. (1974). Aphasia rehabilitation resulting from melodic intonation therapy. *Cortex, 10,* 303–316.

Sproat, R. (1985). Welsh syntax and VSO structure. *Natural Language and Linguistic Theory, 3,* 173–216.

Sproat, R. (1986). Competence, performance, and agrammatism: A reply to Grodzinsky. *Brain and Language, 27,* 160–167.

Steffensen, M. S. (1978). Satisfying inquisitive adults: Some simple methods of answering yes/no questions. *Journal of Child Language, 5,* 221–236.

Stevenson, A. (1893). The speech of children. *Science, 21,* 118–120.

Stevick, E. (1976). *Memory, meaning, and method.* Rowley, MA: Newbury.

Stokoe, W. C. (1960). *Sign language structure, Studies in Linguistics Occasional Papers 8.* Buffalo: University of Buffalo Press.

Stokoe, W. (1980). Sign language structure. *Annual Review of Anthropology, 9,* 365–390.

Stokoe, W. C. (1983). Apes who sign and critics who don't. In J. de Luce & H. T. Wilder (Eds.) *Language in primates: Perspectives and implications.* New York: Springer-Verlag.

Sudhalter, V., & Braine, M. S. (1985). How does comprehension of passive develop? A comparison of actional and experiential verbs. *Journal of Child Language, 12,* 455–470.

Supalla, T., & Newport, E. (1978). How many seats in a chair? The derivation of nouns and verbs in American Sign Language. In P. Siple (Ed.), *Understanding language through sign language research.* New York: Academic Press.

Suppes, P. (1976). Syntax and semantics of children's language. In S. R. Hanrad, H. D. Steklis, & J. Lancaster (Eds.), *The origins and evolution of speech.* New York: New York Academy of Sciences.

Swinney, D. A., Zurif, E. B., & Cutler, A. (1980). Effects of sentential stress and word class upon comprehension in Broca's aphasics. *Brain and Language, 10,* 132–144.

Terrace, H. S. (1979). *Nim: A chimpanzee who learned sign language.* New York: Knopf.

Terrace, H. S. (1983). Apes who "talk": Language or projection of language by their teachers? In J. de Luce & H. T. Wilder (Eds.), *Language in primates: Perspectives and implications.* New York: Springer-Verlag.

Terrace, H. S., Petitto, L. A., Sanders, R. J., & Bever, T. G. (1979). Can an ape create a sentence? *Science, 206,* 819–902.

Terell, T. (1976). The inherent variability of word final /s/ in Cuban and Puerto Rican Spanish. In B. Valdés & R. García Moya (Eds.), *Teaching Spanish to the Spanish speaking: Trends and perspectives.* San Antonio: Trinity University Press.

Terrell, T. (1978a). Sobre la aspiración y elisión de la /s/ implosiva y final en el español de Puerto Rico [On the aspiration and elision of preconsonatal and final /s/ in the Spanish of Puerto Rico]. *Nueva revista de filología hispánica, 27,* 24–38.

Terrell, T. (1978b). Constraints on the aspiration and deletion of final /s/ in Cuban and Puerto Rican Spanish. *The Bilingual Review, 4,* 325–326.

Thompson, C. R., & Church, R. M. (1980). An explanation of the language of a chimpanzee. *Science, 208,* 313–314.

Uber, D. R. (1981). *A perceptual and acoustic study of syllable-final and word-final* -s *and* -n *in*

Puerto Rican Spanish. Unpublished doctoral dissertation, University of Wisconsin, Madison, WI.

Umiker-Sebeok, D. J., & Sebeok, T. A. (1981). Clever Hans and smart simians. *Anthropos, 76,* 89–165.

Van Cantfort, T. E., & Rimpau, J. B. (1982). Sign language studies with children and chimpanzees. *Sign Language Studies, 34,* 15–72.

Van der Geest, A. J. M. (1975). *Some aspects of communicative competence and their implications for language acquisition.* Assen, The Netherlands: Van Corcum.

Van Valin, R. D., Jr., & Foley, W. A. (1980). Role and reference grammar. In E. A. Moravcsik & J. R. Wirth (Eds.), *Syntax and semantics* (Vol. 13). New York: Academic Press.

von Glaserfeld, E. (1976). The development of language as purposive behavior. In S. R. Harnad, H. D. Steklis, and J. Lancaster (Eds.), *The origins and evolution of speech.* New York: New York Academy of Sciences.

von Glaserfeld, E. (1977). The Yerkish language and its automatic parser. In Rumbaugh (Ed.), *Language learning in a chimpanzee.* New York: Academic Press.

von Stockert, T. R. (1972). Recognition of syntactic structure in aphasic patients. *Cortex, 8,* 323–354.

von Stockert, T. R., & Bader, L. (1976). Some relations of grammar and lexicon in aphasia. *Cortex, 12,* 49–60.

Weigl, E. (1968). On the problem of cortical syndromes. In M. Simmel (Ed.), *The reach of mind: Essays in memory of Kurt Goldstein.* New York: Springer.

Weigl, E. (1970). A neuropsychological contribution to the problem of semantics. In M. Bierwisch & K. E. Heidolph (Eds.), *Progress in linguistics.* The Hague: Mouton.

Weigl, E. (1974). Neuropsychological experiments on transcoding between spoken and written language structures. *Brain and Language, 1,* 227–240.

Weigl, E., & Bierwisch, M. (1970). Neuropsychology and linguistics: Topics of common research. *Foundations of Language, 6,* 1–18. (Reprinted in H. Goodglass & S. Blumstein, (Eds.), *Psycholinguistics and aphasia.* Baltimore: Johns Hopkins University Press.

Weisenburg, T. M., & McBride, K. E. (1935). *Aphasia, a clinical and psychological study.* New York: Commonwealth Fund.

Wells, C. G. (1979). Learning and using the auxiliary verb in English. In V. Lee (Ed.), *Cognitive development: Language and thinking from birth to adolescence.* London: Croom Helm.

Whitaker, H. A. (1971). *On the representation of language in the human brain.* Edmonton, Alberta: Linguistic Research.

Wilbur, R. B. (1979). *American Sign Language and sign systems: Research and applications.* Baltimore: University Park Press.

Wing, C. S., & Scholnick, E. K. (1981). Children's comprehension of pragmatic concepts expressed in *because, although, if* and *unless. Journal of Child Language, 8,* 347–365.

Wood, C. C. (1982). Implications of simulated lesion experiments for the interpretation of lesions in real nervous systems. In M. A. Arbib, P. Caplan, & J. C. Marshal (Eds.), *Neural models of language processes.* New York: Academic Press.

Woolford, E. (1979). The developing complementizer system of Tok Pisin: Syntactic change in progress. In K. C. Hill (Ed.) *The genesis of language.* Ann Arbor: Karoma.

Yeager, C., O'Sullivan, C., & Autry, D. (1981, August). *Communicative competence in pan troglodytes: Rising (or falling) to the occasion.* Paper presented at Meeting of American Psychological Association, Los Angeles.

Zurif, E. B., & Caramazza, A. (1976). Psycholinguistic structures in aphasia: Studies in syntax and semantics. In H. Whitaker & H. A. Whitaker (Eds.), *Studies in neurolinguistics* (Vol. 1). New York: Academic Press.

Zurif, E. B., Caramazza, A., & Myerson, R. (1972). Grammatical judgments of agrammatic aphasics. *Neuropsychologia, 10,* 404–417.

Author Index

Subject Index

S

T

U

V

W

Y

For Product Safety Concerns and Information please contact our
EU representative GPSR@taylorandfrancis.com Taylor & Francis
Verlag GmbH, Kaufingerstraße 24, 80331 München, Germany